CECIL DREEME

Q19: The Queer American Nineteenth Century
Christopher Looby, Series Editor

Queer is a good nineteenth-century American word, appearing almost everywhere in the literature of the time. And, as often as not, the nineteenth-century use of the word seems to anticipate the sexually specific meanings it would later accrue. Sometimes *queer* could mean simply *odd* or *strange* or *droll*. But at other times it carried within itself a hint of its semantic future, as when Artemus Ward, ostensibly visiting a settlement of "Free Lovers" in Ohio, calls them "some queer people," or when the narrator of Constance Fenimore Woolson's "Felipa" refers to the eponymous child, who wears masculine clothing, as "a queer little thing," or when Herman Melville, writing of the master-at-arms Claggart in *Billy Budd*, tells us that young Billy, sensitive to Claggart's attentively yearning yet malicious behavior toward him, "thought the master-at-arms acted in a manner rather queer at times." *Q19: The Queer American Nineteenth Century* makes available again a set of literary texts from the long American nineteenth century in which the *queer* appears in all its complex range of meanings. From George Lippard's *The Midnight Queen*: "'Strange!' cried one. 'Odd!' another. 'Queer!' a third."

CECIL DREEME

Theodore Winthrop

Edited and with an introduction by
Christopher Looby

PENN

University of Pennsylvania Press
Philadelphia

Publication of this volume was aided by gifts from the UCLA Friends of English
and the UCLA Dean of Humanities.

Published by
University of Pennsylvania Press
Philadelphia, Pennsylvania 19104-4112
www.upenn.edu/pennpress

Printed in the United States of America on acid-free paper
10 9 8 7 6 5 4 3 2 1

A catalogue record for this book is available from the Library of Congress.
ISBN 978-0-8122-2365-1

CONTENTS

INTRODUCTION

—•—

Cecil Dreeme and the Misfortune of Sexuality

Christopher Looby

It's always fascinating to come upon a record of an actual reader's lively encounter with a book. Here is a story about a real nineteenth-century reader and his fraught engagement with the novel you are holding, Theodore Winthrop's *Cecil Dreeme*. On January 10, 1875, a young man named Henry Blake Fuller was enduring a dismal stint as a clerk in Ovington's crockery store in Chicago. He had turned eighteen years old the day before, and he confided moodily to his diary (to which he gave the grandiloquent title "A Legacy to Posterity") that he felt he would always look back upon himself at eighteen "as a boy in bad health, & who wished to be somewhere else. In short as a discontented young person. Unfortunate!" Fuller felt acutely conscious, he told his diary, of his many personal inadequacies, which he tallied in self-deriding terms reflecting the standard novelistic clichés of the time: "Harry Fuller at eighteen would never serve as a romantic hero. No olive complexion, no hair in graceful curves and black as the raven's wing; no commanding figure, no fascinating presence, no woman's tenderness with a man's courage.—but why torment myself by prolonging the list of my own deficiencies. Yes, I may set myself down as quite an ordinary person." Then suddenly the diarist's attention turned from morose self-examination, rendered in familiar novelistic terms, to a novel he had just read—this very novel. "Read Cecil Dreeme yesterday. A peculiar book. Not a profound observation. A book that interests me greatly."[1] (There is a truly uncanny echo here of the novel's narrator, Robert Byng, who explains to Cecil Dreeme his attraction to the alluring villain Densdeth: "He interests me greatly" [124].) Versions of many of the romantic clichés with which he had just berated himself would, in fact, have been ready to hand in the florid "Biographical Sketch of the Author" by George W. Curtis that prefaces *Cecil Dreeme* (included here as an integral part of this "peculiar" book). Fuller would have read there of Winthrop's "keen gray eye" and "clustering fair hair" (1), would have learned that Winthrop's "sensitive seriousness grew sometimes morbid" (4) and that he was afflicted with "an ill-health that colored all his life" (4); that he had "a flower-like delicacy of temperament" characterized by "the curious, critical introspection which marks every sensitive and refined nature" (6), but that his "womanly grace of temperament merely enhanced the unusual manliness of his character and impression" (6). Fuller would have found, in other words, someone whose "ill-health" matched his own "bad health," but who was somehow a paragon of the "romantic hero" he felt he was not. He would have found a model for his own morbid self-castigation, but perhaps also an image of something less "ordinary" that he might aspire toward.

Many questions arise here. The teenaged Fuller was certainly a great reader: the diary in question is full of references to novelists and novels, poets and poetry, as well as histories and other literary genres. Wilkie Collins (July 12, 1874), Charles Dickens—he reported reading *David Copperfield* and *Dombey and Son* (July 14), *Nicholas Nickleby* (Aug. 23), and *Bleak House* (Nov. 22)—Goethe's *Iphigenie auf Tauris* and Schiller's *Maid of Orleans* (July 17), Longfellow's "Wayside Inn" (July 20), Johnson's *Rasselas* (Aug. 30), Bulwer's *The Last Days of Pompeii* (Sept. 27), Gibbon's *Decline and Fall of the Roman Empire* (Jan. 28, 1875), Scott's *The Lay of the Last Minstrel* and *The Lady of the Lake* (Nov. 25), and Macaulay's *Essays* (Dec. 25)—Fuller mentioned all of these and more. About many of them he had substantive critical observations to make, as a future novelist very well might. Some of them he read patiently over an extended period of time, and returned to for rereading and reconsideration. But about *Cecil Dreeme*, which he evidently read in one day—on his eighteenth birthday, no less, and in a state of deep discontent—he could not muster anything that would satisfy him as "a profound observation." Something about *Cecil Dreeme* left him nonplussed, but at the same time intrigued. "A peculiar book," he wrote. "A book that interests me greatly."

How did *Cecil Dreeme* come to Fuller's attention? What did he find "peculiar" about it, and why did it interest him so "greatly"? Did someone who had responded to its peculiarity—and who thought its peculiarity would interest Fuller—recommend it to him? We probably cannot know. Fuller went on to become a noted writer himself, and many decades later he would write one of the earliest unmistakably queer American novels, *Bertram Cope's Year* (1919).[2] The fact of this later literary performance, and the knowledge that Fuller was also an avid lover of men, perhaps licenses us to infer that the great and baffled interest that his teenaged self took in the "peculiar book" *Cecil Dreeme* must have had something to do with its (and his) incipient queerness.

The single word Fuller used to describe the novel, the mere epithet *peculiar*, is a curious one, having served over the years prior to the invention of homosexual identity as one of the many vague euphemisms that could evoke what was not yet, in 1875, as firmly conceived, securely denoted, or publicly recognized as it would soon come to be: a style of sexual personhood that had not yet coalesced into a defined social identity, did not yet have a label, had not yet become a description under which people could act and could understand themselves and others to exist. *Cecil Dreeme*'s narrator, Robert Byng, tellingly refers at one point to the "*peculiar* power" that the dangerously magnetic Densdeth exerted over him, and at another place to the "too *peculiar* a tenderness" he himself felt for his beloved Cecil Dreeme (194, 281, emphasis added). A decade earlier Nathaniel Hawthorne's narrator, Miles Coverdale, teased his friend Hollingsworth in *The Blithedale Romance* (1852) by reading to him some suggestive passages from the writings of Charles Fourier, and explaining to him ("as modestly as I could") the radical sexual arrangements that Fourier advocated. Coverdale then provocatively asked Hollingsworth whether he thought they could introduce these "beautiful pecularities" into their own communal practice.[3] At roughly the same time as Winthrop published *Cecil Dreeme* another adventurous novelist, Margaret J. M. Sweat, had the eponymous protagonist of *Ethel's Love-Life* (1859) describe to her fiancé Ernest the "peculiar relationship" she had with a woman named Leonora: "Women often love each other with as much fervor and excitement as they do men," Ethel patiently explained, and although Leonora has been banished from Ethel's life their "subtle essences mingled and assimilated too thoroughly ever to be entirely disunited."[4]

Fuller in 1875 may not yet have had any sense of a firm sexually categorical possibility for himself or for a character in a novel. But he was certainly aware of the bent of his own desires, and of his unsuitedness for the role of romantic hero if it would entail an erotic interest in women. Naturally, then, he would have taken a great interest in a novel that, among many other things that might have appealed to him, featured a passionate friendship apparently between two men, described unabashedly (and repeatedly) as "more precious than the love of women" (139), "a love passing the love of women" (163). But that passionate friendship, forthrightly depicted in 1861 by Theodore Winthrop as something that did not entail categorization as "homosexual," would have been at least somewhat more likely by 1875, when Fuller read the novel, to have had such an implication. But then again, it would not yet certainly have had this implication: many readers and reviewers at the time did not detect any such suggestion. Same-sex romantic friendship was then in the midst of a long late nineteenth-century transition from a perfectly normal and even celebrated form of personal attachment to a suspect and eventually deviant form of desire.[5] What we have, in the encounter between Henry Blake Fuller and *Cecil Dreeme*, then, is a neat vignette exhibiting a book written and published before what is often called the "invention" of the homosexual (indeed, the invention of the heterosexual too) and an act of reading coming in an uncertain, slightly later moment when that incomplete invention may or may not have been clearly known to this particular young reader.[6] The book's transitional status, and the liminal quality of this scene of reading, both contribute to what Fuller called "peculiar" about *Cecil Dreeme.* What he called "peculiar" corresponds to what we might today call *queer.*

Queer is a term in use today to suggest a broad range of erotic tastes, inclinations, attachments, and desires that do not fall neatly into the binary categories the dominant culture still frequently deploys for the sake of distinguishing between the normal (heterosexual) and the ab-normal (homosexual). It seems fair, then, to describe *Cecil Dreeme* as a queer novel, since it doesn't entirely observe or respect that binary distinction (and certainly doesn't frame that distinction in the rigid way that later generations would do). *Cecil Dreeme* depicts some "peculiar" ways of feeling and desiring, relatively unfamiliar to us today, and registers the profound effects of what may have seemed to its author like the faintly incipient and unwelcome emergence of sexual taxonomies that (as it happens, because Theodore Winthrop was killed in the Civil War) he would not live to see put firmly in place. Unlike his reader Henry Blake Fuller (1857–1929), whose life began before the homosexual had fully become, in Michel Foucault's famous phrase, "a species," a recognized type of person,[7] but who did live to see that historical emergence play itself out, Winthrop died in 1861 just as that process of sexual emergence was faintly beginning to get traction. Fuller's youthful recognition of this quality in *Cecil Dreeme*—what he was able in 1875 to call "peculiar" and what we might today call *queer*—hints at the role Winthrop's novel may have played in the lives of other readers who recognized in it something that interested them greatly but that they could not precisely describe. And it suggests as well the agency *Cecil Dreeme* may have exercised in beginning to articulate modern forms of disciplinary sexual identity (the novel taints some forms of desire as "perverse," and there is, after all, a faint odor of suspicion attached to Fuller's adjective "peculiar") as well as articulating countervailing literary resources for erotic dissidence ("It interests me greatly").

At the same time, then, as *Cecil Dreeme* takes its historical place in a genealogy of emergent sexual identities, it also takes its place in a history of resistance to that emergence, because of the share it takes in the devoted preservation of what Peter Coviello has nicely called "all the errant possibilities for imagining sex that have sunk into a kind of muteness with the advent of modern sexuality."[8] *Cecil Dreeme* regrets what it senses as the imminent "deployment of sexuality," in Foucault's terms—the stringent necessity people would soon be under to sign up for (or be assigned to) one sexual category or another.[9] *Cecil Dreeme* thus takes us back to a time before "homosexuality" and "heterosexuality" fully existed—indeed, even before a crisp distinction came to be made between the realms of the sexual and the nonsexual as such.[10] Perhaps the queerest thing about *Cecil Dreeme* is its tense negotiation of the fuzzy boundaries between the realms of the senses that it would designate as, on the one hand, morally blameworthy "sensuality" (184), and, on the other, those it would celebrate as innocent pleasures of the senses.

If you have ever wondered how and why the unnecessary institution of heterosexuality emerged in history, *Cecil Dreeme* has a provocative answer. The novel's date, as I have suggested, is fairly close to one of the usual chronological markers of the advent of heterosexual/homosexual differentiation, that is, the first appearance of the term *homosexual* in print—in German—in 1869 or so.[11] Many historians of sexuality have pointed out how the articulation of one category of sexual existence, homosexuality, implies the existence of its opposite, heterosexuality. *Cecil Dreeme* evocatively captures the feeling of the fraught moment when this strange new thing, heterosexuality, appeared on the historical scene as an untested and not universally welcomed phenomenon—one whose cunning attractions, it appeared to some, might not outweigh its punitive exactions. Heterosexuality, this novel forthrightly claims, is a poor substitute for passionate love between men—and heterosexuality's historical emergence in the nineteenth century is consequently, *Cecil Dreeme* laments, a grave misfortune.

But if we must resign ourselves to the unhappy fate of heterosexuality's emergence and eventual dominance, *Cecil Dreeme* further implies, then perhaps something can be done to make it a tolerable form of life. If only it could be infused, the novel finally suggests, with the passionate intensity that had belonged principally to male same-sex attachments, heterosexuality might then prove to be a more or less satisfactory arrangement. (Readers who don't want the plot's twists to be revealed should postpone reading the rest of this introduction). This is the meager hope with which the novel's narrator, Robert Byng, is left when the man he loved (known to him as Cecil Dreeme) turns out to be a woman (Clara Denman) in male disguise. This revelation creates for Byng a vexatious problem. Can his cherished same-sex love be transmuted, somehow, into heterosexual attachment? Perhaps it can—although Byng continues to refer to his beloved mostly as "he" and "him" and "Cecil Dreeme" even after Clara's true sex and actual name have been revealed (197ff.). "Every moment it came to me more distinctly that Cecil Dreeme and I could never be Damon and Pythias again" (204), Byng laments. He continues: "And now that the friend proved a woman, a great gulf opened between us" (204). "But thinking of what might start up between Cecil Dreeme and me, *and part us*," Byng rues, "I let fall the hand I held" (204, emphasis added). If something were now to "start up" between them—and if Byng could reconcile himself to recognizing her as "Clara," which he continues to be unable or unwilling fully to do even at the novel's end—it seems it would always be an attachment troubled by the sacrifice it exacts from its practitioners, the compulsory abandonment of the prior institution of same-sex friendship.[12] Robert's love for Cecil was fundamentally predicated on his being a man—although, to be sure, a peculiar man, "a man of another order, not easy to classify" (82). If he could now love the woman, Clara, it would be a love always haunted by its need to draw upon and, if possible, transmute the charisma of homoerotic attachment into heterosexual desire.

Here is how it goes. Having been surprised and dismayed by the discovery that the man he loved dearly—the delicately enchanting young painter Cecil Dreeme—was in fact, all along, a young woman in disguise, the novel's narrator is left at the tale's close with a melancholy task ahead of him—converting his powerful love for Cecil into a different, derivative, and denatured kind of love, the love of the woman Clara Denman, who had been masquerading as Cecil. The man Byng has called his "friend of friends" (136, 172), "dearer to me than a brother" (175), "part of my heart" (190)—"this friend closer than a brother was [now] a woman" (197). What can happen to a friendship "more precious than the love of women" (139), "a love passing the love of women" (163), when its object now turns out to be—a woman? It is a bit like what Millamant says to Mirabell in William Congreve's *The Way of the World* (1700), setting out her conditions for consenting to marry him: if he will agree to her various stipulations, she says, it is possible that she "may by degrees dwindle into a wife."[13] *Cecil Dreeme* leaves Robert Byng to wonder what it would mean, and whether he can consent, to dwindle into a husband and, perforce, reconcile himself to being in effect a heterosexual. Byng has spent a considerable portion of his tale describing his never very enthusiastic or strenuous attempts to convince himself to fall in love with a woman ("I loved, or thought I loved, or wished that I loved" another character, he avers, the enchanting Emma Denman [138]; "I had fancied I loved" her, he later admits [166]). But he has all the while been more apt to worry about the dire prospect of being "imprisoned for life in matrimony" (43). It is as if we see him, then, when the gender of his love object has been suddenly switched, internalizing the new coercions of heterosexuality before our eyes. To the revealed Clara he says, "I talked to you and thought of you, although I was not conscious of it, as man does to woman only" (199). Again: "Ignorantly I had loved my friend as one loves a woman only" (204).

One easy mistake to make about this novel's plot, however, is to judge that the eventual revelation of Cecil Dreeme's female identity constitutes a wary retreat from the queer potential that the novel has created. It might seem, to be sure, that Winthrop's novel about a man's love for another man is fatally compromised—or, as some recent readers would have it, rescued—by the belated revelation that one of them is in fact (sigh of relief) a woman. One commentator, for example, writes of Byng and Dreeme that "gradually their comradeship deepens into something more: a friendship 'more precious than the love of women,' reminiscent of the Greek lovers Damon and Pythias." But then he adds, not very coherently, "At last, to the narrator's relief, his heterosexuality is reaffirmed—more or less—when it turns out that the delectable roommate is a woman in disguise."[14] (That "more or less" is a nasty touch: it amounts to a homophobic sneer.) The novel, as I have emphasized, portrays Byng as emphatically *not* relieved to discover that Dreeme is a woman but as in fact quite the opposite: surprised, disappointed, confused, and dismayed. Nor is his "heterosexuality" reaffirmed by this revelation—it is anachronistic to think of him as securely possessing a quality of "heterosexuality" that would be satisfyingly "reaffirmed" by the revelation of Dreeme's female sex. It would be more accurate to say that with the revelation that Cecil is really Clara, the unwelcome fate of heterosexuality is rudely forced upon him.

In a similar vein, another commentator has written that when Dreeme is revealed to be a woman in masculine disguise, "the revelation is startling to Robert who now has an explanation for his sexual attraction to the young man."[15] Again, this gets things desperately— one wants to say deliberately, perversely—wrong. Byng has not been at all troubled by his romantic attraction to Cecil Dreeme; on the contrary, he has felt personally gratified and even morally strengthened by it. Thus he has never felt any need of an "explanation" for this attraction; such a claim betrays, again, an anachronistic imposition of later ideas of sexual normalcy upon a very different nineteenth-century set of assumptions about the moral value and intrinsic beauty of same-sex intimacies. And it prejudicially assumes, to boot, that heterosexual attraction is natural and proper and that its hidden motivating presence here would somehow justify Byng's otherwise inexplicable erotic attraction to another man. *Cecil Dreeme* does not think that there is anything wrong with same-sex passion, that it needs "explanation" or that one would naturally be relieved to have an opportunity to disown it. Could this in fact be what Henry Blake Fuller found so "peculiar" and yet so interesting about it?

Cecil Dreeme's liminal historical position, on the cusp of the invention of sexuality, can be measured by the kinds of responses it began to engender in the decades after its initial popularity and Fuller's intrigued but slightly nervous response to it. Julian Hawthorne in 1887 reviewed "Theodore Winthrop's Writings" and found himself baffled and perturbed by the greater popularity of *Cecil Dreeme* as compared to Winthrop's other novels, which he considered superior. *John Brent*, he writes, is "more mature" in style and "quality of thought," and "its tone is more fresh and wholesome."[16] Hawthorne ratchets up the suggestive moralizing a few pages later on: in *Cecil Dreeme* "the love intrigue is morbid and unwholesome," and the characters are "artificial and unnatural." And there is more: "Cecil Dreeme herself [Hawthorne, unlike Byng, has no trouble assigning her the correct gendered pronoun] never fully recovers from the ambiguity forced upon her by her masculine attire."[17] Tellingly, Winthrop's "unwholesome" production reminds the younger Hawthorne of his father Nathaniel's *Blithedale Romance*, which, as we have hinted, had its own interest in the "beautiful peculiarities" of sexual irregularity.

Theodore Winthrop's other novels—Fuller would have found them all quite "peculiar" too, despite Julian Hawthorne's insistence that they were not "unwholesome" like *Cecil Dreeme*—are ripe with suggestions of same-sex and other queer desires that do not conform to either Winthrop's contemporaries' emergent norms or to what have become ours. *Edwin Brothertoft* (1862), for example, is a historical romance of the American Revolution, in which the narrator is fascinated by nothing so much as the magnificent and evidently locally celebrated moustache that one of the tale's heroes, the patriot Major Peter Skerrett, wears. "On his nut-brown face his blonde moustache lay lovingly curling," we are told.[18] When Skerrett disguises himself as a redcoat officer as part of a plot to rescue Edwin Brothertoft's estranged daughter Lucy—whose coarse and dishonest mother, having deceived Brothertoft into marriage, now intends to marry her daughter unwillingly to an oafish British officer named Kerr—the patriotic destruction of this fabled moustache is called for, since its widespread celebrity would otherwise give Skerrett's true identity away. But Skerrett at the same time fears—because he is dreaming romantically of Lucy, whom he has yet to meet—that without his beauteous and "lovingly curling" moustache he will not make the best first impression on her when he achieves her rescue.

Lucy, for her part, is actively conjuring a mental image of her fondly awaited handsome rescuer and his anticipated virtues: "Truth, Virtue, Courage and the sister qualities, Lucy had dimpled into the bronzed cheeks, as a sailor pricks an anchor, or Polly's name, into a brother tar's arm with Indian ink" (240). It is tempting to say that something like a fantasy of heterosexual romance is being metaphorically converted here into a moment of pricking intimacy between two sailors for whom "Polly" is just the generic name for a little-regretted absence. In *Edwin Brothertoft* nearly every realized affiliation between a man and a woman is ugly and deformed, characterized by treachery and horror; even the promising match between Peter Skerrett and Lucy Brothertoft, once he (sans moustache) does rescue her, is left conspicuously unrealized and strenuously uncertain at the end. "It *seems* the fair beginning of a faithful love" (emphasis added), we hear from the narrator, but he asks nervously whether this love will "end in doubt, sorrow, shame, and forgiveness; or in trust, joy, constancy and peace" (369). That pregnant question is the very last line of the novel, and no answer is given—unless the discouraged answer lies, only partially hidden, in the near-homonymy between "brother tars" and "Brothertoft."

Winthrop's other completed novel, *John Brent* (1862), has an even weirder and richer queer subtext. The first-person narrator, Richard Wade, early in the Western portion of the tale acquires a magnificent black stallion that no one has yet been able to tame and ride. But Wade himself is able to domesticate the steed using the methods of love. "I loved that horse as I have loved nothing else yet, except the other personage for whom he acted,"[19] prefiguring the heroic horse's later crucial mediation of his relationship with the eponymous John Brent, a dear college friend with whom Wade was once intimate and with whom he is now to be reunited. "Brent was [then] a delicate, beautiful, dreamy boy" (41), Wade recalls; he reappears suddenly in Nevada ten years later when Wade, who has been seeking gold, is packing up to return east and care for his widowed—and now dead—sister's two orphaned children. When the long-lost Brent rides toward him Wade first mistakes him at a distance for a handsome Indian brave of the kind that James Fenimore Cooper's pen might have drawn in his lustrous beauty: "'The Adonis of the copper-skins!' I said to myself." And then Wade unabashedly confides to the page: "I wish I was an Indian myself for such a companion; or, better, a squaw, to be made love to by him" (38).

But as Brent draws nearer, Wade begins to recognize him as a deeply tanned white man—"not copper, but bronze" (38)—and, indeed, soon hails him as his beloved school friend, whereupon their interrupted intimacy is resumed and they set out across the prairie together. Brent has changed—those ten years, we learn, have involved struggle and pain, due to a woman's perfidy—but those difficulties, in Brent's own words, "have taken all the girl out of me" (39). And to explain Wade's initial misrecognition, he adds—here it comes again—"'Ten years have presented me with this for a disguise,' said he, giving his moustache a twirl" (39). The moustache aside, however, this doesn't explain Wade's fantasy of being a "squaw" so that he might be "made love to" by a handsome Indian brave; in Winthrop's world, this desire evidently needs no explanation at all.

Although Brent ends up at the novel's end with an anticipated marriage to a fine woman, abetted by his loyal friend Wade, the latter is left alone for the moment with his bated love for Brent—whom he loved, he tells us, "as mature man loves man. I have known no more perfect union than that one friendship. Nothing so tender in any of my transitory loves for women" (57). When this same Richard Wade appears again in another piece of Winthrop's fiction, a long story published in the *Atlantic Monthly*, "Love and Skates" (1862), he is somewhat older and now expressly in search of a wife of his own: he is judged to be "incomplete and abnormal" because he's unmarried.[20]

Wade eventually, like Brent earlier, finds his own excellent woman to marry, but not until he has a peculiarly intense passage with one Bill Tarbox, a rough worker in the Hudson River Valley iron factory Wade has been sent to superintend. Wade and Tarbox are both thirty years old, described as each other's matching physical counterparts, each a "Saxon six-footer" (137, 139). Wade first establishes his managerial authority and manly dominance by beating Tarbox in a fistfight; Tarbox thenceforth respects and admires Wade, and becomes his devoted ally—as well as avid ice-skating partner. When the river freezes over one Christmas Day, and the entire town goes out for a frolic on the ice, Wade and Tarbox have an opportunity to demonstrate their well-rehearsed skill as a figure-skating pair: "Wade backwards, Bill forwards, holding hands . . . both dropped into a sitting posture, with the left knee bent, and each with his right leg stretched out parallel to the ice and fitting compactly by the other man's leg. In this queer figure they rushed through the laughing crowd" (154). A "queer figure" indeed, holding hands face to face and with legs interlaced, but with sharp blades extended in each other's vicinity too—their tense rivalry and their tight attachment both expressed in this peculiar posture.

I have thus far concentrated on representing Winthrop's depiction of same-sex love as a mainly positive phenomenon—and something that threads through many of his published writings—in order to correct a few egregious misrepresentations of *Cecil Dreeme*. But it must be conceded after all that this is itself a rather one-sided account of queer relations in it. This is a novel that presents what I will call a "stereoscopic" picture of male-male love. There are two same-sex love plots in it, one of which I have discussed (involving Byng and Dreeme), which is understood to be beautiful and healthy, while the other (between Byng and a seductive character named Densdeth) is condemned as morbid and suspect. The two queer love plots share the space of the novel uneasily, we might say; the one fits within the literary tradition of exalted same-sex romantic friendship, the other within a competing tradition that Eve Kosofsky Sedgwick has called the "paranoid gothic," characterized by its melodramatic depiction of "homosexual panic."[21]

I borrow the term "stereoscopic" from the novel itself (88). One of the peculiarities of the tale has to do with Byng's nonrecognition of Clara Denman when she is first presented to him in male disguise. This obtuseness may seem implausible to some readers. After all, Byng knew Clara and her sister Emma intimately in childhood, even played "little husband and little wife" with them (112), but oddly he doesn't at all recognize Clara now. True, Byng has been told that Clara is dead, so he does not expect ever to meet her; she is also in masculine disguise, apparently quite convincing; he has been prepared by others in various ways to meet a young man, an artist named Cecil; the room where they first meet is dark; Cecil is pale and wasted with lack of nourishment; and ten years have passed since they last met (when he was fifteen and Clara was several years younger). Clearly Winthrop labors to make this nonrecognition seem passably believable under the circumstances. At several moments in the story Byng *almost* thinks he has seen Cecil before, but he cannot quite remember where or when. Later, Clara says that she recognized him instantly: "I knew you as my old playmate from the first moment" (204). But because he does not appear to recognize her in that first moment, she doesn't reveal herself to him. She is relieved, also, to be able to go unrecognized, since she is in hiding from Densdeth, living in deep fear of being located by him. Dreeme's reclusiveness argues that he has a secret of some kind, and this putative secret continues to stimulate Byng's curiosity even as he feels duty-bound to respect its privacy—but still he never brings himself to recognize Clara in Cecil.

There is certainly something willful in Byng's nonrecognition, as he later comes to admit: "And every moment fancies drift across my mind that I actually know his secret, and am blind, purposely blind to my knowledge, because I promised when we first met that I would be so" (126). When he first encounters Cecil Dreeme, famished and half-conscious, he forbears to look directly at him, thinking it would be rude to stare at someone who was only half awake and too weak to resist uninvited inspection: "Curiosity urged me to study the face more in detail. But that seemed disloyal to the sleeper. . . . I therefore stopped intentionally short of a thorough analysis of his countenance" (81). When Dreeme does become fully conscious, however, Byng looks intently at him, "eye to eye" (87), and he has one of his fleeting sensations of half-recognition: "As we regarded each other earnestly, I perceived the question flit across my mind: 'Had I not had a glimpse of that inspired face before?'" (88). He already knows that Dreeme is a painter, so he immediately thinks of likely places he might have caught sight of him plying his trade in the past (here is where the image of a stereoscope comes in): "I may have seen him copying in the Louvre, sketching in the Oberland, dejected in the Coliseum, elated in St. Peter's, taking his coffee and violets in the Café Doné, whisking by at the Pitti Palace ball. He may have flashed across my sight, and imprinted an image on my brain to which his presence applies the stereoscopic counterpart" (88). The stereoscope (also called a stereograph) was a technology, widely popular in the nineteenth century, for creating the illusion of three-dimensional depth in a photographic image. A pair of almost identical pictures was printed side by side on a single paper card, one a right-eye view and the other a left-eye view of the same scene (that is, the images were captured from fractionally divergent perspectives, as a person's two eyes would see a scene from very slightly different angles). The photographic card was inserted into a viewer (a hand-held viewer, sometimes called a Holmes Stereoscope, after its inventor, Oliver Wendell Holmes, who made this entertainment device affordable for the American market). The parallax effect of the two slightly offset images required that the viewer's brain combine them, as it combined the visual sensations from a viewer's own two slightly divergent eyes, thus producing the appearance of three-dimensional depth of field.[22] Used metaphorically by Winthrop (or, rather, by the narrator Byng), the idea of having seen Dreeme fleetingly once, somewhere in the past, and now having a second image to complete, as it were, the stereoscopic effect, should logically *lead* to recognition rather than stymie it.

But instead of recognizing his old playmate, Byng cannot (or will not) do so, even as he observes that Dreeme appears to recognize him:

> *When he glanced up at me anew, I fancied I saw an evanescent look of recognition drift across his face.*
>
> *This set me a second time turning over the filmy leaves of the book of portraits in my brain. Was his semblance among those legions of faces packed close and set away in order there? No. I could not identify him. The likeness drifted away from me, and vanished. (89)*

As readers we must take *Cecil Dreeme* stereoscopically, as it were: the two queer romances (one beautiful, one sinister) are each other's slightly mismatched counterparts, which, if taken together, produce a historical reality effect. The "stereoscopic counterpart" of the plot of glorious romantic friendship in *Cecil Dreeme* is the counterplot of sinister same-sex attraction centered in the figure of Densdeth. And just as Byng cannot bring his two images of Cecil together, the novel, we might say, does not bring its two homoerotic love plots into a single focus. This is not, in my view, a deficiency at all—rather, it is one of the qualities that makes *Cecil Dreeme* such a powerfully queer witness to the contradictions of its historical moment, its suspension between a prior historical deployment in which same-sex passion was uncontroversial and celebrated and an emerging historical deployment that would soon stigmatize same-sex love as morbid, unwholesome, indecent, and perverse.

Roland Barthes in his classic essay "From Work to Text" (1971) elaborated upon the concept of the *text* (which he famously distinguished from the *work*) by saying that the essential plurality of the *text* will make it seem "stereographic," written from multiple directions and thus necessarily read from multiple angles. "The stereographic plurality of the text" is produced, he said, not merely by the ambiguity of its contents but by the irreducible multiplicity of its "weave of signifiers."[23] This image of the stereographic text also appeared in his *S/Z: An Essay* (1970), where Barthes referred to "the stereographic space of writing."[24] By this he meant to foreground the way in which all writing (understood as *text*) is characterized not by the peaceable coexistence of different meanings but by their irrefragable heterogeneity, their dissemination of meaning. One senses that *Cecil Dreeme* fits the description very well, and not only because, like the Balzac story "Sarrasine" that is Barthes's object of textual analysis in *S/Z*, Winthrop's text too involves gender masquerade. And not only because, as the notes to the present edition show, *Cecil Dreeme* is woven of countless quotations, allusions, and intertexts, from the Bible to ancient mythologies to the Western classics to contemporary literature.

Cecil Dreeme is "stereoscopic" (and slyly tells us that about itself) because its queer-affirmative "romantic friendship" love plot and its gothic "homosexual panic" love plot are so deeply at odds with one another and yet so intimately allied.[25] Byng tells us that Densdeth aims at "perverting" him (39), as he "perverts" Mr. Denman (116), as he has in the past perverted the decrepit college janitor Locksley, and as he is currently trying to pervert another young man, Raleigh. Trying to characterize his magnetic attraction to the darkly handsome Densdeth, Byng reports that he felt "a hateful love for his society" (109). When Densdeth lies dying, stabbed and bleeding, Byng says he knelt down, "raised Densdeth's head" (194), and gently "parted the black hair from his forehead" (195). "There was the man whom I should have loved if I had not hated" (195). "Should have hated if I had not loved" would have done equally well here.

Chapter XX, "A Nocturne," is as good a place as any to observe this "stereoscopic" textuality in a short compass. Robert and Cecil have a habit of taking long walks together at night, when the reclusive painter feels relatively safe from public observation. But on this night the city seems ominous: "Night! When the gas-lights, relit, reawaken harmful purposes, that had slept through all the hours of honest sunshine in their lairs; when the tigers and tigresses take their stand where their prey will be sure to come; when the rustic in the peaceful country, with leaves whispering and crickets singing around him, sees a glow on the distant horizon, and wonders if the bad city beneath it be indeed abandoned of its godly men, and burning for its crimes. Night! The day of the base, the guilty, and the desolate!" (142). The evocation here of Sodom and Gomorrah, the cities of the plain understood to be given over to the carnal wickedness to which the name sodomy was therefore given, destroyed by the Lord, who rained "brimstone and fire" upon them (Genesis 19:24), cannot be accidental. And yet we are also given the thought of a young man in the rural countryside, looking toward what he has been told is the "bad city," and wondering whether it is in fact really "abandoned of its godly men, and burning for its crimes." It is in this very chapter that Dreeme and Byng first touch each other: "He dropped his cloak and took my arm. It was the first time he had given me this slight token of intimacy" (143). The gesture seals their love; they are now "Orestes and Pylades" (144), as they will be "Damon and Pythias" (204), two exemplary classical pairs of same-sex lovers. But then they have a fateful encounter with Densdeth outside a theater, and he recognizes (but conceals his recognition of) Clara Denman in the guise of Cecil Dreeme. The two love plots (the romantic and the sinister) meet and gaze at one another, so to speak—we might almost say *cruise each other*—on the nocturnal streets of New York City.

Editor's Note

Cecil Dreeme has been reproduced here from its first printing (Boston: Ticknor and Fields, 1861) and has not been modernized except in one incidental respect. Contractions have been closed up (e.g., *is n't* becomes *isn't*, *he 's* becomes *he's*, *did n't* becomes *didn't*, *I 've* becomes *I've*, *should n't* becomes *shouldn't*). A few minor typographical errors have also been silently corrected.

The notes to the text at the back of the book, keyed to page numbers, identify quotations and many literary allusions; provide classical, biblical, biographical, and other historical references; translate non-English words and phrases; and provide other kinds of supplementary information.

Engraved by J. C. Buttre.

MAJ THEODORE WINTHROP

THEODORE WINTHROP

From Lillian C. Buttre, *The American Portrait Gallery: With Biographical Sketches of Presidents, Statesmen, Military and Naval Heroes, Clergymen, Authors, Poets, Etc., Etc.*, Vol. II (New York: J. C. Buttre, 1877), n.p.

CECIL DREEME

Biographical Sketch of the Author

George William Curtis

Theodore Winthrop's life, like a fire long smouldering, suddenly blazed up into a clear, bright flame, and vanished. Those of us who were his friends and neighbors, by whose firesides he sat familiarly, and of whose life upon the pleasant Staten Island, where he lived, he was so important a part, were so impressed by his intense vitality, that his death strikes us with peculiar strangeness, like sudden winter-silence falling upon these humming fields of June.

As I look along the wooded brook-side by which he used to come, I should not be surprised if I saw that knit, wiry, light figure moving with quick, firm, leopard tread over the grass,—the keen gray eye, the clustering fair hair, the kind, serious smile, the mien of undaunted patience. If you did not know him, you would have found his greeting a little constrained,—not from shyness, but from genuine modesty and the habit of society. You would have remarked that he was silent and observant, rather than talkative; and whatever he said, however gay or grave, would have had the reserve of sadness upon which his whole character was drawn. If it were a woman who saw him for the first time, she would inevitably see him through a slight cloud of misapprehension; for the man and his manner were a little at variance. The chance is, that at the end of five minutes she would have thought him conceited. At the end of five months she would have known him as one of the simplest and most truly modest of men.

And he had the heroic sincerity which belongs to such modesty. Of a noble ambition, and sensitive to applause,—as every delicate nature veined with genius always is,—he would not provoke the applause by doing anything which, although it lay easily within his power, was yet not wholly approved by him as worthy. Many men are ambitious and full of talent, and when the prize does not fairly come they snatch at it unfairly. This was precisely what he could not do. He would strive and deserve; but if the crown were not laid upon his head in the clear light of day and by confession of absolute merit, he could ride to his place again and wait, looking with no envy, but in patient wonder and with critical curiosity, upon the victors. It is this which he expresses in the paper in the July number of the Atlantic Monthly Magazine, "Washington as a Camp," when he says, "I have heretofore been proud of my individuality, and resisted, so far as one may, all the world's attempts to merge me in the mass."

It was this which made many who knew him much, but not truly, feel that he was purposeless and restless. They knew his talent, his opportunities. Why does he not concentrate? Why does he not bring himself to bear? He did not plead his ill-health; nor would they have allowed the plea. The difficulty was deeper. He felt that he had shown his credentials, and they were not accepted. "I can wait, I can wait," was the answer his life made to the impatience of his friends.

We are all fond of saying that a man of real gifts will fit himself to the work of any time; and so he will. But it is not necessarily to the first thing that offers. There is always latent in civilized society a certain amount of what may be called Sir Philip Sidney genius, which will seem elegant and listless and aimless enough until the congenial chance appears. A plant may grow in a cellar; but it will flower only under the due sun and warmth. Sir Philip Sidney was but a lovely possibility, until he went to be Governor of Flushing. What else was our friend, until he went to the war?

The age of Elizabeth did not monopolize the heroes, and they are always essentially the same. When, for instance, I read in a letter of Hubert Languet's to Sidney, "You are not over-cheerful by nature," or when, in another, he speaks of the portrait that Paul Veronese painted of Sidney, and says, "The painter has represented you sad and thoughtful," I can believe that he is speaking of my neighbor. Or when I remember what Sidney wrote to his younger brother,—"Being a gentleman born, you purpose to furnish yourself with the knowledge of such things as may be serviceable to your country and calling,"—or what he wrote to Languet,—"Our Princes are enjoying too deep a slumber: I cannot think there is any man possessed of common understanding who does not see to what these rough storms are driving by which all Christendom has been agitated now these many years,"—I seem to hear my friend, as he used to talk on the Sunday evenings when he sat in this huge cane-chair at my side, in which I saw him last, and in which I shall henceforth always see him.

Nor is it unfair to remember just here that he bore one of the few really historic names in this country. He never spoke of it; but we should all have been sorry not to feel that he was glad to have sprung straight from that second John Winthrop who was the first Governor of Connecticut, the younger sister colony of Massachusetts Bay,—the John Winthrop who obtained the charter of privileges for his colony. How clearly the quality of the man has been transmitted! How brightly the old name shines out again!

He was born in New Haven on the 22d of September, 1828, and was a grave, delicate, rather precocious child. He was at school only in New Haven, and entered Yale College just as he was sixteen. The pure, manly morality which was the substance of his character, and his brilliant exploits of scholarship, made him the idol of his college friends, who saw in him the promise of the splendid career which the fond faith of students allots to the favorite classmate. He studied for the Clark scholarship, and gained it; and his name, in the order of time, is first upon the roll of that foundation. For the Berkeleian scholarship he and another were judged equal, and, drawing lots, the other gained the scholarship; but they divided the honor.

In college his favorite studies were Greek and mental philosophy. He never lost the scholarly taste and habit. A wide reader, he retained knowledge with little effort, and often surprised his friends by the variety of his information. Yet it was not strange, for he was born a scholar. His mother was the great-granddaughter of old President Edwards; and among his relations upon the maternal side, Winthrop counted six Presidents of colleges. Perhaps also in this learned descent we may find the secret of his early seriousness. Thoughtful and self-criticising, he was peculiarly sensible to religious influences, under which his criticism easily became self-accusation, and his sensitive seriousness grew sometimes morbid. He would have studied for the ministry or a professorship, upon leaving college, except for his failing health.

In the later days, when I knew him, the feverish ardor of the first religious impulse was past. It had given place to a faith much too deep and sacred to talk about, yet holding him always with serene, steady poise in the purest region of life and feeling. There was no franker or more sympathetic companion for young men of his own age than he; but his conversation fell from his lips as unsullied as his soul.

He graduated in 1848, when he was twenty years old; and for the sake of his health, which was seriously shattered,—an ill-health that colored all his life,—he set out upon his travels. He went first to England, spending much time at Oxford, where he made pleasant acquaintances, and walking through Scotland. He then crossed over to France and Germany, exploring Switzerland very thoroughly upon foot,—once or twice escaping great dangers among the mountains,—and pushed on to Italy and Greece, still walking much of the way. In Italy he made the acquaintance of Mr. W. H. Aspinwall, of New York, and upon his return became tutor to Mr. Aspinwall's son. He presently accompanied his pupil and a nephew of Mr. Aspinwall, who were going to a school in Switzerland; and after a second short tour of six months in Europe he returned to New York, and entered Mr. Aspinwall's counting-house. In the employ of the Pacific Steamship Company he went to Panama and resided for about two years, travelling, and often ill of the fevers of the country. Before his return he travelled through California and Oregon,—went to Vancouver's Island, Puget Sound, and the Hudson Bay Company's station there. At the Dalles he was smitten with the smallpox, and lay ill for six weeks. He often spoke with the warmest gratitude of the kind care that was taken of him there. But when only partially recovered he plunged off again into the wilderness. At another time he fell very ill upon the plains, and lay down, as he supposed, to die; but after some time struggled up and on again.

He returned to the counting-room, but, unsated with adventure, joined the disastrous expedition of Lieutenant Strain. During the time he remained with it his health was still more weakened, and he came home again in 1854. In the following year he studied law and was admitted to the bar. In 1856 he entered heartily into the Fremont campaign, and from the strongest conviction. He went into some of the dark districts of Pennsylvania and spoke incessantly. The roving life and its picturesque episodes, with the earnest conviction which inspired him, made the summer and autumn exciting and pleasant. The following year he went to St. Louis to practise law. The climate was unkind to him, and he returned and began the practice in New York. But he could not be a lawyer. His health was too uncertain, and his tastes and ambition allured him elsewhere. His mind was brimming with the results of observation. His fancy was alert and inventive, and he wrote tales and novels. At the same time he delighted to haunt the studio of his friend Church, the painter, and watch day by day the progress of his picture, the Heart of the Andes. It so fired his imagination that he wrote a description of it, in which, as if rivalling the tropical and tangled richness of the picture, he threw together such heaps and masses of gorgeous words that the reader was dazzled and bewildered.

The wild campaigning life was always a secret passion with him. His stories of travel were so graphic and warm, that I remember one evening, after we had been tracing upon the map a route he had taken, and he had touched the whole region into life with his description, my younger brother, who had sat by and listened with wide eyes all the evening, exclaimed with a sigh of regretful satisfaction, as the door closed upon our story-teller, "It's as good as Robinson Crusoe!" Yet, with all his fondness and fitness for that kind of life, or indeed any active administrative function, his literary ambition seemed to be the deepest and strongest.

He had always been writing. In college and upon his travels he kept diaries; and he has left behind him several novels, tales, sketches of travel, and journals. The first published writing of his which is well known is his description, in the June (1861) number of the Atlantic Monthly Magazine, of the March of the Seventh Regiment of New York to Washington. It was charming by its graceful, sparkling, crisp, offhand dash and ease. But it is only the practised hand that can "dash off" effectively. Let any other clever member of the clever regiment, who has never written, try to dash off the story of a day or a week in the life of the regiment, and he will see that the writer did that little thing well because he had done large things carefully. Yet, amid all the hurry and brilliant bustle of the articles, the author is, as he was in the most bustling moment of the life they described, a spectator, an artist. He looks on at himself and the scene of which he is part. He is willing to merge his individuality; but he does not merge it, for he could not.

So, wandering, hoping, trying, waiting, thirty-two years of his life went by, and they left him true, sympathetic, patient. The sharp private griefs that sting the heart so deeply, and leave a little poison behind, did not spare him. But he bore everything so bravely, so silently,—often silent for a whole evening in the midst of pleasant talkers, but not impertinently sad, nor ever sullen,—that we all loved him a little more at such times. The ill-health from which he always suffered, and a flower-like delicacy of temperament, the yearning desire to be of some service in the world, coupled with the curious, critical introspection which marks every sensitive and refined nature and paralyzes action, overcast his life and manner to the common eye with pensiveness and even sternness. He wrote verses in which his heart seems to exhale in a sigh of sadness. But he was not in the least a sentimentalist. The womanly grace of temperament merely enhanced the unusual manliness of his character and impression. It was like a delicate carnation upon the cheek of a robust man. For his humor was exuberant. He seldom laughed loud, but his smile was sweet and appreciative. Then the range of his sympathies was so large, that he enjoyed every kind of life and person, and was everywhere at home. In walking and riding, in skating and running, in games out of doors and in, no one of us all in the neighborhood was so expert, so agile as he. For, above all things, he had what we Yankees call faculty,—the knack of doing everything. If he rode with a neighbor who was a good horseman, Theodore, who was a Centaur, when he mounted, would put any horse at any gate or fence; for it did not occur to him that he could not do whatever was to be done. Often, after writing for a few hours in the morning, he stepped out of doors, and, from pure love of the fun, leaped and turned summersaults on the grass, before going up to town. In walking about the island, he constantly stopped by the road-side fences, and, grasping the highest rail, swung himself swiftly and neatly over and back again, resuming the walk and the talk without delay.

I do not wish to make him too much a hero. "Death," says Bacon, "openeth the gate to good fame." When a neighbor dies, his form and quality appear clearly, as if he had been dead a thousand years. Then we see what we only felt before. Heroes in history seem to us poetic because they are there. But if we should tell the simple truth of some of our neighbors, it would sound like poetry. Winthrop was one of the men who represent the manly and poetic qualities that always exist around us,—not great genius, which is ever salient, but the fine fibre of manhood that makes the worth of the race.

Closely engaged with his literary employments, and more quiet than ever, he took less active part in the last election. But when the menace of treason became an aggressive act, he saw very clearly the inevitable necessity of arms. We all talked of it constantly,—watching the news,—chafing at the sad necessity of delay, which was sure to confuse foreign opinion and alienate sympathy, as has proved to be the case. As matters advanced and the war-cloud rolled up thicker and blacker, he looked at it with the secret satisfaction that war for such a cause opened his career both as thinker and actor. The admirable coolness, the promptness, the cheerful patience, the heroic ardor, the intelligence, the tough experience of campaigning, the profound conviction that the cause was in truth "the good old cause," which was now to come to the death-grapple with its old enemy, Justice against Injustice, Order against Anarchy,—all these should now have their turn, and the wanderer and waiter "settle himself" at last.

We took a long walk together on the Sunday that brought the news of the capture of Fort Sumter. He was thoroughly alive with a bright, earnest forecast of his part in the coming work. Returning home with me, he sat until late in the evening talking with an unwonted spirit, saying playfully, I remember, that, if his friends would only give him a horse, he would ride straight to victory. Especially he wished that some competent person would keep a careful record of events as they passed; "for we are making our history," he said, "hand over hand." He sat quietly in the great chair while he spoke, and at last rose to go. We went together to the door, and stood for a little while upon the piazza, where we had sat peacefully through so many golden summer-hours. The last hour for us had come, but we did not know it. We shook hands, and he left me, passing rapidly along the brook-side under the trees, and so in the soft spring starlight vanished from my sight forever.

The next morning came the President's proclamation. Winthrop went immediately to town and enrolled himself in the artillery corps of the Seventh Regiment. During the two or three following days he was very busy and very happy. On Friday afternoon, the 19th of April, 1861, I stood at the corner of Courtland Street and saw the regiment as it marched away. Two days before, I had seen the Massachusetts troops going down the same street. During the day the news had come that they were already engaged, that some were already dead in Baltimore. And the Seventh, as they went, blessed and wept over by a great city, went, as we all believed, to terrible battle. The setting sun in a clear April sky shone full up the street. Mothers' eyes glistened at the windows upon the glistening bayonets of their boys below. I knew that Winthrop and other dear friends were there, but I did not see them. I saw only a thousand men marching like one hero. The music beat and rang and clashed in the air. Marching to death or victory or defeat, it mattered not. They marched for Justice, and God was their captain.

From that moment he has told his own story until he went to Fortress Monroe, and was made acting military secretary and aid by General Butler. Before he went, he wrote the most copious and gayest letters from the camp. He was thoroughly aroused, and all his powers happily at play. In a letter to me soon after his arrival in Washington, he says:—

"I see no present end to this business. We must conquer the South. Afterward we must be prepared to do its police in its own behalf, and in behalf of its black population, whom this war must, without precipitation, emancipate. We must hold the South as the metropolitan police holds New York. All this is inevitable. Now I wish to enroll myself at once in the *Police of the Nation,* and for life, if the nation will take me. I do not see that I can put myself—experience and character—to any more useful use. . . . . . My experience in this short campaign with the Seventh assures me that volunteers are for one purpose and regular soldiers entirely another. We want regular soldiers for the cause of order in these anarchical countries, and we want men in command who, though they may be valuable as temporary satraps or proconsuls to make liberty possible where it is now impossible, will never under any circumstances be disloyal to *Liberty,* will always oppose any scheme of any one to constitute a military government, and will be ready, when the time comes, to imitate Washington. We must think of these things, and prepare for them. . . . . . Love to all the dear friends. . . . . . This trip has been all a lark to an old tramper like myself."

Later he writes:—

"It is the loveliest day of fullest spring. An aspen under the window whispers to me in a chorus of all its leaves, and when I look out, every leaf turns a sunbeam at me. I am writing in Viele's quarters in the villa of Somebody Stone, upon whose place or farm we are encamped. The man who built and set down these four great granite pillars in front of his house, for a carriage-porch, had an eye or two for a fine *site*. This seems to be the finest possible about Washington. It is a terrace called Meridian Hill, two miles north of Pennsylvania Avenue. The house commands the vista of the Potomac, all the plain of the city, and a charming lawn of delicious green, with oaks of first dignity just coming into leaf. It is lovely Nature, and the spot has snatched a grace from Art. The grounds are laid out after a fashion, and planted with shrubbery. The snowballs are at their snowballiest. . . . . . Have you heard or—how many times have you used the simile of some one, Bad-muss or Cadmus, or another hero, who sowed the dragon's teeth, and they came up dragoons a hundred-fold and infantry a thousand-fold? *Nil admirari* is, of course, my frame of mind; but I own astonishment at the crop of soldiers. They must ripen awhile, perhaps, before they are to be named quite soldiers. Ripening takes care of itself; and by the harvest-time they will be ready to cut down.

"I find that the men best informed about the South do not anticipate much severe fighting. Scott's Fabian policy will demoralize their armies. If the people do not bother the great Cunctator to death before he is ready to move to assured victory, he will make defeat impossible. Meanwhile there will be enough outwork going on, like those neat jobs in Missouri, to keep us all interested. . . . . . Know, O comrade, that I am already a corporal,—an acting corporal, selected by our commanding officer for my general effect of pipe-clay, my rapidity of heel and toe, my present arms, etc., but liable to be ousted by suffrage any moment. *Quod faustum sit,* . . . . . I had already been introduced to the Secretary of War. . . . . . I called at ———'s and saw, with two or three others, ——— on the sofa. Him my prophetic soul named my uncle Abe. . . . . . But in my uncle's house are many nephews, and whether nepotism or my transcendent merit will prevail we shall see. I have fun,—I get experience,—I see much,—it pays. Ah, yes! But in these fair days of May I miss my Staten Island. War stirs the pulse, but it wounds a little all the time.

"Compliment for me Tib [a little dog] and the Wisterias,—also the mares and the billiard-table. Ask —— to give you t' other lump of sugar in my behalf. . . . . . Should —— return, say that I regret not being present with an unpremeditated compliment, as thus,—'Ah! the first rose of summer!' . . . . . I will try to get an enemy's button for ——, should the enemy attack. If the Seventh returns presently, I am afraid I shall be obliged to return with them for a time. But I mean to see this job through, somehow."

In such an airy, sportive vein he wrote, with the firm purpose and the distinct thought visible under the sparkle. Before the regiment left Washington, as he has recorded, he said good-by and went down the bay to Fortress Monroe. Of his unshrinking and sprightly industry, his good head, his warm heart, and cool hand, as a soldier, General Butler has given precious testimony to his family. "I loved him as a brother," the General writes of his young aid.

The last days of his life at Fortress Monroe were doubtless also the happiest. His energy and enthusiasm, and kind, winning ways, and the deep satisfaction of feeling that all his gifts could now be used as he would have them, showed him and his friends that his day had at length dawned. He was especially interested in the condition and fate of the slaves who escaped from the neighboring region and sought refuge at the fort. He had never for an instant forgotten the secret root of the treason which was desolating the land with war; and in his view there would be no peace until that root was destroyed. In his letters written from the fort he suggests plans of relief and comfort for the refugees; and one of his last requests was to a lady in New York for clothes for these poor pensioners. They were promptly sent, but reached the fort too late.

As I look over these last letters, which gush and throb with the ful-ness of his activity, and are so tenderly streaked with touches of con-stant affection and remembrance, yet are so calm and duly mindful of every detail, I do not think with an elder friend, in whom the wisdom of years has only deepened sympathy for all generous youthful impulse, of Virgil's Marcellus, "Heu, miserande puer!" but I recall rather, still haunted by Philip Sidney, what he wrote, just before his death, to his father-in-law, Walsingham,—"I think a wise and constant man ought never to grieve while he doth play, as a man may say, his own part truly."

The sketches of the campaign in Virginia, which Winthrop had commenced in the Atlantic Monthly Magazine, would have been continued, and have formed an invaluable memoir of the places, the men, and the operations of which he was a witness and a part. As a piece of vivid pictorial description, which gives the spirit as well as the spectacle, his "Washington as a Camp" is masterly. He knew not only what to see and to describe, but what to think; so that in his papers you are not at the mercy of a multitudinous mass of facts, but understand their value and relation.

●   ●   ●   ●   ●

The disastrous day of the 10th of June, at Great Bethel, need not be described here. It is already written with tears and vain regrets in our history. It is useless to prolong the debate as to where the blame of the defeat, if blame there were, should rest. But there is an impression somewhat prevalent that Winthrop planned the expedition, which is incorrect. As military secretary of the commanding general, he made a memorandum of the outline of the plan as it had been finally settled. Precisely what that memorandum (which has been published) was, he explains in the last letter he wrote, a few hours before leaving the fort. He says: "If I come back safe, I will send you my notes of the plan of attack, part made up from the General's hints, part my own fancies." This defines exactly his responsibility. His position as aid and military secretary, his admirable qualities as adviser under the circumstances, and his personal friendship for the General, brought him intimately into the council of war. He embarked in the plan all the interest of a brave soldier contemplating his first battle. He probably made suggestions some of which were adopted. The expedition was the first move from Fort Monroe, to which the country had been long looking in expectation. These were the reasons why he felt so peculiar a responsibility for its success; and after the melancholy events of the earlier part of the day, he saw that its fortunes could be retrieved only by a dash of heroic enthusiasm. Fired himself, he sought to kindle others. For one moment that brave, inspiring form is plainly visible to his whole country, rapt and calm, standing upon the log nearest the enemy's battery, the mark of their sharpshooters, the admiration of their leaders, waving his sword, cheering his fellow-soldiers with his bugle voice of victory,—young, brave, beautiful, for one moment erect and glowing in the wild whirl of battle, the next falling forward toward the foe, dead, but triumphant.

On the 19th of April, 1861, he left the armory-door of the Seventh, with his hand upon a howitzer; on the 21st of June his body lay upon the same howitzer at the same door, wrapped in the flag for which he gladly died as the symbol of human freedom. And so, drawn by the hands of young men lately strangers to him, but of whose bravery and loyalty he had been the laureate, and who fitly mourned him who had honored them, with long, pealing dirges and muffled drums, he moved forward.

Yet such was the electric vitality of this friend of ours, that those of us who followed him could only think of him as approving the funeral pageant, not the object of it, but still the spectator and critic of every scene in which he was a part. We did not think of him as dead. We never shall. In the moist, warm midsummer morning, he was alert, alive, immortal.

Chapter I

Stillfleet and His News

Home!

The Arago landed me at midnight in midwinter. It was a dreary night. I drove forlornly to my hotel. The town looked mean and foul. The first omens seemed unkindly. My spirits sank full fathom five into Despond.

But bed on shore was welcome after my berth on board the steamer. I was glad to be in a room that did not lurch or wallow, and could hold its tongue. I could sleep, undisturbed by moaning and creaking wood-work, forever threatening wreck in dismal refrain.

It was late next morning when a knock awoke me. I did not say, "Entrez," or "Herein."

Some fellows adopt those idioms after a week in Paris or a day in Heidelberg, and then apologize,—"We travellers quite lose our mother tongue, you know."

"Come in," said I, glad to use the vernacular.

A Patrick entered, brandishing a clothes-broom as if it were a shillalah splintered in a shindy.

"A jontlemin wants to see yer honor," said he.

A gentleman to see me! Who can it be? I asked myself. Not Densdeth already! No, he is probably also making a late morning of it after our rough voyage. I fear I should think it a little ominous if he appeared at the threshold of my home life, as my first friend in America. Bah! Why should I have superstitions about Densdeth? Our intimacy on board will not continue on shore. "What's Hecuba to me, or I to Hecuba?"

"A jontlemin to see yer honor," repeated the Pat, with a peremptory flourish of his weapon.

"What name, Patrick?"

"I misremember the name of him, yer honor. He's a wide-awake jontlemin, with three mustasshes,—two on his lip, and one at the pint of his chin."

Can it be Harry Stillfleet? I thought. He cannot help being wide-awake. He used to wear his beard *à la* three-moustache mode. His appearance as my first friend would be a capital omen. "Show him up, Pat!" said I.

"He shows himself up," said a frank, electric voice. "Here he is, wide-awake, three moustaches, first friend, capital omen. Hail Columbia! beat the drums! Robert Byng, old boy, how are you?"

"Harry Stillfleet, old boy, how are you?"

"I am an old boy, and hope you are so too."

"I trust so. It is the best thing that can be said of a full-grown man."

"I saw your name on the hotel book," Stillfleet resumed. "Rushed in to say, 'How d' ye do?' and 'Good-bye!' I'm off to-day. Any friends out in the Arago?"

"No friends. A few acquaintances,—and Densdeth."

"Name Densdeth friend, and I cut you bing-bang!"

"What! Densdeth, the cleverest man I have ever met?"

"The same."

"Densdeth, handsome as Alcibiades, or perhaps I should say Absalom, as he is Hebrewish?"

"That very Alcibiades,—Absalom,—Densdeth."

"Densdeth, the brilliant, the accomplished,—who fascinates old and young, who has been everywhere, who has seen everything, who knows the world *de profundis,*—a very Midas with the gold touch, but without the ass's ears? Densdeth, the potent millionnaire?"

"Yes, Byng. And he can carry a great many more adjectives. He has qualities enough to make a regiment of average men. But my friends must be built of other stuff."

"So must mine, to tell the truth, Harry. But he attracts me strangely. His sardonic humor suits one side of my nature."

"The cynical side?"

"If I have one. The voyage would have been a bore without him. I had never met and hardly heard of him before; but we became intimate at once. He has shown me much attention."

"No doubt. He knows men. You have a good name. You are to be somebody on your own account, we hope. Besides, Densdeth was probably aware of your old friendship with the Denmans."

"He never spoke of them."

"Naturally. He did not wish to talk tragedy."

"Tragedy! What do you mean?"

"You have not heard the story of Densdeth and Clara Denman!" cried Stillfleet, in surprise.

"No. Shut up in Leipsic, and crowding my studies to come home, I have not heard a word of New York gossip for six months."

"This is graver than gossip, Byng. It happened less than three months ago. Densdeth was to have married Clara Denman."

"The cynical Densdeth marry that strange child!"

"You forget your ten years' absence. The strange child grew up a noble woman."

"Not a beauty,—that I cannot conceive."

"No; but a genius. Once in a century Nature sends such a brave, earnest, tender, indignant soul on this low earth. All the men of genius were in love with her, except myself. But Densdeth, a bad genius, seemed to have won her. The wedding-day was fixed, cards out, great festivities; you know how a showy man like Denman would seize the occasion for splendor. One night she disappeared without sign. Three days afterward she was floated upon the beach down the bay,— drowned, poor thing!"

"What!" cried I, "Clara Denman, my weird little playmate! Dead! Drowned! I did not imagine how tenderly I had remembered her."

"I was not her lover," said Harry, "only a friend; but the world has seemed a mean and lonely place since she passed away so cruelly."

The mercurial fellow was evidently greatly affected.

"She had that fine exaltation of nature," continued he, "which frightens weak people. They said her wild, passionate moods brought her to the verge of madness."

"A Sibylline soul."

"Yes, a Sibyl who must see and know and suffer. Her friends gave out that she had actually gone mad with a fever, and so, while her nurse was asleep, she stole out, erred about the city, fell into the river, and was drowned."

"Not suicide!"

"Never! with such a healthy soul. Yet some people do not hesitate to say that she drowned herself rather than be forced to marry Densdeth."

"These are not the days of forced marriages."

"Moral pressure is more despotic than physical force. I fancy our old friend Churm may think there was tyranny in the business, though he never speaks of it. You know he was a supplementary father and guardian of those ladies. He was absent when it all happened."

"And the Denmans,—how do they seem to bear it?"

"Mr. Denman was sadly broken at first. I used to meet him, walking about, leaning feebly on Densdeth's arm, looking like a dead man, or one just off the rack. But he is proud as Lucifer. He soon was himself again, prouder than before."

"And Emma Denman?"

"I have had but one glimpse of her since the younger sister's death. Her beauty is signally heightened by mourning."

"Such a tragedy must terribly blight her life. Will they see me, do you think? I should like to offer my sympathy, for old friendship's sake."

"As an old friend, they will see you, of course. In fact, conspicuous people, like the Denmans, cannot long shelter themselves behind a sorrow. But come, old fellow, I have been talking solemnly long enough. Tell me about yourself. Come home ripe? Wild oats sowed? Ready to give us a lift with civilization?"

"Ripe, I hope. Not raw, as I went. Nor rotten, as some fellows return. Wild oats? I keep a few handfuls still in my bag, for home sowing. As to civilization; let me get my *pou stô* and my handspike set, and I will heave with a will, lift or no."

"Suppose you state your case in full, as if you were a clown in the ring, or a hero on the stage."

I had been dressing while he talked. My toilette was nearly done. I struck an attitude and replied, "My name is Robert Byng, 'as I sailed.'"

"Name short, and with a good crack to it; man long and not whipper-snapper. Name distinguished; bearer capable. State your age, Byng the aforesaid."

"Twenty-six."

"The prisoner confesses to twenty-six. The judge in the name of the American people demands, 'Why then haven't you been five years at the bar, or ten years at the desk? Why are you not in command of a clipper ship, or in Congress, or driving an omnibus, or clearing a farm? Where is your door-plate? Where is your wife? What school does your eldest son go to? Where is your mark on the nineteenth century?'"

"Bah, Harry! Don't bore me with your Young Americanism! I know it is not sincere. Let me mature, before you expect a man's work of me!"

"The culprit desires to state," says Stillfleet, as if he were addressing an audience, "that he was born to a fortune and a life of idleness and imbecility, that he would gladly be imbecile and idle now, like *nous autres;* but that losing his parents and most of his money at an unsophisticated age, while in Europe, he consulted the Oracle how he should make his living. 'What is that burn on your thumb?' asked the Oracle. 'Phosphorus,' replied Master Bob. 'How came that hole in your sleeve?' Oracle inquires. 'Nitric acid,' Byng responds. 'It was the cat that scratched your face?' says Oracle. 'No,' answers the youth, 'my retort burst before it was half full of gas.' 'Phosphorus on your thumb,' Oracle sums up, 'nitric acid on your sleeve, and your face clawed with gas explosions,—there is only one thing for you to do. Be a chemist!' Which he became. Is that a straight story, Byng?"

"Near enough!" said I, laughing at my friend's rattling history of my life.

"And here he is, fellow-citizens," Stillfleet continued. "He has seen the world and had his fling in Paris, where he picked up a little chemistry and this half-cynical manner and half-sceptical method, which you remark. He has also got a small supply of science and an abundance of dreaminess and fatalism in Germany. But he is a fine fellow, with a good complexion, not dishonest blue eyes, not spoilt in any way, and if America punishes him properly, and puts his nose severely to the grindstone, he may turn out respectable. I'll offer you three to two, Byng, the Devil don't get you. Speak quick, or I shall want to bet even."

"You rascal!" said I. "I would go at you with an analysis after the same fashion, if I were not too hungry. Come down and breakfast."

"Here is a gentleman from Sybaris!" cried Stillfleet. "'Come and breakfast!' says he, lifting himself out of his bed of rose-leaves at midday. Why, man! I breakfasted three hours ago. I've been up to the

Reservoir and down to the Exchange and over to Brooklyn since. That's the style you have to learn, twenty thousand miles an hour, hurrah boys! go ahead! 'En avant, marrche!' 'Marrrrche!' Yes; I took breakfast three hours ago,—and a stout one,—to fortify me for the toil of packing to go to Washington. But I'll sit by and check your come-ashore appetite."

CHAPTER II

Chrysalis College

Stillfleet escorted me down to the long, desolate dining-room of my hotel, the Chuzzlewit.

The great Chuzzlewit dined there on his visit to America, and damned his dinner with such fine irony, that the proprietor thought himself complimented, and re-baptized his hotel.

"Here you are," said my friend, "at a crack house on the American plan. You can breakfast on fried beefsteak, hard eggs, *café au delay,* soggy toast, flannel cakes, blanket cakes, and wash-leather cakes. You can dine on mock soup, boiled porpoise, beef in the raw or in the chip, watery vegetables, quoit pies, and can have your choice at two dollars a bottle of twelve kinds of wine, all mixed in the same cellar, and labelled in the same shop. You can sup on soused tea, dusty sponge-cake, and Patrick *à discrétion.* How do you like the bill of fare?"

"Marine appetites are not discriminating. But, Harry," I continued, when I had ordered my breakfast, "you spoke of going to Washington. I thought only raff—Congressmen, contractors, and tide-waiters—went there."

"Civilization makes its missionaries acquainted with strange lodgings. They are building a big abortion of a new Capitol. I go, as an architect, to expunge a little of the Goth and the Vandal out of their sham-classic plans."

"Beware! Reform too soon, and you risk ostracism. But before you go, advise me. Where am I to live? Evidently not here at the Chuzzlewit. Here the prices are large, and the rooms little. I must have a den of my own, where I can swing a cat, a longish cat."

"Why not take my place off my hands? It is big enough to swing a royal Bengal tiger in. I meant to lock it up, but you shall occupy and enjoy, if you like. It's a grand chance, old fellow. There's not such another Rubbish Palace in America."

"Excellent!" said I. "But will you trust me with your plunder?"

"Will I trust *you?* Haven't we been brats together, lads together, men together?"

"We have."

"Haven't we been comrades in robbing orchards, mobbing tutors, spoiling the Egyptians of mummies, pillaging the Tuileries in '48. Haven't we been the historic friends, Demon and Pythagoras,—no, Damon and Pythias? Answer me that!"

"We have."

"Well, then, enter my shop, studio, palace, and use and abuse my tools, rubbish, valuables, as you like. Really, Byng, it will be a great favor if you will fill my quarters, and keep down the rats with my rat rifle, while I am in Washington trying to decorate the Representative Chamber so that it will shame blackguards to silence."

"Now," said I, after a pause, and a little stern champing over a tough Chuzzlewit chop, "all ready, Harry; conduct me to your den."

We left the Chuzzlewit by the side door on Mannering Place, and descended from Broadway as far as Ailanthus Square. On the corner, fronting that mean, shabby enclosure, Stillfleet pointed out a huge granite or rough marble building.

"There I live," said he. "It's not a jail, as you might suppose from its grimmish aspect. Not an Asylum. Not a Retreat. No lunatics, that I know of, kept there, nor anything mysterious, guilty, or out of the way."

"Chrysalis College, is it not?"

"You have not forgotten its monastic phiz?"

"No; I remember the sham convent, sham castle, modern-antique affair. But how do you happen to be quartered there? Is the College defunct?"

"Not defunct; only without vitality. The Trustees fancied that, if they built roomy, their college would be populous; if they built marble, it would be permanent; if they built Gothic, it would be scholastic and mediæval in its influences; if they had narrow, mullioned windows, not too much disorganizing modern thought would penetrate."

"Well, and what was the result?"

"The result is, that the old nickname of Chrysalis sticks to it, and whatever real name it may have is forgotten. There it stands, big, battlemented, buttressed, marble, with windows like crenelles; and inside they keep up the traditional methods of education."

"But pupils don't beleaguer it?"

"That is the blunt fact. It stays an ineffectual high-low school. The halls and lecture-rooms would stand vacant, so they let them to lodgers."

"You are not very grateful to your landlords."

"I pay my rent, and have a right to criticise."

"Who live there besides you?"

"Several artists, a brace of young doctors, one or two quiet men about town, Churm, and myself."

"Churm! How is that noble old fellow? I count upon reclaiming his friendship."

"How is Churm? Just the same. Tranquil sage; headlong boy. An aristocratic radical. A Timon without gall. Says the wisest things; does the kindest. Knows everything; and yet is always ready for the new truth that nullifies the old facts. He cannot work inside of the institutions of society. He calls them 'shingle-cells,' tight and transitory. He cannot get over his cynical way of putting a subject, though there is no cynic in his heart. So the world votes him odd, and lets him have his own way."

"Lucky to get liberty at cost of a nickname! Who would not be called odd to be left free?"

"If Churm were poor, he would be howled at as a radical, a destructive, an infidel."

"I suppose he is too rich and powerful to be harmed, and too intrepid to care."

"Yes; and then there is something in Churm's vigor that disarms opposition. His generosity hoists people up to his level. But here we are, Byng, at the grand portal of the grand front."

"I see the front and the door. Where is the grandeur?"

"Don't put on airs, stranger! We call this imposing, magnifique, in short, pretty good. Up goes your nose! You have lived too long in

Florence. Brunelleschi and Giotto have spoilt you. Well, I will show you
something better inside. Follow me!"

We entered the edifice, half college, half lodging-house, through a
large doorway, under a pointed arch. The interior was singularly ill-
contrived. A lobby opened at the door, communicating with a dim corridor running through the middle of the building, parallel to the front.
A fan-tracery vaulting of plaster, peeled and crumbling, ceiled the
lobby. A marble stairway, with iron hand-rails, went squarely and
clumsily up from the door, nearly filling the lobby.

Stillfleet led the way up-stairs.

He pointed to the fan-tracery.

"This of course reminds you of King's College Chapel," said he.

"Entirely," replied I. "Pity it is deciduous!" and I brushed off from
my coat several flakes of its whitewash.

The stairs landed us on the main floor of the building. Another
dimly lighted corridor, answering to the one below, but loftier, ran from
end to end of the building. This also was paved with marble tiles. Large
Gothicish doors opened along on either side. The middle room on the
rear of the corridor was two stories high, and served as chapel and
lecture-room. On either side of this, a narrow staircase climbed to the
upper floors.

By the half-light from the great window over the doorway where we
had entered, and from a small single mullioned window at the northern
end of the corridor, there was a bastard mediævalism of effect in Chrysalis, rather welcome after the bald red-brick houses without.

"How do you like it?" asked Stillfleet. "It's not old enough to be romantic. But then it does not smell of new paint, as the rest of America
does."

We turned up the echoing corridor toward the north window. We
passed a side staircase and a heavily padlocked door on the right. On
the left was a class-room. The door was open. We could see a swarm
of collegians buzzing for such drops of the honey of learning as they
could get from a lank plant of a professor.

We stopped at the farther door on the right, adjoining the one so
carefully padlocked. It bore my friend's plate,—

H. STILLFLEET,

ARCHITECT.

CHAPTER III

————◆————

Rubbish Palace

Stillfleet drew a great key, aimed at the keyhole, and snapped the bolt, all with a mysterious and theatrical air.

"Now," said he, "how is your pulse?"

"Steady and full. Why shouldn't it be?"

"Shut your eyes, then! Open sesame! Eyes tight? Enter into Rubbish Palace!"

He led me several steps forward.

"Open!" he commanded.

"Where am I?" I cried, staring about in surprise.

"City of Manhattan, corner of Mannering Place and Ailanthus Square, Chrysalis College Buildings."

"Harry," said I, "this is magic, phantasmagoria. Outside was the nineteenth century; here is the fifteenth. When I shut my eyes, I was in a seedy building in a busy modern town; I open them, and here I am in the Palazzo Sforza of an old Italian city, in the great chamber where there was love and hate, passion and despair, revelry and poison, long before Columbus cracked the egg."

"It is rather a rum old place," said Stillfleet, twisting his third moustache, and enjoying my surprise.

"Trot out your Bengal tiger. Let me swing him, and measure the dimensions."

"Tiger and I did that long ago. It is thirty feet square and seventeen high."

"Built for some grand college purpose, I suppose."

"As a hall, I believe, for the dons to receive lions on great occasions. But lions and great occasions never come. So I have inherited. It is the old story. '*Sic vos non vobis ædificatis ædes.*' How do you like it? Not too sombre, eh? with only those two narrow windows opening north?"

"Certainly not too sombre. I don't want the remorseless day staring in upon my studies. How do I like it? Enormously. The place is a romance."

"It is Dantesque, Byronic, Victor Hugoish."

"Yes," said I, looking up. "I shall be sure of rich old morbid fancies under this ceiling, with its frescoed arabesques, faded and crumbling."

"You have a taste for the musty, then," said Harry.

"Anything is better than the raw. The Chuzzlewit has given me enough of that. Well, Harry, your den is my den, if you say so."

"Yours to have and to hold while I am gone, and much romance may you find here. Let me show you the whole. Here's my bath-room, 'replete,' as the advertisements say, 'with every convenience.' Here, alongside, is my bedroom."

He opened doors in the wall opposite the windows.

"A gilded bedstead!" said I.

"It was Marshal Soult's, bought cheap at his sale."

"A yellow satin coverlet!"

"Louis Philippe's. Citizen Sabots stole it from the Tuileries in '48 and sold it to me."

"But what is this dark cavern, next the bedroom?" I asked. "Where does that door at the back open?"

"Oh! that is my trash room. Those boxes contain 'Raphaels, Correggios, and stuff.' I was jockeyed with old masters once, as my compatriots still are. I don't hang them up and post myself for a greenhorn."

"But that door at the back?"

"What are you afraid of, Byng?"

"I ask for information."

"Your voice certainly trembled. No danger. Rachel will never peer through and hiss '*Le flambeau fume encore.*' No Lady Macbeth will march in, wringing her hands that never will be clean."

"I hope not, I am sure."

"It is clear you expect it. Your tone is ominous."

"Indeed. A Palazzo Sforza style of place inspires Palazzo Sforza fancies, perhaps. But really, Harry, where does the door open?"

"It does not open, and probably will not till doomsday. It is bolted solid on my side, whatever it be on the other. It leads to a dark room."

"A dark room! that is Otrantoish."

"A windowless room, properly an appendage to this. But there is another door on the corridor. You may have noticed it, closed with a heavy padlock. The tenant enters there, and asks no right of way of me."

"The tenant, who is he? I should know my next neighbor."

"You know him already."

"Don't play with my curiosity. Name."

"Densdeth."

"Densdeth," I repeated, aware of a slight uneasiness. "What use has he for a dark room?—here, too, in this public privacy of Chrysalis?"

"The publicity makes privacy. Densdeth says it is his store-room for books and furniture."

"Well, why not? You speak incredulously."

"Because there is a faint suspicion that he lies. The last janitor, an ex-servant of Densdeth's, is dead. None now is allowed to enter there except the owner's own man, a horrid black creature. He opens the door cautiously, and a curtain appears. He closes the door before he lifts it. Densdeth may pestle poisons, grind stilettos, sweat eagles, revel by gas-light there. What do I know?"

"You are not inquisitive, then, in Chrysalis."

"No. We have no *concierge* by the street-door to spy ourselves or our visitors. We can live here in completer privacy than anywhere in Christendom. Daggeroni, De Bogus, or Mademoiselle des Mollets might rendezvous with my neighbor, and I never be the wiser."

"Well, if Densdeth is well bolted out of my quarters, I will not pry into his. And now I'll look about a little at your treasures."

"Do; while I finish packing. I cannot quite decide about taking clean shirts to Washington. In a clean shirt I might abash a Senator."

"Abash without mercy! the country will thank you," said I. "But, old fellow, what a wealth of art, virtu, and rococo you have here!"

"I have sampled all the ages of the world. No era has any right to complain of neglect," says Stillfleet, patronizingly. "You will find specimens of the arts from Tubal Cain's time down. One does not prowl about Europe ten years without making a fair bag of plunder. How old Churm enjoys my old books, old plates, and old *objets!*"

"I hope he will not desert the place when its proper master is gone. Where are his quarters in Chrysalis?"

"Story above, southwest corner, with an eye to the sunset. Odd fellow he is! He lurks here in a little hermit cell, when he might live in a gold house with diamond window-panes."

"Is he so rich?"

"Crœsus was a barefooted pauper to him."

"Not a miser,—that I know."

"No; he spends as a prairie gives crops. But always for others. He would be too lavish, if he were not discretion itself. Only his personal habits are ascetic."

"Perhaps he once had to harden himself sternly against a sorrow, and so asceticism grew a habit."

"Perhaps. He is a lonely man. Well, here I am, packed, abashing shirts and all! Come down now. I must exhibit you, as my successor, to Locksley, the janitor of Chrysalis,—and a capital good fellow he is."

CHAPTER IV

The Palace and Its Neighbors

Stillfleet and I passed out into the chilly marble-paved corridor.
The young Chrysalids in the class-room seemed to be in high revolt. They were mobbing their lank professor. We could see the confusion through the open door.

"He takes it meekly, you see," said Stillfleet. "He knows that the hullabaloo isn't half punishment enough for his share in the fiction of calling the place a college."

We descended the main stairway. The whitewashed fan-tracery snowed its little souvenir on us as we passed. On the ground floor, a few steps along the damp corridor, was the door marked "Janitor."

Stillfleet pulled the bell. A cheerful, handsome, housewifely woman opened.

"Can we come in, Mrs. Locksley?" said my friend.

"You are always welcome, Mr. Stillfleet."

We entered a compact little snuggery. There was something infinitely honest and trusty in the effect and atmosphere of the place.

Three junior Locksleys caught sight of Stillfleet. They rushed at him, with shouts and gambols enough for a dozen.

I love to see children kitten it securely about a young man. They know friends and foes without paying battles and wounds for the knowledge. They seem to divine a sour heart, a stale heart, or a rotten heart, by unerring instinct. If a man is base metal, he may pass current with the old counterfeits like himself; children will not touch him.

"The world has smoked and salted me," said Stillfleet, "and tried to cure me hard as an old ham. But there is a fresh spot inside me, Byng, and juveniles always find it. I've come to say good-bye, children," he continued; "but here's Mr. Bob Byng, he'll take my place. His head is full of fairy stories for Dora. His fingers make windmills and pop-guns almost without knowing it. Think of that, Hall!"

Dora, a pretty damsel of twelve, and Hall, a ten-year-old male and sturdy, inspected me critically. Was I bogus? Their looks said, they thought not.

"As for Key Locksley here," said Harry, "all he wants is romp and sugar-plums. This is Mr. Byng, Key. 'Some in his pocket and some in his sleeve, he's made of sugar-plums I do believe.'"

So Master Key, a toddler, accepted me as his Lord Chief Confectioner.

"Now, children," said Stillfleet, with mock gravity, "be Mr. Byng's monitors. Require him to set you a good example. Tell him young men generally go to the bad without children to watch over them."

"Many a true word is spoken in jest," said Mrs. Locksley.

"But where is your husband?" my friend asked. "I must exhibit his new tenant to him."

"Coming, sir!" said a voice from the bedroom adjoining.

I had heard a rustling and crackling there, as if some one was splitting his way into a starchy clean shirt.

At the word, out came Locksley, a bristly little man. His hair and beard were so stiff that I fancied at once he could discharge a volley of hairs, as a porcupine shoots quills at a foe. This bristliness and a pair of keen black eyes gave him a sharp, alert, and warlike look, as if he were quick to take alarm, but not likely to be frightened. No danger of the hobbledehoys of Chrysalis, the College, riding roughshod over such a janitor.

I detected him as a man who had seen better days, and hoped to see them again, by his shirt-collars. They were stiff as Calvinism and white as Spitzbergen. Such collars are the badge of men who, though low in the pocket, are not down in the mouth. So long as there is starch in the shirt, no matter how little nap the coat wears; but limp linen betokens a desponding spirit, and presently there will be no linen and despair.

"Locksley," said Stillfleet, in his rattling, Frenchy way, "here's my friend Byng, Robert Byng, Esquire, of Everywhere and Nowhere. I pop out and he pops in to Rubbish Palace. He's been a half-century in Europe and knows no more of America than the babe unborn. Protect his innocence in this strange city. Save him from Peter Funk. Don't let him stay out after curfew. He must not make any low acquaintances in Chrysalis. He has a pet animal, the Orgie, picked up in Paris, very noisy and bites; don't allow him to bring it into these quiet cloisters. Well, I trust him to you and Mrs. Locksley. I'm off for Washington. Good by, all!"

He shook hands with janitor and janitress, kissed Dora, tweaked the boys, and fled riotously.

I saw him and his traps into a carriage and off,—off and out of the era of my life which I describe in these pages. With him I fear the merry element disappears from a sombre story.

I perceived what a lonely fellow I was, as soon as I lost sight of Stillfleet.

"Every man has his friends, if he can only find them," I said to myself. "But here I am, a returned absentee, and not a soul knows me, except Densdeth. *Exit* Harry Stillfleet; *manet* Densdeth. I believe I will look him up. Why should I make a *bête noir* of such an agreeable fellow? He won't bite. He's no worse than half the men I've known. But first I must transfer myself bag and baggage to Chrysalis."

The Chuzzlewit unwillingly disgorged me and my traps, after so short a period of feeding upon us. The waiter, specially detailed to keep me waiting if my bell rang, handled his clothes-broom, when he saw me depart, as if he would like to knock me down, lock me up, and make me pay a princely ransom for my liberty.

I escaped, however, without a skirmish or the aid of a policeman, and presently made my formal entry into Rubbish Palace.

"Great luck!" thought I, beginning to unpack and arrange, "to find myself at home the first day."

"Dreadful bore, to beat through this great city on a house-hunt!"

I picked up a newspaper on Stillfleet's table, and read the advertisements.

"Lodgings for a single gentleman of pious habits."

"Fine suite of apartments to let. N. B. Dodsley's Band practises next door, and can be heard *free of expense*, at all hours of day or night."

"Parlor and bedroom over Dr. Toothaker's office in Bond Street. Murderers, Coroners, Banjoists, and District Attorneys need not apply."

I was glad to have escaped inquiring into such places, and to tumble into luxury at once.

And comfort? I asked myself. How as to comfort?

My new quarters were almost too grandiose for comfort. That simple emotion was hardly sufficiently ambitious for an apartment big enough to swing a tiger, fifteen feet from tip to tip, in. There was no chimney, and therefore none of the domestic cheerfulness of an open fire. But an open fire would have interfered with the Italian aspect of the chamber. To keep the temperature up to Italy, I had a mighty stove, a great architectural pile of cast-iron, elaborate as if Prometheus had been a mediæval saint, and this were his shrine.

I looked about my great room, and it seemed to me more and more as if I were tenanting the museum of some old virtuoso Tuscan marquis, the last habitable chamber of his palazzo, the treasury where he had huddled all the heirlooms of the race since they were Counts of Etruria, long before Romulus cubbed it with wolves and Remus scorned earth-works.

It is idle to say that the scenery about a man's life does not affect his character. It does so just in proportion to his sensitiveness. A clown, of course, might inhabit the Palace of Art, with the Garden of Eve in front and the Garden of Armida behind, and still never have any but clownish thoughts in his clown's noddle.

Whatever else I was, I was certainly not a clown. My being was susceptible to every touch and every breath of influence. My new home and its scenery took me at once in hand, and began to string me to harmony with itself. I fell into a spiritual mood befitting the place.

A romantic place.

And Stillfleet's collection heightened the romantic effect. Stillfleet was a fellow of the practical and artistic natures well combined, with a bizarre slash, a bend dexter of oddity running through him. Fact, beauty, and fun were all represented in his museum.

He had, as he said, sampled all the ages. The ages when beings were brutes, and did nothing but feed and drink and fight and frisk and die, leaving no sign but an unwieldy skeleton, were represented in this Congress by a great thighbone, which a shambling mammoth had spent his days in exaggerating.

The fossil stood to symbolize the first kick of animal life against chaos. From that beginning the series went on rapidly. The times when Art put its fancies into amorphous, into grotesque, into clumsy forms, had all contributed some typical object.

Then of things of beauty, joys forever, there was abundance. There were models of the most mythological temples, and the most Christian spires and towers. There were prints and pictures, old and young. There were curiosities in iron and steel, in enamel and ivory, in glass and gem, in armor and weapons.

I will not attempt at present to catalogue this museum, or give any distinct impression of it. On that first afternoon I did not pause to analyze. I should have plenty of time in future, and now I had my own traps to arrange. That must be done systematically, so that I should be a settled man from the start.

I felt, however, as I proceeded with my unpacking and bestowing, a fine sense of order in the apparent whimsical disorder of the objects about me. The pictures had not alighted on the walls merely at the first convenient perch. There was method in all the contrasts and confusions of the place.

That modern French picture, for example, of masquers—a painting all vigor, all *abandon,* all unterrified and riotous color—had not without spiritual, as well as artistic significance, ranged itself beside a scene of a meagre Franciscan in a cavern, contemplating a scourge, a cup, and a crust. There was propriety in setting a cast of the Venus of Milo in a corner with the armor of a knight and the pike of a Puritan.

As I went on putting my chattels to rights and making myself at home in a methodic way, the atmosphere of the spot more and more affected me. I am careful in stating this dreamy influence. A certain romantic feeling of expectation took possession of me. I had no definite life before me. I was passive, and awaiting events. A man at work resists emanations and miasms; a man at rest is infected.

I looked about the room. Everything in it seemed watching me. I fancied that the ancient objects were weary of being regarded as dead curiosities, as fossils. They seemed to reclaim their former semi-animation, to desire to be the properties of an actual drama, to long to sympathize with joy and sorrow, as they had dumbly sympathized long ago.

I felt myself becoming a dramatic personage, but with no *rôle* yet assigned.

"Here is the stage," I thought. "Here is the scenery. Here is such a hall as conspirators, when there were conspirators, would have held tryst in. But the vindictive centuries are dead and gone. There is no Vehm to sit here in sombre judgment. And if there were a Vehm, the age of crime is over. I dare say I shall lead a commonplace life enough here,—study, smoke, sleep, just as if the room were not thirty feet square, dimly lighted with mullioned windows, and hung with pictures grim with three centuries of silent monitorship.

"Lucky that I'm not superstitious!" my thought continued. "I never shall peer behind the bed for ghosts, or for fiends into the coal-bin. A superstitious man might well be uneasy here. If I wanted to give a timid fellow the horrors, I would shut him up in this very room for a single night without light and without cigars. I don't believe a guilty man could stand it at all. If one had fathered villain purposes, those bastards of the soul's begetting would be sure to return and plague their parent in these lodgings. No, a guilty man could never live here a day.

"Densdeth, now,—how would he like to be quartered in Rubbish Palace? I forget that he does occupy the next room. By the way, I will see whether the door to his dark room is fast on my side."

I crowded between the piles of packing-cases in Stillfleet's lumber-closet to examine. Unless Densdeth were a spirit, and could squeeze through a keyhole, I was safe from a visit by that entrance. Stillfleet had screwed on this door a grand piece of ancient ironmongery, a bolt big enough to hold the gate of a condemned cell.

As I stooped to admire the workmanship of the old bolt, I was aware of the faint fragrance of a subtle and luxurious perfume. Stillfleet's boxes were musty enough. The scent was only perceptible at the door. It must come from the other side.

"Odor of boudoir, not store-room," I thought. "But perhaps he keeps a box of some precious nard stored here, and it has sprung a leak. Never mind, Mr. Byng; keep your nose for your own Cologne-bottle. Boudoir or magazine, remember it is Densdeth's, a man you mistrust."

I shut the closet-door, left the coffins of Stillfleet's Old Masters in their dark vault, and returned to my work.

In another half-hour all my traps had found their places. Everything, from boots to Bible, was where it would come to hand at need. I laid my matches so that I need not grope about in the formidable dimness of my chamber when I entered at night.

It was five o'clock. I felt a great want of society, and an imperative appetite for dinner.

"Why not venture," I asked myself, "to knock at Mr. Churm's door up-stairs? Perhaps he will dine with me at the Chuzzlewit, or show me a better place. He will not think me impertinent, I am sure, in making myself known anew to him."

I took the nearest staircase for the floor above, expecting to find there another corridor running the whole length of the building, as below. A locked door, however, at the left of the landing obstructed my passage towards Churm's side of Chrysalis. At the right also was a door, cutting off that portion of the corridor. It stood ajar.

As I was turning to descend, and find my way by the other staircase to Churm's lodgings, the question occurred to me, "Have I a neighbor overhead? Densdeth beside me,—who is above? By what name shall I chide him, if in dancing his breakdowns he comes crashing through the centre-piece of my ceiling? I should be glad to have a fine fellow close at hand to serve me as a counterblast to Densdeth. I *must* have friends, and if I can find one in my neighbor, so much the better."

I pushed open the door, and entered the little hall; it was lighted, as below, by a narrow mullioned window,—only half-lighted at that hour of a winter's afternoon.

A lonely, dismal place. The ceiling, instead of showing a tidy baldness under recent combings by a housemaid's broom, was all hairy with cobwebs. I was surprised that no spider had slung himself across the doorway, making the lobby a cave of Adullam.

There were two doors on the right. Each was labelled "To Let." The light was so faint by this time that I was obliged to approach close to satisfy myself that "To Let" was not the name of a tenant.

On the left the same unprofitable nonentity occupied the room over Densdeth's. The fourth door, corresponding to my own, remained. I inspected that in turn.

An ordinary visiting-card was tacked to the door. It bore a name neatly printed by hand.

I deciphered it with difficulty by the twilight through the grimy window: —

CECIL DREEME,
PAINTER.

A modest little door-plate. Its shyness interested me at once. Some men force their name and business on the world's eye, as the vulgar and pushing announce their presence by a loud voice and large manner. A person of conscious power will let his works speak for him. Take care of the work, and the name will take care of itself.

"Mr. Cecil Dreeme," I said to myself, "is some confident genius, willing to have his name remain in diminutive letters on a visiting-card until the world writes it in big capitals in Valhalla. Here he lurks and works, 'like some poet hidden in the realm of thought.' By and by a great picture will walk out through this cobwebby corridor.

"Cecil Dreeme," I repeated. "My neighbor overhead has a most musical, most artistic name. Dreeme,—yes; the sound, if not the spelling, fits perfectly. A painter's life, if common theories be true, should be all a dream. Visions of Paradises and Peris should always be with him. No vulgar, harsh, or cruel realities should shatter his placid repose. Cecil, too,—how fortunate that those liquid syllables were sprinkled upon him by the surplice at the font. Tom or Sam or Peter would have been an unpardonable discord."

Cecil Dreeme! The melodious vagueness of the name gently attracted me. It was to mine what the note of a flute is to the crack of a rifle.

Cecil Dreeme—Robert Byng.

"There is a contrast to begin with," I thought. "Our professions, too, are antagonistic. Chemistry—Art. Formulas—Inspirations. Analysis—Combination. I work with matter; he with spirit. I unmake; he makes. I split atoms, unravel gases; he grafts lovely image upon lovely image, and weaves a thousand gossamers of beauty into one transcendent fabric."

As these fancies ran through my brain, I began to develop a lively curiosity in my neighbor overhead.

Remember that I was a ten years' absentee, without relatives, without sure friends, wanting society, and just now a thought romanticized by the air and scenery of Rubbish Palace.

I began to long to be acquainted with this gentleman above me, this possible counterblast to Densdeth, this possible apparition through my ceiling at the heel of a breakdown.

"Does he, then, dance breakdowns?" I thought. "Is he perhaps a painter of the frowzy class, with a velvet coat, mop of hair and mile of beard, pendulous pipe and a figurante on the bowl, and with a Düsseldorf, not to say Bohemian, demeanor. Is he a man whose art is a trade, who paints a picture as he would daub the side of a house? Or is he the true Artist, a refined and spiritualized being, Raphael in look, Fra Angelico in life, a man in force, but with the feminine insight,—one whose labor is love, one whose every work is a poem and a prayer? Which? Shall I knock and discover? An artist generally opens his doors hospitably to an amateur.

"No," I decided, "I will not knock. We shall meet, if Destiny has no objection. Two in the same Chrysalis, we cannot dodge each other without some trouble. If I am lonely by and by, and yearn for a friend, and he does not dance through my centre-piece, I will fire a pistol-ball through his floor. Then apology, laugh, confession, and sworn friendship,—that is, of course, if he is Raphael-Angelico, not Bohemian-Düsseldorf."

These fancies, so long in the telling, flashed rapidly through my mind.

I turned away from the door, with its quiet announcement of the name and business of a tenant, not precisely evading, but certainly not inviting notice.

I made my way down, and up again by the other staircase to the same floor. Here I found the same arrangement of rooms, but more population and fewer cobwebs. The southern exposure was preferred to the northern, in that chilly structure.

I knocked at Mr. John Churm's door in the southwest corner of the building.

No "Come in." I must dine alone at the Chuzzlewit.

As I stepped from Chrysalis, I gave a look to Ailanthus Square in front.

"This will never do!" I exclaimed.

It was a wretched place, stiffly laid out, shabbily kept, planted with mean, twigless trees, and in the middle the basin of an extinct fountain filled with foul snow, through which the dead cats and dogs were beginning to sprout at the solicitation of the winter's sunshine.

A dreary place, and drearily surrounded by red brick houses, with marble steps monstrous white, and blinds monstrous green,—all destined to be boarding-houses in a decade.

"This will never do!" I exclaimed again. "Outdoor life offers no temptation. I am forced inward to indoor duties and pleasures. Objects in America are not attractive. I must content myself with people. And what people? My first day wanes, Stillfleet is off, and I have made no acquaintance but a musical name on a door in a dusty corner of Chrysalis."

CHAPTER V

Churm Against Densdeth

I had hardly taken my first spoonful of lukewarm mock soup at the long, crowded dinner-table of the Chuzzlewit, when General Blinckers, a fellow-passenger on the Arago, caught sight of me. He bowed, with a burly, pompous, militia-general manner, and sent me his sherry. It was the Chuzzlewit Amontillado, so a gorgeous label announced, and sunshine, so its date alleged, had ripened it a score of years before on an aromatic hill-side of Spain. But the bottle was very young for old wine, the label very pretentious for famous wine, and my draught, as I expected, gnawed me cruelly.

In a moment came a bow from Governor Bluffer, also fellow-passenger, and his bottle of the Chuzzlewit champagne,—label prismatic and glowing, bubbles transitory, wine sugary and vapid.

Bluffer was of Indiana, returning from a trip to Europe as a railroad-bond placer. He had placed his bonds, second mortgages of the Muddefontaine Railroad, with great success. His State would now become first in America, first in Christendom. He was sure of it. And by way of advancing the process, he had proposed to me to become "Professor of Science" in the Terryhutte University,—salary five third mortgages of the Muddefontaine per annum.

Blinckers was of Tennessee, wild-land agent. He had been urgent all the passage that I should take post as Professor in the Nolachucky

State Polytechnic School,—salary a thousand acres per annum of wild land in the Cumberland Mountains.

Both of these offers I had declined; but I was obliged to the two gentlemen. I bowed back to their bows, and sipped the liquids they had sent me without mouthing.

Presently, as I glanced up and down the table, I caught sight of Densdeth's dark, handsome face. He had turned from his companion, and was looking at me. He lifted his black moustache with a slight sneer, and pointed to untasted glasses of Blinckers and Bluffer standing before him.

"See!" his glance seemed to say. "Libations at the shrine of Densdeth, the millionnaire. Those old chaps would kiss my feet, if I hinted it."

Then he held up his own private glass, as if to say, with Comus,—

> *"Behold this cordial julep here,*
> *That flames and dances in his crystal bounds!"*

A dusty magnum stood beside him, without label, but wearing a conscious look of importance. He carefully filled a goblet with its purple contents, and despatched it to me by his own servant.

Densdeth was a coxcomb, partly by nature, partly for effect. He liked to call attention to himself as the Great Densdeth. He always had special wines, special dainties, and special service.

"It pays to be conspicuous," he said to me, on board the steamer. "I don't attempt to humbug fellows like you, Byng,"—and at this I of course felt a little complimented,—"but we must take men as we find them. They are asses. I treat them as such. Ordinary people adore luxury. They love to see it, whether they share it or not. A little quiet show and lavishness on one's self is a capital thing to get the world's confidence.

"Besides, Byng," he continued, "I love luxury for its own sake. I mean to have the best for all my senses. I keep myself in perfect health, you see, for perfect sensitiveness and perfect enjoyment. Why shouldn't I take the little trouble it requires to have the most delicate wine, and other things the most delicate, always at command? Life is short. *Après, le déluge,* or worse."

While I was recalling these remarks, Densdeth's servant had deposited the wine at my right. He was an Afreet creature, this servant, black, ugly, and brutal as the real Mumbo Jumbo. Yet sometimes, as he stood by his master, I could not avoid perceiving a resemblance, and fancying him a misbegotten repetition of the other. And at the moments when I mistrusted Densdeth, I felt that the Afreet's repulsive appearance more fitly interpreted his master's soul than the body by which it acted.

I raised the goblet to my mouth. The aroma was delicious.

"Densdeth," I thought, "must have had a cask of the happiest vintage of Burgundy's divinest juice hung in gimbals, and floated over the Atlantic in the June calms."

I put the fragrant draught to my lips, and bowed my compliments.

Densdeth was studying me, with a covert expression,—so I felt or fancied. I interpreted his look,—"Young man, I saw on the steamer that you were worth buying, worth perverting. I have spent more civility than usual on you already. How much more have I to pay? Are you a cheap commodity? Or must I give time and pains and study to make you mine?"

Do these fancies seem extravagant? They must justify themselves hereafter in this history.

I set down Densdeth's glass, untasted.

"What does it mean," thought I, "this man's strange fascination? When his eyes are upon me, I feel something stir in my heart, saying, 'Be Densdeth's! He knows the mystery of life.' I begin to dread him. Will he master my will? What is this potency of his? How has he got this lodgment in my spirit? Is he one of those fabulous personages who only exist while they are preying upon another soul, who are torpid unless they are busy contriving a damnation? Why has he been trying to turn me inside out all the voyage? Why has he kept touching the raw spots and the rotten spots in my nature? I can be of no use to him. What does he want of me? Not to make me better and nobler,—that I am sure of. No; I will not touch his wine. I will keep clear of his attentions."

By the way of desperate evasion, I seized and tossed off, first, Governor Bluffer's mawkish champagne, and then the acrid fabrication with which Blinckers had honored me.

Of course the rash and feeble dodge was futile. I was not to be let off in that way.

There stood Densdeth's wine, attracting me like some magic philter. It became magnetic with Densdeth's magnetism. I could almost see an imp in the glass,—not the teetotaller's bottle-imp, but a special sprite, urging me, "Drink, and let the draught symbolize renewed intimacy with Densdeth! Drink, and accept his proffered alliance. Be wise, and taste!"

The vulgar scenery of the long dining-room faded away from my eyes. The vulgar, dressy women, the ill-dressed, vulgar men, the oleaginous waiters, all became distant shadows. I heard the clatter and bustle and pop about me, as one hears the hum of mosquitos outside a bar at drowsy midnight. I was conscious of nothing but the wine—the philter—and him who had poured it out.

Absurd! Yes; no doubt. But fact. Certainly a Chuzzlewit dining-room is a shrine of the commonplace; but even there such a mood is possible under such an influence. Densdeth was exceptional.

I sat staring at the silly glass of wine, and began to make an unwholesome test of my self-control. I recalled the typical legend of Eve and the apple, and exaggerated the moral importance of my own incident after the same fashion.

"If I resist this symbolic cup," thought I, "I am my own man; if I yield, I am Densdeth's."

When a man is weak enough to put slavery and freedom thus in the balance, it is plain that he will presently be a slave.

"Bah!" I thought. "What harm, after all, can this terrible person do me? Why shouldn't I accept his alliance? Why shouldn't I study him, and learn the secret of his power."

My slight resistance was about to yield to the spiritual enticement of the wine, when suddenly an outer force broke the spell.

A gentleman had just taken a vacant chair at my right. Absorbed in the *mêlée* of my own morbid fancies, I had merely perceived his presence, without noticing his person.

Suddenly this new-comer took part in the drama. He flirted his napkin, and knocked Densdeth's wine-glass over into my plate. The purple fluid made an unpleasant mixture with my untouched portion of fish.

"Thank you!" I exclaimed, waking at once from my half-trance, my magnetic stupor, and feeling foolish.

I turned to look at my unexpected ally. Perhaps some clumsy oaf who had never brandished a napkin before, and struck wide, like a raw swordsman.

No. My neighbor was a gentleman. He held out his hand cordially.

"Have I waked you fully, Byng?" he asked.

"Mr. Churm?" said I.

He nodded. We shook hands. The touch dissipated my brief insanity.

"You have been in a state of coma so long over that wine," said he, "that I thought I would give you a fillip of help."

I tried to laugh.

"No," resumed Churm. "Only escaped dangers show their comic side. You are not safe from Densdeth yet. You would have yielded just now if I had not spilled the glass."

"Yielded!" I rejoined. "Not exactly; I was proposing to test his mysterious influence."

"Never try that! Don't dive into temptation to show how stoutly you can swim. Once fairly under water in Acheron, and you never come to the top again."

"Face Satan, and he flies, is not your motto, then."

"Face him when you must; fly him when you may."

"But really,—Devil and Densdeth; is it quite polite to identify them?" I asked.

"If you do not wish to see them melt into one, keep yourself from both."

"And stay in a pretty paradise of innocence?"

"I cannot jest about this, Byng. I knew a fresh, strong, pure soul,—fresher, stronger, purer than the fairest dreams of perfection. It was the destiny of such a soul to battle with Densdeth and be beaten. Yes; defeated, and driven to madness or despair."

"You are speaking of Clara Denman."

"I am."

As he replied, I looked up and caught Densdeth's eye. He took my glance and carried it with his to the upper end of the table. A flamboyant demirep was seated there. Densdeth marked that I observed her, and then smiled sinister, as if to say: "Byng, the romantic, there is the type of American women; look at her, and correct your boyish ideal."

Churm noticed this by-play.

"But better madness and death for my dear child," said he, sadly, "than Densdeth!"

Then waiving the subject, he continued: "You were surprised to find me at your side."

"It was an odd chance, certainly."

"No chance. Locksley told me that you had moved in from the Chuzzlewit, as Stillfleet's successor. I knocked at Rubbish Palace door. You were out. I thought you might be dining here. I looked in, saw you, and took my seat at your side. I did not hurry recognition. I was curious to see if you would know an old friend."

"I have called upon you already," said I. "I am a big boy, but I wanted to put myself under tutelage."

"Well, we are in the same Chrysalis; we will try to take care of each other till our wing."

My lively interest in the name Cecil Dreeme recurred to me.

"Are there others worth knowing in Chrysalis?" I asked.

"No. Bright fellows like brighter places. Only an old troglodyte like myself burrows in such a cavern. Nobody but Stillfleet could have kept in jolly health there. Take care it does not make you sombre."

"It will suit my sober, plodding habits. But tell me, do you know anything of a Mr. Dreeme, a painter, fellow-lodger of ours? I saw his name on a door as I was looking for yours? Is he a rising genius? Must I know him?"

As I asked these questions, it happened that Densdeth laughed in reply to some joke of his guest.

Densdeth's smile, unless he chose to let it pass into a sneer, was gentlemanly and winning. A little incredulous and inattentive I had found it when I spoke of heroism, charity, or self-sacrifice. It pardoned belief in such whimsies as a juvenility. His laugh, however, expressed a riper cynicism. It was faithless and cruel,—I had sometimes thought brutally so.

Breaking in at this moment, rather loudly for the public place, it seemed to strike at the romantic interest I had felt in the name Cecil Dreeme. What would a man of the world think of such idle fancies as I had indulged apropos of the painter's door-card? I really hoped Churm would be able to reply, "O, Dreeme! He is a creature with a seedy velvet coat, frowzy hair, big pipe,—rank Düsseldorf. Don't know him!"

"There is a young fellow of that name in the building," said Churm. "I have never happened to see him. Locksley says he is a quiet, gentlemanly youth from the country, who lives retired, works hard, and minds his own business."

Neither my friend nor I ventured upon serious topics for the rest of the dinner.

"I have an errand down town," said he. "You shall walk with me, and afterwards we will discuss your prospects over a cigar at Chrysalis."

So we talked Europe—a light subject to Americans—until dessert was over, and the Chuzzlewit guests began to file out, wishing they had not taken so much pie and meringue on top of the salad, and had given to the Tract Society the two dollars now racking their several brains, and rioting in their several stomachs, in the form of sherry or champagne.

Churm and I joined the procession. We were battling for our hats in the lobby with a brace of seedy gents who proposed to appropriate them, when Densdeth came out.

He saluted me cordially and Churm distantly.

No love between these two. Apart from any moral contrast, their temperaments were too opposite to combine. Antagonistic natures do not necessarily make man and woman hostile, even when they are imprisoned for life in matrimony; domestic life stirs and stirs, slow and steady, and at last the two mix, like the oil and mustard in a mayonnaise. But the more contact, the more repulsion, in two men of such different quality as Churm and Densdeth.

Both were quiet and self-possessed, and yet it seemed to me that, if a thin shell of decorum and restraint between them should be broken by any outer force, the two would clash together like explosive gases, and the weaker be utterly consumed away. I had already had hints, as I have stated, that they had causes for dislike. I could not wonder, as I saw them standing side by side. They were as different as men could be and yet be men.

I observed them with a certain premonition that I was to be in some way drawn into the battle they must fight or were fighting. With which captain was I to be ranged?

Densdeth was a man of slight, elegant, active figure, and of clear, colorless, olive complexion. His hair was black and studiously arranged. He was shaved, except a long drooping moustache,—that he could not have spared; it served sometimes to conceal, sometimes to emphasize, a sneer. His nose was a delicate aquiline, and his other fine-cut features corresponded. His eyes were yellow, feline, and restless,—the only restless thing about him. They glanced from your lips to your eyes and back, while you talked with him, as if to catch each winged word, and compare it with the expression perched above. Quick and sidelong looks detect a swarm of Pleiads where the steady gaze sees only six. Densdeth seemed to have learnt this lesson from astronomy; he shot his glance across your face to catch expressions which fancied themselves latent. Keen eyes Densdeth's to recognize a villain.

Churm was sturdy and vigorous; well built, one would say, not well made; built for use, not made for show. His Saxon coloring of hair and complexion were almost the artistic contrast to Densdeth's Oriental hues. He wore his hair and thick brown beard cut short. His features were all strongly marked and finished somewhat in the rough, not weakened by chiselling and mending. His eyes were blue, frank, and earnest. He looked his man fair and square in the face, and never swerved until each had had his say. Keen enough, too, Churm's eyes. They were his lanterns to search for an honest man and friend, not for a rogue and tool.

These men's voices also proclaimed natures at war.

In wild beasts the cry reveals the character. So it does in man,—a cross between a beast and a soul. If beast is keeping soul under, he lets the world know it in every word his man speaks. The snarl, the yelp, and the howl are all there for him that has ears to hear. If the soul in the man has good hope and good courage, through all his tones sound the song of hope and the pæan of assured victory.

Churm's voice was bold and sweet, with a sharp edge. He was outspoken and incisive. Any mind, not muffled by moss or thicket, would hear itself echo when he spoke. His laugh, if it made free to leap out for a holiday, was a boy's laugh, frank, merry, and irrepressible. There was, however, underneath all his cheerful, inspiring, and forgiving tones, a stern Rhadamanthine quality, as of one to whom profound experience has given that rare, costly, and sorrowful right,—the right to judge and condemn.

Densdeth spoke with a delicate lisp, or rather Spanish softness. There was a snarl, however, beneath these mild, measured notes. He soothed you; but you felt that there was a claw curled under the velvet. As to his laugh, it was jackal,—a cruel, traitorous laugh, without sympathy or humor,—a sneer given voice. But this ugly sound it was impossible to be much with Densdeth and not first echo and then adopt.

The same general contrast of nature was visible in the costumes of these gentlemen. Even a coat may be one of the outward signs by which we betray the grace or disgrace that is in us.

Churm was in fatigue dress. He looked water-proof, sun-proof, frost-proof. No tenderness for his clothes would ever check him from wading a gutter or storming a slum, if there were man to be aided or woman to be saved. He dressed as if life were a battle, and he were appointed to the thick of the fight, too well known a generalissimo to need a uniform.

Densdeth was a little too carefully dressed. His clothes had a conscious air. His trousers hung as if they felt his eye on them, and dreaded a beating if they bagged. His costume was generally quiet, so severely quiet that it was evident he desired to be flagrant, and obeyed tact rather than taste. In fact, taste always hung out a protest of a diamond stud, or an elaborate chain or eye-glass. Still these were not glaring errors, and Densdeth's distinguished air and marked Orientalism of face made a touch of splendor tolerable.

I sketch a few of the external traits of these two. I might continue the contrast at length. Even at that period of my acquaintance they had become representative personages to me. And now, as I look back upon that time, I find that I divined them justly. They in some measure personified to me the two opposing forces that war for every soul.

As they bowed coldly to each other in the hall of the Chuzzlewit, and turned to me, I seemed at once to become conscious of their rival influences. My dual nature felt the dual attraction.

"Glad to see you again, Byng," said Densdeth, offering his hand. "Will you walk into my parlor? I am quartered here for a day or two. Come; I can give you an honest cigar and a thimbleful of Chartreuse."

"Thank you," I replied. "Another time, if you please. Just now I am off with Mr. Churm."

"*Au revoir!*" says Densdeth. "But let me not forget to mention that I have seen our friends, Mr. and Miss Denman. They hope for a call from you, for old friendship's sake. If I had known of your former intimacy there, we should have had another tie on board the steamer."

His yellow eyes came and went as he spoke, exploring my face to discover, "What has Churm told him of me and Clara Denman? What has he heard of that tragedy? Something, but how much?"

"Miss Denman will be at home to-morrow, at one," he continued. "I took the liberty to promise that you would accept my guidance, and pay your respects at that hour."

"You are very kind," I of course said. "I will go with pleasure."

"I will call for you, then, at Chrysalis. I heard here at the hotel-office that you had moved into Harry Stillfleet's grand den. I felicitate you."

"You have a den adjoining," said I, my tone no doubt betraying some curiosity.

"O, my lumber-room," he replied, carelessly. "I find it quite a convenience. A nomad bachelor like myself needs some place to store what traps he cannot carry in his portmanteau."

"Well, Mr. Churm," said I, as we walked off together; "you see I cannot evade Densdeth. He is my first acquaintance at home, my next-door neighbor in Chrysalis, and now he takes the superintendence of my re-introduction to old friends. Fate seems determined that I shall clash against him. I am not sure whether my self is elastic enough to throw him off, even if I desire to."

"No self gets a vigorous repelling power until it is condensed by suffering."

"Then I would rather stay soft and yielding," said I, lightly. "But, Mr. Churm, before I call upon the Denmans, you must tell me the whole story of their tragedy, otherwise I may wound them ignorantly."

"I desire to do so, my dear boy, for many reasons. We will have a session presently at your rooms, and talk that history through."

He walked on down Broadway, silent and moody.

"Observe where I lead you," said he, turning to the east through several mean, narrow streets.

"Seems to me," said I, "you have fouler slums here than Europe tolerates."

"If you could see the person I am going to visit, you would understand why. If men here must skulk because they are base, or guilty, or imbecile, they strive to get more completely out of sight, and shelter themselves behind more stenches than people do in countries where the social system partially justifies degradation. But here we are, Byng. I have brought you along with a purpose."

Churm stopped in front of a mean, frowzy row of brick buildings. He led the way through a most unsavory alley into a court, or rather space, serving as a well to light the rear range of a tenement-house. In a guilty-looking entry of this back building Churm left me, while he entered a wretched room.

It is no part of my purpose to describe this dismal place, or to moralize over it. Perhaps at that time in my life I had too little pity for poverty, and only a healthy disgust for filth. I remained outside, smoking and listening to the jackal-voices of the young barbarians crying for supper from cellar to garret of the building.

"You will remember this spot," said Churm, issuing after a few moments, and leading the way out again.

"My poor victimized nose will have hard work to forget it."

"And the name Towner," my friend continued.

"Also Towner," I rejoined. And probably my tone expressed the query, "Who is he?"

"Towner is the tarnished reverse of that burnished medal Densdeth,—Densdeth without gilding."

"Did Densdeth fling him away into this hole?"

"He is lying *perdu* here, hid from Densdeth and the world. He has been a clerk, agent, tool, slave, of the Great Densdeth. The poor wretch has a little shrivelled bit of conscience left. It twinges him sometimes, like a dying nerve in a rotten tooth. He sent for me the other day, by Locksley, saying that he was sick, poor, and penitent for a villany he had done against me, and wanted to confess before he died, and before Densdeth could find him again. This is my third visit. He cannot make up his impotent mind to confession. He must speak soon, or concealment will kill him. I am to come down to-night at eleven and watch with him."

"Till when you will watch with me in Chrysalis."

"Yes; and now I suppose you wonder why I brought you here."

"To teach me that republics are unsavory?"

"Perhaps I want you to take an interest in this poor devil, in case I should be absent; perhaps I wish you to see the result of the Densdeth experiment, when it does not succeed; perhaps—well, Byng, you will promise me to expend a little of your superabundant vitality on my patient, if he needs it?"

"Certainly; but understood, that you pay to have me deodorized and disinfected after each visit."

I could not give a cheerful turn to the talk. Churm walked on, silent and out of spirits.

CHAPTER VI

Churm as Cassandra

We turned from Broadway down Cornwallis Place, parallel to Mannering Place, and entered Chrysalis by the side door upon that street.

"I have a word to say to the janitor," said Churm.

Pretty Dora Locksley admitted us to the snuggery. Lighted up, it was even more cheerful than when I saw it with Stillfleet. The table was set for supper. The bright teapot, the bright plates, the bright knives and forks, had each its own bright reflection of the gas-light to contribute to the general illumination.

Mrs. Locksley, the bright cause of all this brilliancy, was making the first cut into a pumpkin-pie of her own confection, as we entered. It was the ideal pumpkin-pie. Its varnished surface shone with a rich, mellow glow, and all about its marge a ruffle of paste of fairest complexion lifted, like the rim of delighted hills about a happy valley. As Mrs. Locksley's knife cleft the soil of this sweet vale, fragrant incense steamed up into the air. What nose would not sniff away all remembrance of the mephitic odors it had inhaled, to entertain this fresh, wholesome emanation? Mine did at once. I felt myself deodorized from the sour souvenirs of Towner's slum. The moral atmosphere, too, of this honest, cheerful, simple home-scene acted as a moral disinfectant. The healthy picture hung itself up in a good light in my mental gallery. It was well it should be there. Chrysalis owed me this, as a contrast to the serious pictures awaiting me along its dusky halls, as a foil to a sombre tableau hid behind the curtain at the vista's end.

Mrs. Locksley offered a quadrant of her pie to Churm.

"I resign in Mr. Byng's favor," said he.

"Hail Columbia!" cried I, accepting the resignation; and as I eat I felt my Americanism revive.

"I've just seen Towner again," Churm says, "and am to sit up with him."

"Poor fellow!" said Locksley. "Has he any chance?"

"Poor fellow, indeed!" cried Mrs. Locksley, in wrath, evidently sham. "Don't waste 'poors' on him, William. Didn't he as much as kill my poor sister, and ruin us?"

"You don't look very ruinous, Molly. No; you're built up fresh by losing money, and not having an Irish Biddy to feed you on mud-pies. We must not bear malice, wife!"

"We don't, William. And the proof is this jelly I've made for him."

"Right!" says Locksley. "But, Mr. Churm," he continued, and here his bristly aspect intensified, as if a foe were at hand, "Mr. Densdeth is back in the steamer. He's been here to-day, asking for Towner. But he got nothing out of me."

"The sight of Densdeth would kill the man. He shivers at the mere thought of his old master. We must keep him hid until he dies or gets some life into him. Good night."

"A trusty fellow, the janitor," said I, as we walked up stairs.

"Trusty as a steel bolt on an oak door."

"He will keep my secrets, if I have any, as one of his collegians? He won't stand on the corner and button-hole everybody with the news that I never go to bed, and hardly ever get up? He won't put my deeds or misdeeds in the newspapers?"

"No. If you should say to him, 'Locksley, I've got a maggot in my head. I am going to lock myself up in Rubbish Palace and train it. I want to hibernate for three months and not see a soul, except you with my meals. Let me be forgotten!' Locksley would reply, 'Very well, sir!' And you would be as secluded as if you had gone to Kamtschatka."

"You speak as if such things happened in Chrysalis."

"They might, under Locksley."

"How refreshing," said I, "to find such a place and such a person plump in the middle of New York! But tell me, what is Locksley to Towner?"

"Towner married our janitor's wife's sister. Locksley is a very clever machinist. He was a prosperous locksmith, manufacturing locks of a patent of his own, until Towner persuaded him to indorse his paper. Towner had some fine scheme by which he meant to make himself independent of Densdeth, and so escape from his service. His old master had become hateful to him. But Densdeth did not propose to let his serf go free. He made it his business, so both the men think, to spoil the speculation, and ruin the two, financially. Locksley lost everything. I got him this place, until he could look about and take a fresh start."

I opened my door. From the back of the sombre apartment, the great black stove, with its isinglass door, like a red Cyclops eye, stared at the strangers. The gas-light from the street shone faint through the narrow windows.

"Ghostly scenery!" said I, glancing about.

The casts and busts stood white and ghostly in the corners, and by the door of the lumber-room a suit of armor, holding a spiked mace in its fingerless gauntlets, reflected the dull glow of the fire-light.

"Those great carved arm-chairs," said Churm, "stand as if the shadows of so many black-robed inquisitors had just quitted them."

"What a chamber this would have been," I said, "for the sittings of a secret tribunal, a Vehmgericht! Imagine yourself and me enthroned, with crapes over our faces, and Locksley, armed with one of these halberds of Stillfleet's, leading in the culprit."

"Have you selected your culprit?"

"Well, Densdeth is convenient. He might be brought in from that dark room of his, next door. The scene becomes real to me. Come, Mr. Churm, you shall pronounce sentence. Put on the black cap, and speak!"

"I condemn him to bless as many lives as he has cursed."

"A gentle penalty!" said I. "But it may take time. Who knows but you are making a Wandering Jew of our handsome Absalomitish friend? *Fiat lux!*" I continued, striking a match, and lighting my chandelier. "Vanish the Vehm and the halberd! Appear the nineteenth century and the cigar! Take one!"

Churm smoked for some time in grave silence. At last he began.

"I loved your father, Robert, like a brother. For his sake and your own, I wish to be your friend."

His benignant manner, even more than the words, touched me. I felt my eyes fill with tears.

"Thank you," said I, "for my father's sake and my own. I yearn, as only a fatherless man can, for such a friend as you may be. I hoped I might count upon you."

"We have met but those few times in Europe since your boyhood. I think I know something of you. Still I may as well have more facts. What do you think of yourself? Person and character, now, in a paragraph."

"Person you see!" said I, standing up, straight as an exclamation-point. "Harry Stillfleet made me parade this morning, and pronounced me reasonably fit for service, legs, lungs, and looks. Character,—as to my character, it is not yet compacted enough for inspection. My soul grows slow as a century-plant. You can hardly look for blossoms at the end of the first twenty-five years. I am a fellow of good intentions,— that is the top of my claim. But whether I am to be a pavior of hell or a promenader of heaven, is as hell or heaven pleases. It seems to me that my allotted method of forming myself is by passing out of myself into others. I am dramatic. I adopt the natures of my companions, and act as if I were they. When I have become, in my proper person, a long list of *dramatis personœ,* I shall be ready to live my life, be it tragedy, comedy, or romance. And there you have me, Mr. Churm, in a rather lengthy paragraph!"

"I understand. And now you have come home, a working-man, who wishes *'se ranger'?"*

"I should like to find my place."

"Your place to live you have found already. Your place to labor will not be hard to find. Capable men of your trade are in demand. I have no doubt I can settle you to-morrow."

"You are a friend indeed," said I.

"Home and handicraft disposed of;—and now this young absentee, with his place to live and his place to labor arranged, is beginning to think of the other want, namely, somebody to love. How is that, Byng?"

"*'Hoc erat in votis!'*" said I, bashfully.

"It was in mine, when I was, like you, impressible, affectionate, trustful, and in my twenties. My forties have a confidence and a special warning to offer you, Robert, if you will accept it."

"No mature man has ever given me the benefit of his experience. Yours will be most precious."

"I strip off the battens, and slide back the hatches, and show you a cell in my heart which I thought never to uncover. But there comes a time, after a man's grief has become historical to himself, when he owes the lesson of his own tragedy to some other man. You are the man to whom my story belongs."

"Why am I the one?"

"That you must discover for yourself. I tell you my tale. You must adapt it to your own circumstances. You must put in your own set of characters from the people you meet. I point a moral for you; I have no right to impale others upon it."

"You might misunderstand and wrong them?"

"I might. This bit of personal history I am about to give you explains my connection with the Denmans."

"It will lead you then to the mystery of Clara's death?"

"Yes."

CHAPTER VII

Churm's Story

Churm took refuge with his cigar for a moment.

"Twenty-four years ago," he began, jerking his short sentences away as if each was an arrow in his heart,—"twenty-four years ago I was a young man about New York. There came a beautiful girl from the country. Poor! She had rich friends in town. They wanted a flower for their parlors. They took her. Emma—Emma Page was her name."

He repeated the name, as if it was barbed, and would not come from him without an agonized effort.

"She charmed all," he continued. "She fascinated me. Strangely, strangely. I will not analyze her power. You will see what knowledge it implied. I was a simple, eager fellow. Eager to love, as you are."

"*I* only said *willing,*" I interjected.

"The wish soon ripens to frenzy. Presently the lady and I were betrothed. I was a passionate lover. You would not think it to look at me now, with this coat and these clodhopper shoes." He forced a smile.

"Shaggy jackets and thick shoes with an orchestral creak are *de rigueur* for lovers now," rejoined I, trying to lighten the growing gloom of Churm's manner.

"*We* wore smooth black, and paper soles," said he. "Ah, well! I was a loyal, undoubting heart. I loved and I trusted wholly."

He paused, and drew his cigar to a fresh light. Then, as he

remained silent and grew moodier, I recalled him to the subject, and asked, "You lost her? By death?"

"By death, Byng? Yes, by the death of my love. She stabbed it. Shall I tell you how? Poor child! one single poisoned look of hers, one single phrase that proved a tainted nature, stabbed and poisoned my love dead, dead, dead."

Again he was silent. Pity would not let me speak.

"This may seem disloyalty," he by and by resumed. "But she is dead and pardoned long ago. I must be loyal to the living. You may run the risk I ran. I give to you, to you only, to you peculiarly, the warning of my misery. If you are ever harmed as I was, you will owe the same to your son, or your friend."

I was full of youthful, unshaken self-confidence. I saw no danger, anticipated no wound. I could not make the personal application Churm suggested. I listened, greatly touched and interested, but without foreboding.

"A look and a word," Churm began again, "seemed to flash upon me the conviction that the woman I loved was sullied. A foul-minded man may do foul wrong by such a fancy. My mind was pure. My first impulse was to rebel against the agonizing doubt, and be truer and tenderer than before. You comprehend the feeling?"

"Thoroughly. Your impulse would be mine."

"'Love,'" said I to myself, "'tests love,'" Churm continued. "'I mistrust, because I do not love enough. I must beware of being personally base and cruelly unjust to her. My suspicion shall be the evanescent dream of an unwholesome instant,—like Ophelia's song.' But still the anguish and the dread stayed in my heart. What could I do? Wait? Watch? Make myself a spy to examine this seeming sully, and find it an indelible stain? Uncover the bad side of my nature, apply it to hers, and study the kind and degree of the electricity evoked by the contact! Should I protect myself by any such baseness? While these thoughts were tangling in my brain, an outer force cut the knot."

"Some one spilt the philter," said I, thinking of the scene over Densdeth's wine.

"Denman was my unconscious ally," Churm continued, without noticing the interruption. "Denman saved me from the worst, the bitterest fate that can befall a true man,—to marry a woman whose truth and purity he can allow himself to doubt."

"Bitter indeed! A blight of all the bloom and harvest of a life!" said I;—so fancy had taught me.

"Ah, yes! as the 'marriage of true minds' alone gives fragrance and ripeness. I have missed the harvest, I escaped the blight. Denman, rich and handsome, with life clear before him, came back from Europe. Wealth had illusions for Emma Page. She was new to it. I was not poor; but my wealth was only *in posse.*"

"Few divine a young man's *posse,* I fear," said I, as he paused to whiff.

"*Posse* must be put into a pipe and blown into an illustrious bubble, before the world perceives the *esse,*" he rejoined. "But inventive power is the best capital. Mine has made me far richer than Denman. Well; he arrived at the moment of my agonizing doubt. Miss Page was The Beauty of our day. He was charmed. His cruder vision admired the rose and did not miss the dew-drop. She presently allowed me to perceive that he was to be my substitute. I will not tire you with the detail of the stranding and wreck of our engagement."

"No?" said I. "I begin to identify myself strangely with your story."

"No. No detail! To recall talks and looks and tones would be more tragedy than I could bear, even to make my story sharper. So our engagement ended. That slight perfidy was nothing. My wrong was deeper."

"Ah, poor Emma!" he continued, "forgiven long ago! That stain of hers, whether it were taint of being, or fault of nurture, or rash or sober sin, killed faith and hope in me for a time."

He paused again, and the blank seemed to symbolize a blank in his life.

"It was a wide gulf to swim over," he said. "Dark waters, Robert! Dark and broad! and I have seen many souls of men and women drown, that had not force to buffet through, or patience to drift across. But I escaped, and, having paid the price of suffering without despair, the larger hopes and higher faiths were revealed to me."

He struck aside the smoke with a strong, swimmer's gesture of the arm,—a forceful character, as even his motions showed.

"This is sacred confidence, Robert," he said. "I give it to you, as a father warning a son."

"And as a son I take and treasure it."

"Denman," Churm went on, "did not mind the wrong he might have been doing me, had my love not already perished. Denman never heeds any one between him and his object. He looks at the prospect; what is the fly on the pane to him? He has been walking over others all his life, trampling them if they lifted up their heads. But a selfish man gets himself sent first to Coventry, and then, if he does not mend, to St. Helena. Denman, a great merchant by inheritance, has gained money-power at the cost of moral weight. Our best men look coldly on him. He knows it, and grasps at bigger wealth to crush criticism. It is the old story,—vaulting ambition, the Russian campaign. Denman's gigantic schemes are the terror, the wonder, and the admiration of Wall Street. But he seems to a cool student a desperate man. It saddens me to meet him now,—aged, worn, anxious, hardly daring to look me in the face, and, as I fear, wholly in the power of Densdeth."

"Densdeth!" cried I. "Who and what is Densdeth? Does he hold every man's leading-strings to the Devil?"

"What is Densdeth? My story will give you a fact or two in answer to the question. I go on with it rapidly.

"Emma Page married Denman.

"She tried splendor for a year. She was the beautiful wife of the richest young man in town.

"At the year's end, her daughter Emma was born.

"A child is a terrible vengeance to a mother who has ever lowered her womanhood, by thought or act. What tortures she would have endured,—so she now too late thinks,—if she could have purged and made anew the nature she has transmitted to an innocent being! But there it lies before her in the cradle, the embodiment of her inmost thought. There lies the heir, and the waste of his heritage is irreclaimable."

"Don't be so cruelly stern," said I. "You out-Herod Herod, in the converse. You massacre the Innocents because they are guilty. This is the old dead dogma of original sin, *redivivus* and rampant."

"No; the dogma is dead, and science handles the facts without the trammels of an impious theory. Life cures, and Death renews. But Life should be a feast, not a medicine.

"Emma's birth," he continued, "transformed Mrs. Denman. For a year she was a faithful mother.

"Denman did not like his wife so well in this capacity. They diverged

widely. To be handsome for him and showy for the public was his notion of Mrs. Denman's office. The second year flowed rough.

"At the end of it, Clara was born, the child of a woman chastened
and purified.

"A fortnight after her birth, Denman came to me.

"'My wife is desperately ill,' said he. 'She wishes to see you.'

"I went calmly to this farewell interview with my old love. The husband seemed to abdicate in my behalf.

"'I am to die,' she said, almost gayly. 'I have sent for you, because I
trust you wholly. Dear friend, here are my daughters! Befriend them
for my sake! I feel that you will understand the yearnings of young
souls. Make them what you once hoped of me! Will you not be the father of their spiritual life? Forgive me, dear friend, for the old wrong,
for the old wrongs! Prove that you have pardoned *me* by loving mine.
Good-bye.'"

Churm was silent awhile.

He lighted a fresh cigar and smoked steadily. The smoke lifted
slowly in the still room, and hung in wreaths overhead. He sat looking
vaguely into the shifting cloud.

CHAPTER VIII

Clara Denman, Dead

I watched Churm, as he smoked.

Love, disloyalty, penitence, death,—were these all unrealities, that he could speak of them in his own history so calmly? Could a man be hurt as he had been, and overlive unscarred? I had heard cool men say, that "the tragedies of this life become the comedies of another, and that we should some time smile to recall our cruellest battles here, as now we smile to watch the jousts of flies in a sunbeam." Churm's tragedy was still tragedy to him. He had begun to recite it with evident pain. But the pain of his tone became indifference before he closed; and now he sat there smoking, as if he had related gravely, but without emotion, the mishaps of some stranger.

I wondered.

He looked through the smoke, caught my wondering eye, smiled soberly, and said: "Such an experience as I have described is like a shirt of Nessus, which one wears until the prickles of its poisoned serge have thoroughly toughened his skin. When it ceases to gall, he strips it off and hangs it by the highway for whoever runs to take; or if he finds some sensitive friend, like you, Robert, he lays it upon his shoulders, and says, 'Wear this! The edge of its torture is gone. It will harden you for the garment the Fates are weaving for you.'"

"Dear me!" said I, shrugging my shoulders. "Have I got to stand haircloth and venom? Well, if that is the common lot, and I cannot escape, I am much obliged to you for trying to make me pachydermatous. But you have not succeeded very well. The story of another's pain makes my heart softer."

"Sympathy for others is stout armor for one's self. But, Byng, you have heard the first tragedy of the series; listen to the second!"

"The second! Is there a third? Is the series a trilogy?"

"The third is unwritten. The march of events has paused while Densdeth was off. And to-day he steps from behind the curtain with you, a new character, half inclined to be his satellite. Perhaps you have a part to play."

There was a vein of seriousness in this seeming banter.

"Perhaps!" said I, puffing a ring of smoke away. "But pray go on. I am eager to hear the whole."

"After his wife's death, Denman said to me, 'Mr. Churm, Emma told me that you were willing, for old friendship's sake, to give an eye to my two poor girls' education. Suppose you take the whole responsibility off my hands. I will make their million apiece for them. You shall teach them how to spend it.' I gladly accepted this godfatherly post. The girls became to me as my own children.

"I shall say nothing to you," Churm here interjected, "of Emma."

"Why not?" I asked.

"You will see her. Judge for yourself! Clara you will never see. Of her I will speak. But first what do you remember of the sisters?"

"They were my pets when I was a school-boy. Emma I recollect as a lovely, fascinating, caressing little thing. Clara was shy and jealous, full of panics that people disliked her for her ugliness. I might have almost forgotten them, except for a sweet, simple, girlish letter they jointly wrote me upon my father's death. It touched me greatly."

"I remember," said Churm. "Clara consulted me as to its propriety. Dear child! sympathy always swept away her reserve. But you speak of her ugliness, Robert?"

"She was original, unexpected; but certainly without beauty. In fact, ugly and awkward, beside Emma."

"She became beautiful to me by the light that was in her. I could not criticise the medium through which shone so fair a soul. She educated me; not I her. She illuminated for me the new truths, she interpreted the new oracles; and so I have not fallen old and staid among my rudiments, as childless men, with the best intentions, may."

"You give me," said I, "a feeling of personal want and personal robbery by her death."

"Fresh, earnest, unflinching soul!" Churm sadly continued. "How she flashed out of being all the false laws that check the mind's divine liberty! Not the laws of refinement and high-breeding; they, the elastic by-laws of the fundamental law of love, are easy harness to the freest soul. In another house than Denman's, among allies, not foes, what a noble poem her life would have been!"

"Foes!" said I. "Was there no love for her at home?"

"Denman admired his daughters. Love remains latent in him. He has not outgrown his passion for the grosser fictions, wealth, power, show."

"But Emma! The two sisters did not love one another? If not, where was the fault?"

"Nature made them dissonant."

"Their foster-father could not harmonize them?"

"I did my best, Byng. But young women need a mother. I suppose the mothers in society shrug up their shoulders, when they talk of Clara's disappearance and death, and say, 'What could you expect of a young person, whose nurse, governess, and chaperon was that odd Mr. Churm?'"

"You were absent when she disappeared?"

"Away from my post. In England. On some patent business."

"Pity!"

"I curse myself when I think of it. About *this* misery, Robert, I have not learned to be calm."

"You did not approve her proposed marriage with Densdeth,—that I am sure."

"I knew nothing of it."

"What! your ward, your child, did not write, did not consult you on so grave a matter?"

"Her letters had been constant. They suddenly ceased. Her last had been a pleading cry to me to succor her father against his growing intimacy with Densdeth. I wrote that I would despatch my business, and hasten home. I never heard again. There was foul play."

"Suppression of letters?"

"Yes; or I was belied to her."

"Such a woman would not lightly abandon a faith."

"Only some villanous treason could destroy her faith in me. And such I do not doubt there has been. I make no loose charges. But why was I kept in the dark?"

"No rumor of the marriage reached you?"

"A rumor merely. Do you know Van Beester?"

"That banking snob who tries to be a swell? a fellow who talks pro-slavery and fancies it aristocracy? Yes; I was bored with him once at a dinner in Paris."

"Van Beester was put in my state-room on board the steamer when I returned. He had been in England, consummating a railroad job. The old story. Eight per cent third mortgage bonds, convertible. Enormous land grant. Road running over Noman's Land into Nowhere. One of Densdeth's schemes. Denman also had an interest."

"A swindle? Something Muddefontaineish?"

"O no! Noman's Land, the day the road was done, would become Everybody's Farm. Nowhere would back into the wilderness. Up would sprout the metropolis of Somewhere. Swindle, Robert? Your term is crude."

"I suppose Van Beester did not offer it to the English gudgeons under that name."

"It was a mighty pretty bait for them,—two millions in savory portions, a thousand each. I forget whether some large gudgeon's gills had taken the whole at one gulp; or whether a shoal of small fry had nibbled the worms off the bob. But the whole loan had been stomached in London, and Van Beester was going home in high feather."

"A blatant nuisance, of course. And you could not abate or escape him."

"No; unless I shoved him through our porthole, or slipped through myself. Densdeth was the man's hero. He could never talk without parading Densdeth. 'Such talents for finance!' he would exclaim. 'Such knowledge of men! Such a versatile genius! Billiards or banking, all one to him! Never loses a bet; never fails in a project! Such a glass of fashion! Such a favorite with the fair sex!'"

"Pah! 'Fair sex!' I can fancy the loathsome fellow's look and tone," I exclaimed.

"Then, in a pause of his sea-sickness," Churm continued, "he spoke of the Denmans. 'Mr. Denman so princely! Daughters so charming! For his part he admired Emma,'—'Emma,' the scrub called her. 'But then there was something very attractive, very exciting, about Clara, and he didn't wonder that Densdeth had selected *her*,—lucky girl!' 'What do you mean?' cried I, appalled. 'Don't you know?' said the fellow, chuckling over his bit of fashionable intelligence. 'I have it from the best authority, Densdeth himself. Here is his letter. I got it the morning we sailed. He is to be married the twenty-third. Blow, breezes! and we shall get there in time for the wedding.'"

"You could interpret her pleading cry, now," said I.

"I seem to hear it repeated in every blast: 'Help, dear friend, dear father,—for my mother's sake!' A maddening voyage that was! Dark waters, Robert! I shall hate the insolent monotony of ocean all my days. I could do nothing but walk the deck and tally the waves, or stand over the engine and count the turns."

"People would laugh at a fellow of my age," said I, "for such conduct. It is lover-like."

"I loved Clara, as if she were spirit of my spirit. When the pilot boarded us, before dawn on the twenty-third, I was up chafing about the ship. He handed me his newspaper. The first thing I saw was Clara Denman's name among the deaths."

"Cruel!" exclaimed I.

"I thanked God for it. Better death than that marriage!"

"There is still something incomprehensible to me in your horror of Densdeth. I only half feel it myself; Stillfleet more than half feels it. What is it? What is he?"

"We will talk of him another time," Churm replied. "Now I must hasten on. I found, as I said, Clara's name among the deaths, and inside the paper a confused story of her disappearance and drowning.

"I was so eager to hear more, that I smuggled myself ashore in the health-officer's gig, and took the quarantine ferry-boat to town, for speed. While I was looking for a hack at the South Ferry, the return coaches of a funeral to Greenwood drove off a boat just come into the slip.

"In the foremost coach I saw the Denmans and Densdeth.

"I pulled open the door and sprang in.

"I can never forget Denman's look when he saw me. He blenched and shrank into his corner of the carriage, cowed.

"There sat Densdeth, colorless and impassive, opposite me. By my side was Emma, weeping under a heavy veil, and Denman, with a mean and guilty look, beside her.

"'It is not my fault,' Denman said, feebly stretching out both his hands, as if he expected a blow from me. 'I acted for the best, as I thought, so help me God!'

"Densdeth interposed. His smooth, cool manner always puts roughness in the wrong.

"'This is a sad pleasure, Mr. Churm,' said he, 'If we had looked for your return, we would have deferred this sorrowful ceremony.'

"'Denman!' said I.

"He started, and held out his hands in vague terror.

"'Denman!' I repeated. 'Here has been some crime. What have you done with that innocent girl? Who or what murdered her?'

"'No,' said he, drearily. 'She is dead. That is bitter enough. Not murdered! O, not murdered! Do not be so harsh with an old friend!'

"'Denman,' said I, 'an older friend than you committed her daughter into my hands on her death-bed. In her name I accuse you. I say, you have tried to crowd this poor child into a marriage she abhorred. I say you drove her to death. I say you murdered her,—you and Densdeth.'

"He gave me a dull look,—a pitiful look, for that proud, stately man,—and turned appealingly to his supporter.

"'Mr. Churm,' said Densdeth, 'it is not like you to talk in this hasty way. I refuse to be insulted. My own distress shows me how the shock may have unbalanced you. But this heat and these baseless charges are poor sympathy for a parent, a sister, and a betrothed, coming from the funeral of one dear to them. Is it manly, Mr. Churm, to assail us? I appeal to your real generosity not to sharpen our grief by such cruelty.'

"Of course he was right. I was a brute if they were not guilty. I was silenced, not satisfied.

"Densdeth went on, with thorough self-possession. The man's olive skin is a mask to him.

"'You have a right, Mr. Churm,' said he, 'to hear all the facts of Clara's death. I will state them. Ten days ago she took a sharp fever from a cold. One afternoon she became a little light-headed. But at evening she was doing well, and in such a healthy, quiet sleep that we thought she needed no watching. Indeed, we believed her recovered from the trifling attack. In the morning she was gone,—gone, and left no clew. We instantly organized search, with all the care that the tenderest affection could suggest.'

"'Yes, yes! we did our best!' Denman eagerly interrupted.

"'Four days ago,' continued Densdeth without pause, 'her body was found, floated ashore on Staten Island. It was disfigured by the chances of drowning, but there were no marks of injury before death. She was fully identified. We suppose, and the doctor concurs, that at night her fever and light-headedness returned, that she left the house, strayed toward the river, fell from some dock, and was drowned.'

"Denman shivered as Densdeth concluded his curt, business-like statement.

"'Yes, yes, Churm!' said he again. 'I did my best. Do not say murder, again! Do not be so harsh with an old friend! Tell him, Densdeth, tell him how we spent care and time and money to recover the poor child. Do not let him think anything was neglected.'

"He looked feebly from Densdeth to me. Then he turned to his daughter.

"'Speak, Emma!' said he, almost peevishly. 'Why do you not help justify your father? Tell Mr. Churm that your sister's death is only a misery, no fault of ours.'

"Emma made no reply, but sobbed uncontrollably behind her veil."

"Poor girl!" I interjected, as Churm paused to look at his watch. "A dark beginning of life for her! I pity her most tenderly."

"It is almost eleven," said Churm. "I must go to my patient, Towner, without delay. And now I can say to you, that I believe he knows something of Clara's tragedy. When he speaks, I shall learn where the guilt lies."

"You suspect guilt then?" I asked. "The facts do not satisfy you? Have you a theory on the subject?"

"I have no doubt the final facts are as Densdeth gave them. But what are the precedent facts? What crazed my child? What unbalanced her healthy organization of mind and body? No trifling influenza. No bashful bridal panic of a girl. No, Byng; among them, they had hurt her heart and soul. There is the murder! Her father I believe to be in Densdeth's power."

"How?" I asked.

"How I can only divine from parallel cases. Denman has perhaps overstepped honesty to clutch wealth. Densdeth knows it. Densdeth has said, 'Give me your daughter, or be posted as a rogue!' Denman has made the common mistake, that, if he could elude the shame of detection, he would escape the remorse of guilt."

"So they took advantage of your absence to use *quasi* force with the lady?"

"Yes; and they belied me, or Clara would have awaited my protection. Ah, Robert, I dread some crushing infamy was revealed to her in that house. No common shame, no common sorrow, would have maddened her to wander off and die. And now good night, Robert! Keep this tragedy in mind—in both its parts. One such story, well meditated with the characters in view, may be the one needful lesson and warning of a life. And let the whole be a sacred confidence with you alone!"

"It shall be. Good night."

He wrung my hand and went out.

Let me recall him as he turns away.

A sturdy, not clumsy, man of middle height; fair skin, ruddy, not too red; nose resolute, not despotic; firm upper lip, gentle lower; glance keen, not astute, nor vulpine; expression calm, not cold; smile humorous and sympathetic; voice and laugh of the heart, hearty; a thoroughly lovable man,—the man of all others to be husband and father.

Besides, a man of vast ability and scope. Nature seemed to have no secrets from him. He handled the mechanic forces, he wielded social forces, with the same masterly grasp. Wherever civilization went, it bore his name as an inventor, an organizer and benefactor to mankind. He was skill, order, and love.

And yet he lived alone and weary; his life, as he had told me tonight, all desolated by the shadow of a sin.

CHAPTER IX

Locksley's Scare

Churm's steps went echoing along the corridor, echoing down the stairs. The front door of Chrysalis clanged to after him. Rumbling echoes of the clang marched to and fro along the halls, and fumbled for quiet nooks in the dark distances of the building. There I could hear them lie down to repose, and whisper, 'Silence.'

Silence and sleep reigned.

I was little disposed to sleep. I lighted a fresh cigar and fell into a revery.

Why, I first asked myself, had Churm so urged the history of his unhappy love personally upon me? Why was he so earnest and emphatic in his warning? The two tragedies were detached. He might have simply recalled the fact of his guardianship, and then described the fate of his ward. But he had gone back and forced himself to uncover his wound,—why? Not for my sympathy. No; he had outlived the need of sympathy. Besides, no loyal man would betray the error of a woman once loved, for pity's sake. No; some strong sense of duty had compelled him to take a father's place, and say to me, "Beware!"

I puzzled myself awhile, inquiring, What did he see in my temperament or my circumstances to make this warning needful? No solution of the question came to me. I dismissed the subject, and thought with a livelier interest over the Denman tragedy.

I began to perceive how much I had unconsciously counted upon the friendship of the Denmans. It was a rough shock to learn that I must doubt of Denman's thorough worth. He, too, was a friend of my father. His was an important figure in the background of my boyish recollections. A large, handsome man I remembered him, a little conscious in his bearing, but courteous, hospitable, open-handed, using wealth splendidly,—in fact, my ideal of what a rich man should be. It was a grave disappointment to me to be forced to dismiss this personage, and set up instead in my mind the Denman Churm had described. My hero was, in plain words, a rogue, a coward, and a slave.

I perceived, too, that half unconsciously I had kept alive pretty little romantic fancies about Emma and Clara. Living so many years in Italy and France, among women with minds deflowered by the confessional, and among the homely damsels of Germany, I was eager for the society of fresh, frank, graceful, girlish girls at home. The Denmans had often visited my imagination, companions of my sunniest memories of childhood. The earliest pleasure of my return I had looked for in the revival of this intimacy. But now I found one dead mysteriously, the other's life clouded by a tragedy. My pretty fancies all perished.

I began to dread my interview with Emma Denman to-morrow. Densdeth to be my usher!

What if she, like her father, had deteriorated under Densdeth's influence?

To cure myself of this sorry thought, I looked up among my treasures the letter which the two girls had written me several years ago, upon my father's death. It came to me in a friendless, foreign land, one desolate summer, while I was convalescing from an attack of the same fever that orphaned me.

Precious little childish epistle, now yellow with age! I remembered how I read it, slowly and feebly, one sultry Italian day, when the sluggish heat lay clogged and unrippled in the streets of the furnace-like city. I recalled how I read it, pausing between the sentences, and feeling each as sweet as the cool, soothing touch of the hand of love on a throbbing forehead.

I unfolded the letter, and re-read it reverently, and with a certain tragic interest. Clara was the scribe. These were her quaint, careful characters, her timid, stiff, serious, affectionate phrases.

I pictured to myself the two girls signing this sisterly missive, blushing perhaps with a maidenly shyness, smiling with maidenly confidence, sobered by their gentle sympathy for my grief.

Then, with a sudden shifting of the scenes, there came up before me a picture of the sad drama so lately enacted in Mr. Denman's house. Clara driven to madness or despair, Emma bereaved, Denman lost to self-respect, Churm belied; and in the background a malignant shadow,—Densdeth.

All at once a peremptory knock at my door disturbed me.

A stout knock, thrice repeated. The visitor meant to be heard and answered.

I was fresh from the French theatres, where three great blows behind the curtain announce its lifting.

"What!" thought I, "does the drama march? Is a new act beginning? Am I playing a part in the Denman trilogy? And what new character appears at midnight in the dusky halls of Chrysalis? Who follows Densdeth and Churm? Who precedes Emma Denman?"

I opened the door, wide and abruptly.

Locksley stood there, with fist uplifted to pound again.

The sudden draught put out his candle. The corridor had a sombre, mysterious look.

"Come in," said I.

"Is Mr. Churm here?" he asked, in an anxious tone.

"No; he left me at eleven, to go to his invalid, down town."

"I hoped to catch him. I wanted his advice very much."

He looked at me earnestly, as he spoke, as if studying my face for a solution of some difficulty.

"Come in out of the dark and cold!" said I.

He entered. The bristly man had a worried, doubtful look, quite different from his alert, warlike expression of the morning. He was porcupine still, but porcupine badly badgered. He glanced nervously about the room, with the air of one excited and slightly apprehensive. The suit of armor with the spiked mace, standing sentry at the lumber-room door, gave him a start.

"Empty iron!" said I; "and he can't strike with that billy he holds."

"I've seen the old machine a hundred times," Locksley rejoined. "It only jumped me because I'm all on end with worry."

"Can I help? My advice is at your service, if it's worth having, and you choose to trust a stranger."

"O, I know you're the right sort. We've made up our minds about that, big and little, down to the Janitory. But I don't want to bother you."

"Never mind! What is the trouble? Burglars? Or slow fire?"

"Why, you see, sir," said Locksley, "I'm in considerable of a scare about that young painter up-stairs."

He pointed to the centre-piece of the arabesqued ceiling. I looked up, almost expecting to see a pair of legs dangling through, according to my fancy of the afternoon.

"What?" said I, my interest wide awake. "The one overhead?"

"Yes, sir."

"Mr. Cecil Dreeme? I saw the name on a card above."

"Mr. Cecil Dreeme, and I'm afraid something's come to him."

"Is he missing?"

"No; he's there. But I haven't seen him these two days. Dora went up with his breakfast this morning, and with his dinner. No one answered when she knocked. I've just been up, and hammered a dozen thumps on his door. I couldn't raise a sound inside."

Locksley's voice sank to an anxious whisper as he spoke.

"What do you fear?" said I.

"Sickness or starvation,—one of them I'm afraid has come to him. Or perhaps he's punying away for want of open air and sunshine, and some friend to say 'Hurrah boys!' to him."

"You have a pass-key, of course; why didn't you push in?"

"I would have shoved straight through, and seen what was the matter, if Mr. Dreeme had been like other young fellows. But he isn't. He might be there dying alone, and I shouldn't like to interfere on my own hook, against his particular orders not to be disturbed. What do you say, Mr. Byng? Suppose it's a case of life and death,—shall I break in?"

"It is a delicate matter to advise upon. A gentleman's house is his castle. I must have my facts before I become accomplice to a burglary. What do you know of Mr. Dreeme's health or habits to make you anxious?"

"Not over much. But more than any one else."

"He is reserved then?" My curiosity about the name was increasing, as the slight mystery seemed to thicken.

"Reserved, sir! I don't believe a soul in the city knows a word of him, except us Locksleys. He's one of the owl kind."

"A friendless stranger," said I, recalling my fancies of the afternoon, by his door. "A man with the shyness and jealousy of an artist awaiting recognition. He does not wish to be known at all until he is known to fame."

"That sounds like it, partly," Locksley returned. "But there must be other reasons for his keeping so uncommon dark."

"What! Poverty? Creditors? Crime?"

"Crime and Mr. Dreeme! You'd drop that notion, if you saw him. Not that! No; nor poverty exactly. He can pay his omnibus yet, and needn't go on the steps, and risk a 'Cut behind.'"

"What then?" I asked, unwilling to pry disloyally, and yet eager to hear more.

"I suspicion that something's hit him where he lives, and he's lying by till the wound heals. I know how a man feels when the world's mean to him. He wants to get out of sight, and hide in a den like old Chrysalis. That was the way with me when I failed, and Mr. Densdeth put up my creditors not to let me take the Stillwell. I was mighty near hiding in Hellgate."

"How did he happen to shelter in Chrysalis?" I asked.

"I shall have to tell you all the little I know. I've halted because we Locksleys promised Mr. Dreeme not to be public about him. We've kept it close. But you're one of the kind, Mr. Byng, that a man naturally wants to open his self to."

"I'm not leaky; depend upon that!"

"Well," said Locksley, fairly uncorked at last, and overrunning with his story; "Mr. Dreeme came in, after ten, one night about three months ago, and says he, 'I've just got to town by the late train. The last time I was down, I saw the card out, "Studios to Let." Will you show me what there is?' 'Well,' says I. 'It's pretty well along in the night to be hiring a studio!' 'Yes,' says he, mild as you please, but knowing his own mind; 'but I've got to have one. I'm not hard to satisfy, and if I could move in right off, I should save the money they'd take from me at the Chuzzlewit, or some other costly hotel.' 'You're not so flush as you'd like to be, perhaps,' says I. 'No,' says he, 'if flush means rich, I'm not.'"

"So you got him as a tenant," said I, trying to hurry the narrator.

"Yes; he was such a pleasant-spoken young man that I took to him. Besides, not being flush made him one of my family,—and a big family it is!"

"We must not forget, Locksley, that while we discuss, he may be suffering."

"That's true. I must talk short, and talking short isn't natural to my

trade. Filing iron trains a man to be slow, just as hammering iron practises him to bounce his words like a sledge on an anvil. Well; I took Mr.
Dreeme up-stairs, and showed him the studio overhead. It has closets
and bath, like this room. He said that would do him. He paid me a
quarter in advance, and camped right in, with a small bundle he had."

"Gritty fellow!"

"Grit as the Quincy quarry! or he'd never have stuck there alone for
three months, painting like time, and never stirring out till night."

"That is enough to kill the man! Never till night! Not to meals, or to
buy materials? Not to meet a friend, to see the world?"

"The world and people are what he wants to dodge. I buy him all
his materials. He took the last tenant's furniture just as it stood,—and
it's only about Sing-Sing allowance. He don't seem to need all sorts of
old rubbish to put ideas into him, as the other painters do. I fitted him
out, according to list, with sheets and towels, and clothes too. He said
he couldn't knock off work for no such nonsense as clothes. He must
paint, or he shouldn't have money for clothes or victuals."

"A resolute recluse, concentred upon his art," said I. "And about his
meals?"

"Mother Locksley cooks 'em, and Dora takes 'em up when I'm off. But
he don't eat enough to keep a single-action cockroach on his rounds."

"Poor fellow! I don't wonder he has but a hermit's appetite." I am
ashamed to say that interest in this determined withdrawal from the
world made me forget for a moment that the exile might be in urgent
need of relief.

"Mrs. Locksley," continued the janitor, "has never seen him. He has
had the children up, and drawn their likenesses, like as they can be.
But women he don't seem to want to have anything to do with."

"Ah!" cried I. "Here we have a clew! Some woman has wronged
him; so he is going through a despair. That is an old story. He edits it
with unusual vigor."

"That's what my wife and I think," says Locksley. "He loved some
girl, she went crooked, and so things look black to him."

"What!" thought I. "Is he passing through Churm's 'dark waters'?
Strange if I should encounter at once another illustration of that sorrow!"

After my dramatic fashion of identifying myself with others, I put
myself in Mr. Dreeme's place, and shrank from so miserable a solution
of his exile.

"Perhaps," I propounded, "some flirt has victimized the poor fellow, and he does not yet realize that we all must take our Bachelor of Arts at a flirt's school, to become Master of the Arts to know and win a true woman."

Locksley smiled, then shook his head, and his worried look returned.

"No," said he; "that kind of a girl makes a man want to be among folks and forget her. Mr. Dreeme has had a worse hurt than that. But whatever wounded him, for the last two weeks he's been growing paler and punier every day. Some says the smell of paint is poison. I don't believe there's any strychnine so bad as moping off alone, and never seeing a laugh, and never playing at give and take, rough and smooth, out in the world."

"You're right," said I; "but let us get through our talk, and see what is to be done."

"To-night," continued Locksley, "just as I was wrastling to get off my wet boots,—they stuck like all suction, did them boots, but I couldn't go to bed in 'em,—just then my wife began talking to me about Mr. Dreeme. 'What do you suppose has come to him?' says she. 'No answer when Dora went up with his breakfast; no answer when she knocked with his dinner. I mistrust he's sick,' says she. While she was talking, a scare—the biggest kind of a scare—come to me about him. 'Wife,' says I, 'a scare has come to me about Mr. Dreeme.' 'Is it a prickly scare, William?' says she. 'Prickly outside and in,' says I; 'I feel as if I'd swallowed a peck of teazles, and was rolling in a bin of 'em.' 'William,' says she, 'scares is sent, and the prickly scares calls for hurries. Just you run up, and lay your fist hard against Mr. Dreeme's door, and if he don't speak, and you can't hear him snore through the keyhole, go to Mr. Churm, and whatever he says do, you do! Mr. Churm always threads the eye the first shove.' So I went up, and rapped, and the more I knocked, the emptier and deader it sounded. Mr. Churm is gone. What shall we do, Mr. Byng? The young man may be up there on his back with a knife into him, or too weak to call out, and panting for brandy or opodildoc. My scare gets worse and worse."

"I begin to share it. We will go and break in at once. Light your candle, while I find a bottle of Mr. Stillfleet's brandy."

CHAPTER X

Overhead, Without

Among the other treasures of Rubbish Palace, I had inherited Still-fleet's liqueur-case. It was on a generous scale,—a grand old oaken chest, bristling with griffins' heads and claws, armed with massive iron handles, and big enough to hold all the favorite tipples of a royal household, or to hide a royal pair if they heard a Revolution coming up the stairs.

Stillfleet had traced the pedigree of his chest to within three generations of Ginevra, in her family. He had no doubt that this was the identical coffer which that sportive lady had made her coffin.

"Clip!" said Stillfleet, shutting down the lid as he told me this legend in the afternoon. "Clip! listen to that snap-lock! Fancy her feelings! Taste that gin! *'Genièvre'* from Ginevra's box. I like to keep my nectars in a coffin; it's my edition of the old plan of drinking from a scull. Life is short. 'Come, my lad, and drink some beer!'"

To this grand sarcophagus I proceeded to seek a restorative for Cecil Dreeme. Locksley's alternative, "opodildoc," was not at hand.

Lifting the heavy lid, instead of poor Ginevra's bare bones, I found a joyous array of antique flasks and goblets. They flashed at me as the gas-light struck them, each with the merry wink of a practised bacchanal. I saw the tawny complexion of the brandy shining through a tall bottle, old enough to have figured at the banquet of the Borgia. Around this stately personage, and gaping for the generous juices he might impart, was a circle of glasses, the finest work of the best days of Venice, clear and thin as bubbles, and graceful as the cups of opening flowers.

I took the decanter and a glass, and, thus armed, followed Locksley into the corridor.

His prickly scare had so teazled the poor fellow that he was now quite like a picture of Remorse or Despair. It was entirely dark in the building. Our single candle carried its little sphere of light along with it. Beyond and overhead might have been the vaults and chambers of a cavern, for all we could see.

Passing Densdeth's padlocked door, we turned toward the side staircase. I looked up and down the well of the stairs. No *oubliette* ever showed a blacker void. It almost seemed to my excited imagination that we ought to hear the gurgle of a drowning prisoner, flung down into that darkness by us, his executioners.

"Awful black!" said Locksley, and the shadow of his bristly hair on the wall stiffened with alarm.

By the dim gleam of the candle, the paint of the wood and stucco of the walls of Chrysalis changed to oak and marble. The sham antique vanished. It became an actual place, not mere theatrical scenery. Seen by daylight, the whole edifice was so unreal and incongruous, that I should not have been surprised to see a squad of scene-shifters at work sliding it off and rolling it up, and leaving Ailanthus Square nothing but its bald brick houses to stare at. Now, as we climbed up the stairs, torch-bearer ahead, cup-bearer behind, Chrysalis passed very well for a murky old castle of the era of plots, masks, poison, and vendetta.

"Yes," thought I, "Locksley's three knocks did announce a new act in my drama. Cecil Dreeme is the new actor. He follows Densdeth and Churm, he precedes Emma Denman. Is he in the plot? Is he underplot, counterplot, or episode? I hope, poor lonely fellow, that he has not already passed off the stage, as Locksley dreads. That would be a dismal opening of my life in Chrysalis."

The janitor now pushed open the partition-door from the upper landing into the northern corridor.

The haggard moon, in its last quarter, hung just above a chimney of Mannering Place opposite, like a pale flame struggling up from a furnace. Its weird light slanted across the mullion of the narrow window.

There was just enough of this feeble pallor to nullify the peering light of Locksley's candle. Ghostly, indeed, the spot appeared! My anxiety and my companion's alarm were lively enough to shape a score of ghosts out of a streak of moonshine.

"To Let," the tenant of the left-hand rooms, had no business with us, nor we with him. On the other side was the modest little card:—

CECIL DREEME,
PAINTER.

Destiny had brought us together. I was about to know him, alive or dead.

Alive or dead! That doubt in both our minds made us hesitate an instant. Locksley looked up to me for orders.

"Knock!" whispered I.

He knocked gently. If there were a sick man within, his hearing, sharpened by silence, would abhor a noise.

We both listened, without whisper or sigh. Locksley deposited his candle on the floor and put his ear to the keyhole. The low light flung a queer, distorted shadow of him on the wall. It seemed a third person, of impish aspect, not meddling with our proceedings, but watching them scornfully.

No answer. Not even the weak "Come in" of an invalid.

Locksley "laid his fist to the door," without respect to his knuckles.

"Nothing," whispered he, "except a sound of emptiness."

We now both knocked loudly, and gave the door a rough shake, as if it merited ungentle handling for obstructing the entrance of well-wishers.

After this uproar, dead silence again, except a low grumble of echoes, turning over in their sleep, to mutter anathemas at the disturbers of their repose.

"Locksley," I whispered, "we are wasting time. Try your pass-key."

He introduced the key. His shadow, exaggerated and sinister, bent over him as he worked.

"I must pick it," said he, turning to me with a dogged burglar-look on his honest face. "His key is in the lock inside. But I haven't been poking into keyholes ever since I was knee-high to a katydid for nothing."

He took from his pocket a pair of delicate pincers. He manipulated for a moment. Presently I heard the key rattle and then drop inside.

That unlawful noise should awake any sleeper! We paused and listened. No sound. Awe flowed in and filled the silent stillness. Again we looked at each other, shrinking from an interchange of apprehension.

"I'm afraid he is—not living," Locksley breathed at last.

"Don't stop! Open!"

He put in his pass-key and turned. The bolt of the latch also yielded to this slight pressure. The door opened a crack without warning. Our candle, standing on the floor, bent its flame over, peering through into the darkness within. Before I could snatch it up, the inquisitive little bud of fire had been dragged from its stem by the draught. The candle was out.

By the pallid moonlight we could just see each other's anxious faces. We could also see, through the narrow crack of the door, that the same faint, unsubstantial glimmer filled the room. This ghostly light repelled me more than the darkness. It could show the form, but not the expression of objects; and form without expression is death.

"I have matches," whispered Locksley.

He drew one across the sole of his shoe. It flashed phosphoric, illuminated the breadth of sturdy cowhide upon which the janitor trod, and went out.

"Take time with the next," said I. "I must go in at once."

CHAPTER XI

Overhead, Within

The same door which we had battered and shaken so rudely I now pushed open with quiet, almost reverent hand.

Was I entering into the presence of Death? No sleep but that, it seemed to me, could hug a sleeper so close as to silence his answer or his protest at our noise.

So I stole into the tacit chamber, eagerly, and yet with my nerves in that timorous tremor when they catch influences, as lifting ripples catch sunrise before the calms.

I pushed back the door against the close, repellent atmosphere within. Holding it, still, as it were a shield against some sorrowful shock I was to encounter, I paused a breath to see my way.

The force of the faint moonlight brought it only as far as the middle of the room. There there was a neutral ground, not light, not dark, a vague in which forms could be discerned by intent vision.

I involuntarily closed my eyes, to give sight the recoil before the leap. When I opened them, and flung my look forward to grapple with what it could find, the first object it seized was a small splash of white light, half drowned in the dimness. The moonbeams were also, without much vigor, diving to examine this sunken object. Their entrance, or perhaps my own trembling eagerness, seemed to make a little fluctuation about it. I steadied and accustomed my glance, and presently deciphered the spot as a mass of white drapery in a picture, standing upon an easel.

While I was making this out, I heard behind me the crack and fizz of Locksley's second failure with his matches.

The little sound was both ally and stimulant. I advanced another step, and my groping sight detected a large arm-chair posted before the easel.

Hanging over the arm of the chair, where the moonlight could not reach, I saw another faint, pale spot. It was where a hand would rest. Was it a hand?

Beckoned forward by this doubt, I moved on and saw, flung back in the arm-chair, a shadowy figure. A man? Yes; dim form and deathly face,—a man!

The air of the room was close and sickly. I choked for breath. Life needs a double portion at such moments.

Dead? Is he dead? I seemed to scream the unspoken question to my heart.

It cost me an effort to master the involuntary human shudder at such an encounter. I sprang forward where the pale hand without motion beckoned, and the pale face pleaded for succor.

Nothing of the repellent magnetism of a corpse as my hand approached the forehead.

But as little the responsive thrill of life wakening at life's touch, and renewing with a start the old delicious agony of conscious being.

I laid my hand upon the brow.

Cold! But surely not the cold of death! This was no dead man whom I anxiously, and the moon impassively, were studying. Tranced, not dead, so instinct told me. Life might be latent, but it was there.

I felt tears of relief start into my eyes.

Whoever has lived knows that timely death is the great prize of life; who can regret when a worthy soul wins it? But this untimely perishing of a brother-man, alone and helpless in the dark and cold, was pure waste and ruin.

Locksley now came to my side, sheltering his lighted candle.

"Dead?" gasped he, and stopped silent before the arm-chair.

"No, no," I whispered, and the curdling whisper showed me how deep my horror had been. "No; only fainted, I trust. Open the window! Fresh air is the first want."

"Fresh air he shall have, if there's any blowing," says Locksley, briskly. "Fresh air beats the world for stiddy vittles."

While he worked at the window, I poured a compacter restorative than air out of Stillfleet's flask. I gently forced a few drops of the brandy down the unconscious man's throat, and expended a few sprinkles to bathe his forehead.

"It is the painter, Locksley?" I asked.

"Yes sir."

And so began my acquaintance with Cecil Dreeme.

CHAPTER XII

———•·•———

Dreeme, Asleep

A current of wintry wind flowed in as Locksley lifted the sash. "Fresh air is prime for the inside," said he. "But warm air for the outside is the next best thing. Shall I light a fire in the stove?"

"Do; but first hand me that plaid."

I wrapped my unresisting patient in the shawl. He was a mere dead weight in my hands. I shuddered to think that his life might be drifting away, just out of my reach.

"I hope we are not too late," I said.

"Shall I fetch a doctor?" asked Locksley.

"Fire first. Then doctor—if he does not revive."

"There's no kindling-wood," says Locksley, from the closet. "I'll run down to your place, Mr. Byng, and get some."

"Pray do!"

He hurried off. I was left alone with the tranced man. I repeated the little dose of brandy, and stood aside to let the light of the candle fall upon his face.

"Stop!" said Delicacy. "Respect the young man's resolute incognito."

"Too late!" I thought in reply. "Incognito has nearly murdered him. I shall knock it in the head without ceremony. Besides, Fate has appointed me his physician; how can I doctor him intelligently without feeling the pulse of his soul by studying his face?"

The first question I asked the pale, voiceless countenance was, whether I was not committing the impertinence of trying to force a man to live who had wished to kill himself. Suicide? No; I don't see any blood. I smell no laudanum. Here has been unhappiness, but no despair, no self-disgust. A pure life and a clear intellect,—so the face publishes. Such a youth might wear out with work or a wound; he would never abdicate his birthright to live and learn, to suffer and be strong. Clearly no suicide.

"No," my thought continued rapidly, "Locksley has supplied the theory of Mr. Dreeme's case. His face illustrates and confirms it. A man of genius, ardent, poor, and nursing a wound. The wound may be merely a scratch, he may merely have had the poet's quarrel with vulgar life; but, great or small, the hurt has consigned him to this unwholesome solitude, and here he has lavished his mind and body on his art. No, Cecil Dreeme, you are dying because you have ignorantly lived too intensely. But the world does not willingly let such faces die. I myself feel the need of you. Even with your eyes closed, the light gone, your countenance tells me of the presence of a character and an experience riper and deeper than my own. What have you been taught by suffering, what have you divined by genius, that you wear maturity so patiently upon your sad young face?"

I took the candle and held it to his lips. Did he breathe? The flame flickered. But the air flowing in from without might have caused that; and I would not close the window until the keen northern blast had scourged out every breath of languor from the stifling room.

I withdrew the candle. Curiosity urged me to study the face more in detail. But that seemed disloyal to the sleeper. I had made up my mind that my patient was worthy of all my care. He was not dead, that I should dissect him. While a face can protect itself by the eye,—which is shield to ward, blade to parry, and point to assail,—one feels not much scruple in staring. But what right had I to profit by this chance lifting of the visor of a disarmed man, who wished to do his battle of life unknown?

I therefore stopped intentionally short of a thorough analysis of his countenance. Fair play and my anxiety both made me content with my general impressions. It is error to waste the first look and the first few moments, if one wishes to comprehend a face,—to see into it. No after observations are so sharp and so unprejudiced.

Roughly then,—Cecil Dreeme's face was refined and sensitive, the face of a born artist. Separately, the features were all good, well cut and strong. Their union did not produce beauty. It was a face not harmonized by its construction, but by expression,—by the impression it gave of a vigorous mind, controlling varied and perhaps discordant elements of character into unison. There was force, energy, passion, and no lack of sweetness. Short, thick, black hair grew rather low over a square forehead. The eyebrows were heavy and square. The hollow cheeks were all burnt away by the poor fellow's hermit life. He wore no beard, so that he was as far from the frowzy Düsseldorfer of my fancy as from the pretty, poetic young Raphael. This was a man of another order, not easy to classify. His countenance seemed to interpret his strange circumstances. The face and the facts were consistent, and both faithful to their mystery.

All this while I was chafing his hands, and watching intently for some tremor of revival.

Presently the silence and the lifeless touch grew so appalling, that I was moved to call aloud: "Dreeme! Cecil Dreeme!"

I half fancied that he stirred at this.

Yes! No!

Trance was master still. Life must be patient. If it wrestled too soon, it might get a fatal fall. I dreaded the thought of my invalid giving one gasp, shuddering with one final spasm, and then drooping into my arms—dead.

Locksley now came clattering into the lobby, dropping billets from an over-load of kindling-wood.

He shot down his armful by the stove, and approached the figure in the arm-chair.

"Any pulse?" said he, taking the cold hand in his.

"Is there any?" I asked, eagerly.

"I shouldn't wonder," he replied, "if the blood was starting, just a little, like water under ice in the early spring." Locksley repeated the experiment with the candle.

"He breathes," he whispered.

There was for a moment no draught, and the flame certainly trembled before Dreeme's lips.

"He can't be said to be coming to," again whispered the janitor. "That's too far ahead. But he's out of the woods, and struck the cart-track leadin' to the turnpike."

"Thank God!"

"Ay! that always!" said Locksley, gravely. "Now here goes at the fire! You'll hear a rumblin' in this stove before many minutes that would boost a chimney-sweep."

He heaped in his kindling-stuff, and lighted it. The pleasant noise of fire began. Locksley left the stove, intoning hollow music, like an automaton bassoon, and turned to me: "Looks pretty gritty,—Mr. Dreeme,—don't he? And pretty mild too?"

"Both," said I.

"Not many would have stood it out alone in such a bare barn as this."

For the first time I gave myself an instant to glance about the studio.

A bare barn indeed! Half-carpeted, furnished with a table, a chest of drawers, and two or three chairs. The three doors, corresponding to my bath-room, bedroom, and lumber-room, were the only objects to break the monotony of the unadorned walls. After the lavish confusion of Rubbish Palace, this place looked doubly bleak and forlorn. To paint here, without one single attractive bit of color or form to relieve the eye and subsidize the fancy, was a *tour de force*, like a blind man's writing a Paradise Lost, or a deaf man's composing a symphony.

"He's had to wind his whole picture out of his head," said Locksley, following my glance. "And it ain't so bad either, if you could see it fair by daylight. Look at it there! It's one of those pictures that make a man feel savage and sorry all at once."

Lear and his Daughters,—that was the picture on Dreeme's easel. I glanced at it, as I continued my offices about him.

The faint light of one candle gave it a certain mysterious reality. The background retired, the figures projected. They stirred almost, almost spoke. It seemed that I ought to know them, but that, if I did not catch the likeness at the first look, I could never see it. "That large and imposing figure, the King!—wipe out the hate from his face, and I have surely seen the face. The Regan is in shadow; but the Goneril,—what features do I half remember that scorn might so despoil of beauty? Ah! that is the power of a great artist. His creations become facts. This is not imagination, it is history. At last here is my vague conception of Lear realized."

The Cordelia I recognized at once. "Cecil Dreeme himself. He needed, it seems, but little womanizing. A very noble figure, even as I see it faintly. Tenderness, pity, undying love for the harsh father, for the false sisters, all these Dreeme's Cordelia—Dreeme's self idealized—expresses fully."

These observations, made in the dim light, were interrupted by a little stir and gasp of our patient.

We watched anxiously and in silence. Fresh air, warm wrappings, brandy, and the magnetism of human touch and human presence, were prevailing. Yes; there could be no doubt; he breathed faintly.

The fire in the stove was now roaring loud. That lusty sound and the dismal wind without could not overpower the low, feeble gasps of the unconscious man.

"We've got him, hooray!" said Locksley, in an excited whisper.

We shook hands, like victors after a charge. I could have seized the bristly janitor, and whirled him into a Pyrrhic breakdown, without respect to my ceiling below.

"Air he's got," says Locksley, "and fire he's got, and a friend he's got; now for some food for him! If you say so, I'll just jiff round to Bagpypes, first block in Broadway, and get some oysters. He hasn't touched a mouthful to-day, unless he can eat anthracite out of the coal-bin. Starvation's half the trouble. An oyster is all the world in one bite. Let's get some oysters into him, and we'll build him up higher than a shot-tower in an hour's time!"

"Just the thing!" said I. "But here, take some money!"

"You may go your halves," says the honest fellow. "But, Mr. Byng,"—he hesitated, and looked at me doubtfully,—"suppose he wakes up while I'm gone, and finds a stranger here?"

"I'll justify you. I will show him that I'm a friend before he's made me out a stranger."

"That's right, sir. I think you've got a call here, a loud call. See how things has worked round. You come home, with nobody to look after, you come into Chrysalis, and the very first night a scare is sent to me. I go after Mr. Churm, as is ordered by my wife and the prickles of the scare. I don't find him; I do find you. You don't say, 'Janitor, this is none of my business. Apply at the sign of the Good Samaritan, across the way!' No; you know it's a call. You take hold; and here we are, and the boy a coming to on the slow train. When he gets to the depot, Mr. Byng, I hope you'll stand by him and stick to him."

"I will be a brother to him, Locksley, if he will let me."

"Let or no let, Mr. Byng. You've got a call to pad to him like a soldier-coat to a Governor's Guard. But here I go talkin' off, and where's the oysters?"

He hurried away. I was left alone with Cecil Dreeme.

Locksley's urgent plea was hardly needed. I felt every moment more brotherly to this desolate being, consigned to me by Fate.

"Poor fellow!" I thought. "He, I am sure, will not requite me with harm for saving him, as old proverbs too truly say the baser spirits may."

I wheeled him close to the stove. The room still seemed a dark and cheerless place to come back to life in. I tried to light the gas. It was chilled. There was a little ineffectual sputter as I touched the tube; a few sparks sprang up, but no flame backed them.

"It must be compelled to look a shade more cheerful, this hermit-age!" I thought. So I ran down in the dark to my own quarters for more light.

Rubbish Palace was generous as Fortunatus's purse. Whatever one wanted came to hand. More light was my present demand. I found it in a rich old bronze candelabrum, bristling with candles. More wrappings, too, I thought my patient might require. I flung across my arm a blanket from my bed, and that gorgeous yellow satin coverlet, once Louis Philippe's.

Perhaps, also, Dreeme might fancy some other drink than brandy when the oysters came. There was Ginevra's coffer, again presenting a plenteous choice. I snatched up another old flask, beaming with something vinous and purple, pocketed another Venetian goblet, and, thus reinforced, hastened up-stairs.

Now that the deadly distress of my alarm for the painter was reduced to a healthy anxiety, I could think what a picture I presented marching along, with my antique branch of six lighted candles in one hand, the mass of shining drapery on my arm, and in the other hand the glass, flashing with the red glimmers of its wine. But this walking tableau met no critics on the stairs; and when I pushed open Dreeme's door, he did not turn, as I half hoped he might, and survey the night-scene with a painter's eye.

I deposited my illumination on the table. Then I began to envelop my tranced man in that soft satin covering, whose color alone ought to warm him.

All at once, as, kneeling, I was arranging this robe of state about

Dreeme's feet, I became conscious, by I know not what magnetism, that he had opened his eyes, and was earnestly looking at me.

I would not glance up immediately. Better that he should recognize me as a friend, at a friend's work, before I as a person challenged him, eye to eye.

I kept my head bent down, and let him examine me, as I felt that he was doing, with hollow, melancholy eyes.

Chapter XIII

Dreeme, Awake

I felt that the pale face of Cecil Dreeme was regarding me with its hollow, sad eyes, as I arrayed him in the splendid spoil of the Tuileries.

Saying to himself, perhaps, I thought, "What does this impertinent intruder want? Am I to be compelled to live against my will? I excluded air, rejected food and fire,—must self-appointed friends thrust themselves upon me, and jar my calm accord with Death?"

I might be in a false position after all. My services and my apparatus might be merely officious.

I evaded Dreeme's look, and, moving to the table behind him, I occupied myself in pouring out a sip from the flask I had just brought. The purple wine sparkled in the goblet. In such a glass Bassanio might have pledged Portia.

No sooner had I stepped aside, than Dreeme stirred, and there came to me a voice, like the echo of a whisper: "Do not go."

"No," said I, "I am here."

Thus invited, I came forward and looked at him, eye to eye.

Wonderful eyes of his! None ever shone truer, braver, steadier. These large dark orbs, now studying me with such sad earnestness, completed, without defining, my first impressions of the man. Here was finer vision for beauty than the vision of creatures of common clay.

Here was keener insight into truth; here were the deeper faith, the larger love, that make Genius. A priceless spirit! so I fully discerned, now that the face had supplied its own illumination. A priceless spirit! and so nearly lost to the world, which has persons enough, but no spirits to waste.

As we regarded each other earnestly, I perceived the question flit across my mind: "Had I not had a glimpse of that inspired face before?"

"Why not?" my thought replied. "I may have seen him copying in the Louvre, sketching in the Oberland, dejected in the Coliseum, elated in St. Peter's, taking his coffee and violets in the Café Doné, whisking by at the Pitti Palace ball. Artists start up everywhere in Europe, like butterflies among flowers. He may have flashed across my sight, and imprinted an image on my brain to which his presence applies the stereoscopic counterpart.

This image, if it existed, was too faint to hold its own with the reality. It vanished, or only remained a slight blur in my mind. I satisfied myself that I was comparing Dreeme with his idealized self in the picture.

"You are better," said I.

There came a feeble, flutter-like "Yes," in reply.

He still continued looking at me in a vague, bewildered way, his great, sad eyes staring from his pale face, as if he had not strength to close them.

"I have been giving you brandy," I said; "let me offer a gentler medicine."

I held out the cup. Then, as he made no sign of assent, I felt that he might have a reasonable hesitation in taking an unknown draught from a stranger hand. I sipped a little of the wine. It was fragrant Port with plenty of body and a large proportion of soul. Magnificent Mafra at its royalist banquet never poured out richer juices to enlarge a Portuguese king into manhood. It had two flavors. One would say that the grapes which once held it bottled within the dewy transparency of their rind had hung along the terraces beside the sea, drinking two kinds of sunshine all the long afternoons of ripe midsummer. Every grape had felt the round sun gazing straight and steadily at it, and enjoying his countenance within, as a lover loves to see his own image reflected in his lady's eye. And every grape besides had taken in the broad glow of sunshine shining back from the glassy bay its vineyard overhung, or the shattered lights of innumerable ripples, stirred when the western winds came slinging themselves along the level sunbeams of evening. O Harry Stillfleet! why didn't you have a pipe, instead of a quart, of the stuff? Why not an ocean, instead of a sample?

I sipped a little, like a king's wine-taster.

"Port, not poison, Mr. Dreeme," said I. "This Venice glass would shiver with poison, and crack with scorn at any dishonest beverage."

He seemed to make a feeble attempt at a smile, as I proffered the dose. "Your health!" his lips rather framed than uttered.

I put the glass to his mouth.

An unexpected picture for mid-nineteenth century, and a corner of rusty Chrysalis! a strange picture!—this dark-haired, wasted youth, robed like a sick prince, and taking his posset from a goblet fashioned, perhaps, in a shop that paid rent to Shylock.

Dreeme closed his eyes, and seemed to let the wholesome fever of his draught revivify him. By this time the room was warm and comfortable. The stove might be ugly as a cylindrical fetish of the blackest Africa; but it radiated heat with Phœbus-like benignity.

"How cheerful!" murmured the painter, looking up again, his forlorn expression departed. "Fire! Light! I am a new being!"

"Not a spirit, then!" said I. There was still something remote and ghost-like in the bewildered look of his hollow eyes.

"No spirit! This is real flesh and blood."

I smiled. "Not much of either."

"Have I to thank you that I am not indeed a spirit?" asked he slowly, but seeming to gain strength as he spoke.

"Locksley, the janitor, first, and me, second, you may thank, if life is a boon to you."

"I thank both devoutly. Life is precious, while its work remains undone."

Here he closed his eyes, as if facing labor and duty again was too much for his feebleness. When he glanced up at me anew, I fancied I saw an evanescent look of recognition drift across his face.

This set me a second time turning over the filmy leaves of the book of portraits in my brain. Was his semblance among those legions of faces packed close and set away in order there? No. I could not identify him. The likeness drifted away from me, and vanished, like a perplexing strain of music, once just trembling at the lips, but now gone with the breath, refusing to be sung.

I thought it not best to worry him with inquiries; so I waited quietly, and in a moment he began.

"Will you tell me what has happened? How came I under your kind care? Yours is a new face in Chrysalis."

"I must give the face a name," said I. "Let me present myself. Mr. Robert Byng."

"In return, know me as Mr. Cecil Dreeme. Will you shake hands with your grateful patient, Mr. Byng."

He weakly lifted an attenuated hand. Poor fellow! I could hardly keep my vigorous fist from crushing up that meagre, chilly handful, so elated was I at his recovery and his gratitude.

"I owe you an explanation, of course," said I. "I am a new-comer, arrived from Europe only last night. Mr. Stillfleet, an old comrade, ceded his chambers below to me this afternoon. Locksley came to my door at twelve o'clock, looking for my friend Mr. Churm, who had been sitting with me. Churm had gone. Locksley was in great alarm. I volunteered my advice. He took me into his confidence, so far as this: he said that you were a young painter, living in the closest retirement, for reasons satisfactory to yourself, and that he feared you were dying from overwork, confinement, solitude, and perhaps mental trouble. I said you must be helped at once. We came up, and banged at your door heartily. No answer. We took the liberty to pick your lock and break into your castle. Then we took the greater liberty to put life into you, in the form of air, warmth, and alcohol."

"Pardonable liberties, surely."

"Yes; since it seems you did not mean to die."

"Suicide!" said Dreeme, reproachfully. "No, thank God! You did not accuse me of that, Mr. Byng!"

"When we were knocking at your door, and hearing only a deathly silence, I dreaded that you had let toil and trouble drive you to despair."

"Overwork and anxiety were killing me, without my knowledge."

"And solitude?" said I.

"And that solitude of the heart which is the brother of death. Yes, Mr. Byng, I have been extravagant of my life. But innocently. Believe it!"

There was such eager protest in his look and tone, that I hastened to reassure him.

"When I saw your face, Mr. Dreeme, I read there too much mental life and too much moral life for suicide. I see brave patience in your countenance. Besides, you have too much sense to rush out and tap Death on the cold shoulder, and beg to be let out of life into Paradise before you have earned your entrance fee. You know, as well as I do, that Death keeps suicides shivering in Chaos, without even a stick and a knife to notch off the measureless days, until the allotted dying hour they vainly tried to anticipate comes round."

Dreeme's attention refused to be averted from his own case by such speculations.

"I have been struggling with dark waters,—dark waters, Mr. Byng," said he.

"Churm's very phrase to describe *his* sorrow," I thought. "Who knows but Dreeme's grief is the same?"

"Struggling like a raw swimmer," he continued. "And when I was drowning, I find you sent to give me a friendly hand. It is written that I shall not die with all my work undone. No, no. I shall live to finish."

He spoke with strange energy, and turned toward his easel as he closed.

"You refer to your picture," said I, pleased to see his artist enthusiasm kindle so soon.

"My picture!" he rejoined, a little carelessly, as if it were of graver work he had thought. "How does it promise? I have put my whole heart into it. But hand cannot always speak loud enough or clear enough to interpret heart."

"Hand has not stammered or mumbled here," I replied. "My first glance showed me that. But I must have daylight to study it as it deserves. Am I right in recognizing you as the Cordelia of the piece?"

"For lack of a better model, I remodelled myself, and intruded there in womanly guise. My work is unfinished, as you see; but if you had not interposed to-night, I should have painted no more." He shuddered, and seemed to grow faint again at the thought of that desolate death he had hardly escaped.

"Let me cheer you with a fresh dose of vitality," said I. "A little more Lusitanian sun in crystal of Venice."

This time he was strong enough himself to raise the cup to his lips. He sipped, and smiled gratefully;—and really a patient owes some thanks to a doctor who restores him with nectar smooth and fragrant, instead of rasping his throat and flaying his whole interior with the bitters sucked by sour-tempered roots from vixenish soils.

"It was a happy fate, a kind Providence," said Dreeme, "that sent to me in my extremity a gentleman whose touch to mind and body is fine and gentle as a woman's."

"Thank you," rejoined I. "But remember that I am only acting as Mr. Churm's substitute. I hope you will let me bring him to you in the morning."

"No," said he, almost with rude emphasis.

I looked at him in some surprise. "You seem to have a prejudice against the name," I remarked.

"Why should I? I merely do not wish to add to my list of friends."

"But Mr. Churm is the very ideal friend,—stanch as oak, true as steel, warm and cheery as sunshine, eager as fresh air, tender as midsummer rain. Do let me interest him in you. He is just the man to befriend a lonely fellow."

Dreeme shook his head, resolutely and sadly.

"You seem to mistrust my enthusiasm," I said.

"It is tragic to me," he returned, "to hear a generous nature talk so ardently of its friendships. Have you had no disappointments? Has no one you loved changed and become abased?"

"One would almost say you were trying to shake my faith in my friend."

"Why should I? I speak generally."

Here the partition door of the lobby without opened, and we heard footsteps.

"Friend Locksley, with some supper for you," said I, half annoyed at the interruption of our *tête-à-tête*.

"How kind! how thoughtful of you both!" and tears started in Dreeme's eyes as he spoke.

CHAPTER XIV

A Mild Orgie

Locksley came boldly in, breathlessly.

"All right, I see, Mr. Dreeme," he panted.

"All right, Locksley! thanks to you and Mr. Byng."

"I've been gone," says the janitor, "long enough to make all the shifts of a permutation lock."

He deposited a huge basket on the table.

"Bagpypes's was shut," he continued. "So was De Grope's. I had to go up to Selleridge's. He's an open-all-night-er. Selleridge's was full of fire-company boys, taking their tods after a run. Selleridge couldn't stop pouring and mixing and stirring and muddling. 'Firemen comes first,' says he. 'They've got to have their extinguishers into 'em.' So I jumped up on the counter, and says I, 'Boys, I've got a sick man to oyster up, and if he ain't oystered up on time he'll be a dead shell.' So the red flannels drawed off, like real bricks. I got my oysters, and came away like horse-power."

Locksley took breath, and began to arrange his vivers on the table.

"Six Shrewsburys," he pronounced, bestowing their portly shells before him. "For a roast, if Mr. Dreeme likes. Twelve Blue-Pointers, every one little as a lady's ear. Them for a stew, if Mr. Dreeme likes better. Paper of mixed crackers,—Boston butters, Wilson's sweets, and Wing's pethy. Pad of butter. Plate of slaw, ready vinegared. I wanted to leave the slaw; but Selleridge said, 'No; slaw and oysters was man and wife, and he shouldn't be easy in his mind if he sent one out and kep' the other.' And here's some Scotch ale, in a scrumptious little stone jug, to wash all down."

"You will appall Mr. Dreeme's invalid appetite with these piles of provender," said I.

"On the contrary, my spirits rise with the sight of a banquet and guests to share it," Dreeme returned.

"Nibble on a Wing's pethy," says Locksley, handing the crackers, "while I plant a Shrewsbury to cook in the stove."

"I did not know how ravenous I was," Dreeme said, taking a second "pethy."

"Dora had a hearty cry," says the janitor, "because she couldn't get any word when she came up with your meals to-day, Mr. Dreeme."

"Poor child! I heard her knock in the morning; but I was half asleep, and too weak to answer. All at once my strength, ignorantly overtasked, had failed. Later, I managed to struggle up and dress myself. Then I found my way to this arm-chair before my picture. There I sat all day, sometimes unconscious, sometimes conscious of a flicker of life. Dora came with my dinner. I heard her knock. When I perceived that I could not speak or stir in answer, utter desolation darkened down upon me. I felt myself sink away, and seemed to drown, slowly, slowly, without pain or terror. Immeasurable deeps of space crushed me. But by and by I felt my course reversed. I was rising, slowly as I had sunk. At last I knew the pang and thrill of life. I woke and saw Mr. Byng restoring me."

Dreeme recited this history with strange impassiveness.

"You take it pretty cool," says Locksley. "It seems as if you was making up a tale about somebody else,—holding off your death at arm's length and talking about it."

"Mr. Dreeme speaks as an artist," said I, trying, with a blundering good-humor, to make our parley less sombre. "He already looks at this passage in his life as a peril quite escaped, and so material for dramatic treatment."

"Death and resurrection!" said Dreeme, gravely. "Suppose, Mr. Byng, that you were worn down to die by agony for sins not your own, could you believe that such an incomplete death as mine makes atonement? Could you hope that your strong suffering had purged the guilty souls clean? Could you have faith that their lives would renew and amend, as vital force came back to the life that had sorrowed unto death for them?"

"Solemn questions, Mr. Dreeme," I replied. "Are you quite well enough yet to entertain them?"

Here the Shrewsbury in the stove recalled us to mundane phenomena, by giving a loud wheeze.

"There she blows!" cried Locksley.

He grappled the crustaceous grandee with the tongs, and popped him on a plate. A little fragrant steam issued from the calcined lips, invitingly parted.

"Roast oysters," says Locksley, "always wheezes when they're done to a bulge. If you want 'em done dry, wait till the music's all cooked out of 'em. This is a bulger," he continued, deftly whisking off the top shell. "Down it, Mr. Dreeme, without winking!"

Dreeme obeyed.

Locksley consigned another of the noble race of Shrewsbury to fiery martyrdom. Then he turned again to the painter.

"You won't go and die again?" said he.

Dreeme smiled, and shook his head.

"Not," says the janitor, with queer earnestness of manner, "that I wouldn't come in any time on call and help liven you up, howsever dead you might be. But it ain't good for you; it's unwholesome,—tell him so, Mr. Byng."

"Be informed, then, Mr. Dreeme," said I, "that dying is not good for you. I intend not to let you take any more of it. I prescribe instead a generous life, and I hope you will allow me to aid in administering the remedy."

"That's right," says Locksley, "mix in, Mr. Byng. And now, if you say so, I'll run down and get Mr. Stillfleet's volcano and stew-pan to stew the Blue-Pointers. They're waiting, mild as you please, and not getting a fair show."

The busy fellow bustled off.

"Mixing in is my trade," said I. "I am a chemist. Pardon me if I seem to mingle myself too far and too soon in your affairs."

"I feel no danger from you, Mr. Byng. I accept most gratefully your kind and gentlemanlike interference."

He spoke with marked dignity. Indeed, although the circumstances of our meeting had brought us so near together, the reserve and settled self-possession of his manner kept me at a wide distance. No fear that he would not protect himself against intrusion.

Locksley now reappeared with the stew-pan and alcohol-lamp. He went at his cookery with a blundering frenzy of good-will. It was quite idle for Dreeme to protest that he would be killed by this culinary kindness.

"Just one Blue-Pointer!" says the janitor-cook, forking out a little oyster of pearly complexion from where it lay heads and points among its fellows. "Just one! It'll top off the Shrewsburys, as a feather tops off a commodore."

The bristly fellow's earnestness, as he stood seductively holding up the neat morsel, was so comic, that Dreeme let himself laugh heartily.

I had heard no laugh since Densdeth's at the Chuzzlewit dinner-table. That scoffing tone of his which broke in upon my queries to Churm regarding Cecil Dreeme was still in my ears. The memory of Densdeth's laugh still misrepresented to me all laughter. Laughter, if I took that as its type, was only the loud sneer of a ruthless cynic. Such a laugh made honor seem folly, truth weakness, generosity a bid for richer requital, chivalry the hypocrisy of a knave.

I was hardly conscious how much faith had gone out of me, expelled by his sneering tone, until Dreeme's musical, child-like laugh redressed the wrong. Instantly the wound of Densdeth's cynicism was healed. I was freshened again, and tuned anew to all sweet influences. Honor seemed wisdom; truth the only strength; generosity its own reward; chivalry the expression in manners of a loyal heart. All the brave joyousness of my nature responded to this laugh of Dreeme's, and spoke out boldly in my echoing one. Each of us perceived new sympathy in the other.

Locksley now made his reappearance with the volcano. The oysters crackled in the stove, fizzed and bubbled over the lamp on the table.

The poetic temperament takes in happiness and good cheer as a bud takes sunshine. Dreeme expanded more and more. His silver laugh flowed free in chastened merriment. He seemed to forget that an hour ago he had been dying, friendless and alone; to forget whatever sorrow or terror had driven him to this unnatural seclusion, up in the shabby precincts of Chrysalis College.

We were a merry trio. Reaction after the anxiety of the evening exhilarated me to my best mood. Locksley too was in high feather. His harangue at Selleridge's had loosed his tongue,—never in truth a very tight one,—and he vented no end of odd phrases over the banquet.

Stillfleet's antique flasks and goblets figured decorously at the board. They were spectators rather than actors. The janitor proposed Mr. Dreeme's health.

"I hardly expected, Locksley," said I in reply, "when Stillfleet warned you that I would try to introduce the Orgie here, that you were to be my chief abettor."

"The mildest Orgie ever known!" said Dreeme.

"Rather a feast of thanksgiving. But shall we end it now? I see you grow weary."

"I do, healthily weary. Ah, Mr. Byng! you cannot conceive the blissful revulsion in my life since last night, when I fell asleep alone and without hope,—over-weary with work, weary to death of life."

"Would you like me to camp with a blanket on your floor, in case you should need anything?"

"No," he replied, rather coldly. "I shall do well. I would not incommode you."

"Good night then, my dear Mr. Dreeme. Pray understand that our new friendship must not be slept out of existence."

No doubt my tone betrayed that his sudden cold manner had made me fancy such a result.

"O no!" he said ardently. "I am not a person of many professions, but I do not forget. And I need your kindness still, and shall need it. Pray," continued he, "keep my secret. I do not wish to be known, until my hibernation is over. Locksley has been pretty faithful thus far."

"Until Mr. Byng arrived to make a traitor of me," said the janitor, with compunction.

"Such treachery is higher loyalty," Dreeme rejoined. "You find me hiding my light under a bushel, but don't suspect me, Mr. Byng, of anything worse than a freak, or an ambitious fancy."

Not either of these, I was sure, from his unhappy attempt at a smile as he spoke. But he threw himself upon my good faith so utterly, that I resolved never to open my eyes, to shut them even to any flash of suspicion of his secret that any circumstance might reveal.

"Good night!" And so we parted.

"We've hit the bull's-eye true," said Locksley, as we descended. "You suited him even better than Mr. Churm could have done."

"Mysterious business! Such an odd place to hide in! And his name on the door, too!"

"Who would think of searching for a runaway in a respectable old den like this. Perhaps the name is not his. A wrong name puts people on the wrong scent. It's having *no* name that is suspicious. And if he'd put 'Panther,' instead of 'Painter,' on his door, it wouldn't have kept people away any better. Who goes to a young painter's door? They have trouble enough to get any notice."

"I believe you are right. Will you come in and let me give you a cigar?"

"No I thank you, sir. Miss Locksley has got a natural nose against tobacco. If I go to bed scented, she'll wake up and scallop me with questions. Good night, sir." And we parted at the main staircase.

"A full day," I thought, as I entered my room. No danger of my being bored, if events crowd in this way in America. Here certainly is romance. Destiny has brought Cecil Dreeme and me together without a break-down on his side of the ceiling, or a pistol-shot from me below. Poor fellow! who knows but, even so young, he has had some cruel experience like Churm's? But hold! I must not pry into his affairs. I might strike tragedy, and tragedy I do not love. So to bed, and no dreams of Dreeme.

Chapter XV

A Morning with Densdeth

I slept late after our gentle Orgie, my second night on shore.

A loud rapping awoke me.

I opened. Churm was at the door, stout stick in hand, stout shoes on his feet, stout coat on his back,—the sturdiest man to be seen, search a continent for his fellow! He had the Herculean air of one who has been out giving the world a lift by way of getting an appetite for breakfast.

"Good morning," said he, marching in. "This will never do, my tallish young Saxon, come home to work!"

"What?"

"Nine A. M., and your day's task not begun!"

"I worked too late last night."

"At the mysteries of your trade? I doubt if you encountered a deeper one than I in my watch."

"Perhaps, and perhaps not. What was yours?"

"The heart of a wrong-doer."

"That transcends my trade's methods of analysis."

"And in this case, my powers."

"You are speaking of your *protégé,* Towner," said I, going on with my toilette.

"Of him. He has a confession to make to me. He dares not quite confess. He comes up timorously, like a weak-kneed horse to his leap; then he seems to see something on the other side; he flinches and sheers into a Serbonian bog of lies."

"Afraid of the consequences of confession?"

"Not of the ordinary punishment of guilt, nor of any ordinary revenge from his ancient master in evil."

"Namely, as you allege, Densdeth."

"Densdeth."

"I shall grow perverse enough to take Densdeth's part, and cast my shell to de-ostracize him from his moral ostracism, if I hear him called The Unjust by all the world."

"Don't be Quixotic, Byng. There is more vanity than generosity in that."

"And what dreadful vengeance does your weakling fear?"

"He thinks that, if he betrays his master, he shall never save himself from that master's clutch. Densdeth will pursue him and debase his soul through all the eternities, as he has done in this life."

"Quite a metaphysical distress!"

"Don't laugh at him! It is a real agony with him; and who knows but the danger is real?"

"You do not get at what the poor devil has done in which you are interested?"

"Not at all. And his moral struggle with himself, and defeat, have plunged him back into such pitiable weakness of body, that we have lost all we had gained. The doctor says that it will kill him to see me again for weeks."

"So Densdeth is respited. Well, I will study him in the interval, and find out for myself whether he is *'main de fer, sous patte de velours.'* "

"Very well, Byng; I see you are resolved to buy your experience. Densdeth has magnetized you. He does most young men."

"I don't know yet whether I shall turn to him my positive or negative pole. He may repel, instead of attracting, as soon as I get within his sphere. I acknowledge that I am drawn to him."

"Now then, enough of such topics. My vigils have given me an appetite. I want to reverse *'qui dort dine,'* and read *'qui déjeune dort.'* "

"Where shall we go? Chuzzlewit, Patrick rampant, flannel cakes, and Densdeth?"

"No; a better place. The Minedurt, close by."

"Unpropitious name!"

"Surnames go by contraries. This is old Knickerbocker. It should read 'The Grotto of Neatness,' instead of the 'Minedurt.'"

An avenue—The Avenue—flows up hill, northward, from the middle of Ailanthus Square. Churm conducted me a few blocks along that channel of wealth. He stopped in front of the Minedurt, a hotel with restaurant attached. Respectable could not have been more distinctly stamped upon a building, if it had been written up in a great label across the front, and in a hundred little labels everywhere, like the big red Ten and the little red tens on a bank-bill.

"Notice that large house across the street," said Churm, halting before this respectable establishment.

"I do. It is nearer civilization than anything I have seen. A fine house. Happy the owner! if he appreciates architecture."

"Happy!" said Churm, bitterly. "It is Denman's house! He had ancestral acres here, and was one of the first to perceive that the cream would settle in his grandfather's cow-pasture."

"Stop a moment! The tragedy of my old playmate gives the house a strange sanctity in my eyes."

"It is cursed," said Churm. "No happiness to its tenants,—only harm to its friends, until the wrong done my child there has been expiated."

"Has not her father's grief atoned for his error?"

"You cannot understand my feelings, Byng. You did not know Clara Denman."

I paused to inspect the mansion, sanctified to me by death. Death sanctifies, birth consecrates a home.

Sanctified? But the death here was perhaps a suicide. So some alleged. Can a suicide sanctify? Does it not desecrate? Do not some churches deny the corpse, a self-slayer flung away, its hiding-place in holy ground? No suicide near the sleeping saints! A man may strangle himself with good dinners, or poison himself with fine old Madeira or coarse old Monongahela; a bad conscience, gnawing day and night, may eat away his heart; he may have murdered the woman that once loved him, by judicious slow torture; he may have murdered the friend that trusted him, by a peevish No, when it was help or death; no matter! He will be allowed as comfortable a grave as a sexton can dig, six feet by two in soft soil under green sod, and the priest will dust his dust with all the compliments in the burial service. But let him have put a knife to his throat, or a bullet in his brain, because he could not any longer face the woman he had wronged, or the friend he had betrayed,—what shudders then of sexton and priest! No place for him beside the glutton and the drunkard! The cruel husband or the false friend would shiver in his coffin at such propinquity. Out with him! Out with the accursed thing! To the dogs with the carrion!

Not sanctified,—saddened, I could, without any one's protest, consider Mr. Denman's house. Hundreds, no doubt, every day envied the happy owner. How grand to possess that stately edifice of contrasted freestones, purple and drab; those well-cut pilasters; that dignified roof, in the old chateau manner, fitly capping the whole; that majestic portal; those great windows, heavily draped, but allowing the inner magnificence to peer through, conscious, but not ostentatious;—how grand to stand and call this mine!

Hundreds, no doubt, envied Mr. Denman every day. First in the morning, journeymen, hurrying by with a poor dinner in a tin canister; next, Tittlebat Titmouse, on his way to the counter; then some clerk of higher degree, seller by the piece instead of the yard, by the cargo instead of the pound, bustling down town to his desk; next the poor book-keeper, with twelve hundred a year, and a mouth to every hundred; then the broken-down merchant, who must show himself on the Street, though the Street noted him no more; and so on in order, the financial dignitary, the club-man lounging to his late breakfast or his morning stroll, the country cousin seeing the lions, the woman of fashion driving up to drop a card; and then at sunset the pretty girl walking up town with her lover; and then at night the night-bird skulking by;—all these envied the tenants of the Denman mansion, or at least fancied them fortunate. And all houses announce as little as that the miseries that may dwell within!

"Come, Byng," said my friend, "you cannot see into the heart of that house by staring at it."

We passed in to our breakfast. Over our coffee we glided into cheerful talk. I consulted Churm, and he frankly advised me as to my future.

And so, speaking of my own prospects, we spoke of the hopes and duties of my generation to our country.

"We are the first," said I, "who understand what an absolute Republic means, and what it can do."

"The first as a generation. Individuals have always comprehended it," said Churm.

"And now, acting together, on a larger scale, with a grander co-operation, we will inaugurate the new era for the noblest manhood and the purest womanhood the world has ever known."

I had spoken ardently.

At once, as if in echo to my words, I heard Densdeth's cynic laugh behind me.

My enthusiasm perished.

I turned uneasily. Was Densdeth laughing at my silly boyish fervors?

He was sitting two tables off, breakfasting with a well-known man about town. Densdeth's companion was one of those who have beauty which they debase, talents which they bury, money which they squander. He was a man of fine genius, but genius under a murky cloud, flashing out rarely in a sad or a scornful way. A man sick of himself, sorry for himself. A wasted life, hating itself for its waste, wearing itself out with self-reproach that it was naught. Some evil influence had clutched him after his first success and his first sorrow. Thenceforth his soul was paralyzed. The success had nurtured a lazy pride, instead of an exalting ambition. The sorrow had made him tender to himself and hard to others. What was that evil influence? Could it be in the dark face beside him?

Densdeth nodded to me familiarly, as I turned.

"Don't forget," said he, "our appointment at one. You know Raleigh, I believe."

Mr. Raleigh and I bowed cordially.

We had met in Europe. We had sympathized on art and nature. I had touched only his better side, though I saw the worse. I liked Raleigh, and fancied, as a boy fancies, that I had a certain power over him, and that for good.

We all rose together after our breakfast.

"Are you killing time, or nursing it, Byng?" said Densdeth.

"Killing it for a day or two, until I acclimate to the atmosphere of work."

"Unless you have something better to do, drop over with us to the club. You must know the men. We will have a game of billiards until one."

"Yes, come, Byng," invited Raleigh's sweet voice.

"Thank you," I said. "Business, in the form of Mr. Churm, deserts me. Pleasure woos. I yield."

"Take care!" said Churm to me, as we walked away. "I see you insist upon personal experience."

"O yes! Nothing vicarious for me! I will nibble at our friend. I'll try not to bite, for fear of the poison you threaten."

Churm left us, and walked across Ailanthus Square, on his way down town.

"I must look in at my quarters for a moment," said I to the others; "will you lounge on, and let me overtake you, or honor me with a visit?"

"Let us drop in, Raleigh," said Densdeth. "I am curious to see how the old place looks, with Stillfleet's breezes out and Byng's calms in."

I did the honors, and then, establishing my guests with cigars, I excused myself, and ran upstairs to give good morning to Cecil Dreeme. Churm's presence and a lively appetite together had delayed this duty. Besides, I had felt that he ought not to be disturbed too early.

I knocked, and spoke my name. The recluse might sport oak to the knock alone.

"Coming," responded his gentle voice.

Presently the door opened enough to admit me, but not to display the interior of the chamber to any inquisitive passer.

I was struck, even more than last night, by the singular, refined beauty of the youth. And then his body was so worn and thin, that his soul seemed to get very close to me.

His personal magnetism—that is, the touch of his soul on mine—affected me more keenly than before. It was having cumulative influence. The mighty medicines for soul and body always do.

And so do the poisons.

"You are looking quite vigorous and cheerful this morning," I said, exaggerating a little. "I congratulate you on your leap out of death into full life."

"It is to you I owe it," he said, with deep feeling.

He grasped my hand, and then dropped it suddenly again, as if he feared he was taking a liberty.

(How exactly I remember every word and gesture of those first interviews! Ah, Cecil Dreeme! how little I fancied then what salvage you were to pay me for my succor!)

"You are hard at work again, I see." I pointed to his palette and brushes. "Be cautious! Do not overdo it! You must be under my orders for a while."

I was conscious of claiming this power a little timidly, such was the quiet dignity of the young man.

"I will try to be wiser now, since I have a friend who is willing to admonish me."

"Now," continued he, as if to turn attention from himself, "look at my picture! I want a slashing criticism. You cannot find faults that I do not see myself."

I stepped back to look at it. A work of power! Crude, indeed; but with force enough to justify any crudity.

Its deep tragedy struck me silent.

"Do not spare me," said Dreeme. "Silence is severer than blame. Say, at least, that it is pretty well for a novice,—pretty well considering my years and my practice."

"What has happened to you?" said I, staring at his pale, worn face. "What right have you, in the happy days of youth, to the knowledge that has taught you to paint tragedy thus? What unknown agony have you undergone? Mr, Dreeme, your picture is a revelation. I pity you from my heart."

"You do not believe," said he, evasively, "that imagination can supply the want of experience?"

"Imagination must have experience to transfuse into new facts. You, of course, have not had an unjust father, like your Lear, nor a disloyal sister, like your Goneril; nor have you felt a withering curse, as your Cordelia does. But tyranny and treachery must have touched you. They have initiated you into their modes of action and expression. Do not find inquisitiveness implied in my criticism. I pity you too much for the ability and impulse to paint thus, to be curious how it came."

"Believe, then," said Dreeme, "and it may help you to make allowances for me, that I know in my own life what tragedy means. That experience commands me to do violence to my love of beauty and happy scenes, and paint agony, as I have done there. And now, pray let us be technical. That white drapery,—how does it fall? Are the lines stiff? Is there too much starch in the linen, or too little?"

"Technicality another time. I am uncivil even in delaying so long. Two gentlemen are waiting for me below."

"Your friend, Mr. Churm?" he asked, looking away.

"No. Mr. Densdeth and Mr. Raleigh."

"Densdeth!" said he, with a slight shudder. "You see I have the susceptible nerves of an artist. I tremble at the mere sound of such an ill-omened name. Should you not naturally avoid a person called Densdeth?" And as if the sound fascinated him, he repeated, "Densdeth! Densdeth!"

"Name and man are repulsive; but attractive also. Attractive by repulsion."

"Take my advice, and obey the repulsion. Poisons are not made bitter that we may school ourselves to like them. If this person, with a boding name, repels you, do not taste him, as one tastes opium. Curiosity may make you a slave."

"Odd, that you, a stranger, should have the usual prejudice against Densdeth!"

"Consider that I am as one raised from the dead, and so perhaps clairvoyant. I use my power to warn you, as you have saved me."

"Thank you," said I; "I will see you this evening, and tell you how far I am ruined by a morning with this *bête noir.* If he spoils me, you must repair the harm."

I walked to the door. He released me with a cautious glance into the hall. I ran down stairs and apologized for my delay to my guests.

"It is a privilege to wait, my dear fellow," said Densdeth, "in such a treasure-house. We have been looking at these droll old tapestries of Purgatory and a hotter place. Raleigh insists that the seducing devil, wooing those revellers to hell, is my precise image."

"No doubt of it," says Raleigh. "You must be Mephistophiles himself. Those fifteenth-century fellows have got your portrait to the life. It seems you were at the same business then, as now."

Densdeth laughed. Raleigh and I laughed in answer. Both had caught that mocking tone of his.

"Not only are you the devil of the tapestry," said Raleigh, "but I see myself among your victims."

"You flatter me," said Densdeth, again with his sinister laugh.

"Yes, and Byng too, and certain ladies we know of. I really begin to be lazily superstitious. Don't make it too hot for me, Densdeth, when you get me below. I've only been a negative sinner in this world,—no man's enemy but my own."

Raleigh's jest was half earnest. That and the demonish quality in Densdeth quickened my glance at the old altar-cloth, which hung on the wall, among Stillfleet's prints and pictures.

Under these impressions, I did indeed identify Densdeth with the cloven-hoofed tempter in this characteristic bit of mediæval art. Raleigh was surely there, in the guise of a languid Bacchanal, crowned with drooping vine-leaves. I myself was also there,—a youth, only half consenting, dragged along by an irresistible attraction. And continuing my observations, I recognized other friends, faintly imaged in the throng on the tapestry. An angel, looking sadly at the evil one's triumph and my fall, was Cecil Dreeme's very self. And up among the judges sat Churm, majestic as a prophet of Michael Angelo.

"Come," said Densdeth,—he was by chance standing in the exact attitude of the Tempter in the tapestry,—"come; we shall have but just time for Byng's introduction and our game of billiards."

"Lead on, your majesty!" said Raleigh. "We needs must follow,—to billiards or the bottomless pit."

We walked to the club. It was the crack club then. Years ago it went to pieces. Its gentlemen have joined better. Its legs and loafers have sunk to bar-rooms.

The loungers there were languid when we entered.

No scandal had yet come up from Wall Street; none down from Murray Hill.

The morning was still virgin of any story of disaster to character, financial or social.

The day had not done its duty,—a mere *dies non*, and promising only to be *dies perdita*.

To be sure it was still a young day. It might still ruin somebody, pocket or reputation. Somebody, man or woman, might go to protest, and shame every indorser, before three o'clock.

But everybody at the club had made it seven bells; eight bells would presently strike, and no sign of the day's ration of scandal. They could not mumble all the afternoon over the stale crusts of yesterday; they could not put bubble into yesterday's heel-taps. Everybody was bored. Life was a burden at the windows, by the fire, at the billiard-tables, of that rotten institution.

Densdeth's arrival made a stir.

"See these *gobemouches*," whispered Raleigh to me. "They think Densdeth, the busy man, would never come here at this hour in the morning, unless some ill had happened,—unless there were some new man to jeer, or woman to flout. Now see how he will treat them."

The languid loungers lost their air of nonchalance. There was a general move toward our party. The click of balls upon the tables was still. The players came forward, cue in hand. These unknightly knights of the Long Table stood about us, with the blunted lances of a blunted chivalry, waiting to chuckle over the fate of some comrade in the dust, of some damsel soiled with scorn. Remember, that these were only the baser sort of the members. Heroes may sometimes lounge. Real heroes may play billiards, like the Phelan, and be heroes still.

Densdeth's manner with his auditory was a study.

"Pigs," he seemed to say, "I suppose I must feed you. Gobble up this and this, ye rabble rout! Take your fare and my mental kicking with it."

Soon he tired of the herd, and led the way to a billiard-table, apart.

"I wanted to show you, Byng," said he, with an air of weary disgust, "what kind of men will be your associates among the idlers."

"The busy men are nobler, I hope," said I.

"You shall see. I will give you the *entrée* to the other worlds,—the business world, the literary world, the religious world, all of them. Possibly you may not have quite outlived your illusions. Possibly you may have fancied that men are to be trusted on a new continent. Possibly you may believe in the success of a society and polity based on the assumption that mankind is not an ass when he is not a villain, and *vice versa.*"

"I had some such fancy."

"Better be disenchanted now, than disappointed by and by. *Apropos,* don't suppose I often degrade myself to the level of that swinish multitude of scandal-mongers. But when I saw them so greedy, I could not forbear giving them diet, according to their stomachs."

"What an infernal humbug you are, Densdeth!" said Raleigh, marking a five-shot; "you love to spoil those boys, and keep the men spoilt. If you were out of the world, they would all reform, and go to sucking honey, instead of poison."

"We are all humbugs," rejoined Densdeth; "I want to put Byng on his guard against me and the rest. He might get some unhappy notion, that in America men are brave and women are pure."

I kept my protest to myself, willing to study Densdeth further.

Densdeth led the conversation, as indeed he never failed to do. He was a keen, hard analyzer of men, utterly sceptical to good motives. There is always just such a proportion of selfishness in every man's every act; there must be, because there is a man in it. It may be the larger half, the lesser half, a fraction, the mere dust of an atom, that makes the scale descend. Densdeth always discovered the selfish purpose, put it in focus, held up a lens of his own before it. At once it grew, and spread, and seemed the whole.

Densdeth was the Apostle of Disenchantment. No paradisiacal innocence where he entered. He revealed evil everywhere. That was at the core, according to him, however smooth the surface showed. Power over others consisted in finding that out. And that power was the only thing, except sensuality, worth having.

Thus I condense my impressions of him. I did not know him, in and in, out and out, after this first morning at the club, nor after many such meetings. I learnt him slowly.

Yet I think I divined him from the first. I did not state to my own mind, then, why he captivated me,—why he sometimes terrified me,—why I had a hateful love for his society. In fact, the power of deeply analyzing character comes with a maturity that I had not attained. I was to pay price for my knowledge. Densdeth's shadow was to fall upon me. My danger with evil personified, in such a man as Densdeth, was to sear into me a profound and saving horror of evil. One does not read the moral, until the tale is told.

We played our billiards. One o'clock struck. We left Raleigh to be bored with the world and sick of himself, to knock the balls about, and wish he had been born a blacksmith or a hod-carrier.

Densdeth and I walked to the Denmans.

"You will see a very captivating young lady," he said, with a sharp and rapid glance at me.

I was aware of a conscious look. He caught it also.

"Aha, Byng! a little tenderness for the old playmate! Well, perhaps she has been waiting for you. She has looked coldly on scores of lovers."

There was a familiarity in his tone which offended me. It seemed to sneer away the delicacy I felt towards one with whom I had childish passages of admiration ten years ago. I was angry at his disposing of my destiny and hers at once. In turn, I looked sharply at him, and said, in the same careless tone, "How does Miss Denman compare with her sister?"

Not a spark of emotion in his impassive face. There might have been a slight smile, as if to say, "This boy fancies that he is able to probe me, and learn why I courted the less beautiful sister, and what I did to drive her mad and to death." But the smile vanished, and he said, quietly: "We will not speak of the dead, if you please. Among the living, Miss Denman stands alone. A great prize, Byng! People that pretend to know say that Mr. Denman is a millionnaire. See what a grand house he lives in!"

"Grand houses sometimes make millionnaires paupers," I remarked, thinking of what Churm had told me.

"I am quite sure no pauper owns this," Densdeth said, measuring it with a look, as we walked up the steps.

I remembered what Churm had said, and fancied I saw at least mortgagee, if not proprietor, in my companion's eye. Was he inspecting to see if *his* house needed a trowelful of mortar, or a gutter repaired?

Chapter XVI

———•———

Emma Denman

Densdeth rang. We were admitted at once. The footman introduced us into a parlor fronting on the avenue. The interior of the house was worthy of its stately architecture. I do not describe. People, not things, passions, not objects, are my topics.

Presently, in a mirror at the end of the long suite of rooms, I was aware of the imaged figure of a young lady approaching. Semblance before substance, instead of preparing me for the interview, it almost startled me. I half fancied that shadowy reflection to be the spirit of the dead sister watching. The living sister was coming in the body; the presence of the sister dead tarried in the background, curious to see what would grow from the germ of a childish friendship revived.

In a moment the lady herself stepped forward.

No thought of shadows any more!

She, the substance, took a stand among the foremost figures in my drama.

The effect of the room where I sat was rich and festal, almost to the verge of gorgeousness. Had sorrow dared to intrude among such courtly splendors? Carpets thick with the sunburnt flowers of late summer,—had these felt the trailing step that carries grief on to another moment of grief? Heavy crimson curtains,—must these have uttered muffled echoes when a sigh, outward bound, drifted against their folds? And deep-toned pictures, full of victory and jubilee,—could they not outface the pale countenance of mourning in that luxurious room? It made the power of sorrow and the bitterness of death seem far more giant in their strength, that they had crowded in hither, and hung a dim film of funereal black before all this magnificence.

Crimson was the chief color in carpet, curtains, and walls. This deep, rich background magically heightened the effect of the pale, elegant figure in deep mourning who was approaching.

Emma Denman passed in front of the mirror, erasing her own reflection there. She came forward, and offered her hand to me with shy cordiality. The shyness remembered the old familiar playmate of the days of "little husband and little wife"; the cordiality was for the unforgotten friend.

I found no change, only development, in Emma Denman. Still the same fitful fascination that had been her charm as a child. It seized me at once. I lost my power of quiet discrimination. I can hardly analyze her power even now. These subtle influences refuse to be subject to my chemical methods and my formulas.

It was not the power of beauty, alone. Physical beauty she had, but something higher also. Nor spiritual beauty alone, but something other. The mere flesh-and-blood charms, lilies and roses, the commonplace traits of commonplace women, whose inventory describes the woman, she could afford to disdain. It was a face that forbade all formal criticism. No passport face. Other women one names beautiful for a feature, a smile, or a dimple,—that link between a feature and a smile. Hers was a face suffused with the fine essence of beauty. It seemed to wrong the whole, if one let eyes or mind make any part distinct.

Grace she had,—exquisite grace. Grace is perhaps a more subtle charm than beauty. Beauty is passive; grace is active. Beauty reveals the nature; grace interprets it. Beauty wins; grace woos.

Emma Denman's coloring did not classify her. Her hair was in the indefinite shades between light and dark. One would not expect from her the steadiness of the fair temperaments, nor the ardor of their warmer counterparts in hue. No dismissing her with the label of a well-known type. I must have a new and composite thought in my mind while I curiously studied her.

Her eyes wanted color. They were not blue and constant, not black and passionate. Indeed, but for their sparkle and vivacity, they would have seemed expressionless. Restless eyes! they might almost have taken a lesson from Densdeth's, so rapid were they to come and go, so evanescent and elusive was their glance. But Densdeth's were chasing eyes; hers were flying. Her swift eyes, her transitory smile, her motions, soft as the bend of a branch, light as the spring of a bird, lithe as the turn of a serpent, all were elements in her singular fascination,—it was almost elfin.

She was in deep mourning; and, partly because mourning quickens sympathy, partly because to a person of her doubtful coloring positive contrasts are valuable, it seemed the very dress to heighten her beauty. And yet, as I saw her afterwards, I found that all costume and scenery became thus tributary to her, and all objects and people so disposed themselves, and all lights and shades so fell, as to define and intensify her charm.

Densdeth witnessed our recognition, and then excused himself. "He had business with Mr. Denman in the library, and would join us by and by." We both breathed freer upon his exit. It was impossible not to feel that he was always reading every act and thought; and that consciousness of a ruthless stare turned in upon one's little innocencies of heart is abashing to young people.

Miss Denman had seemed uneasy while Densdeth stayed. She changed her seat, and with it her manner, as he departed. The chair she now took brought her again within range of the distant mirror. Her shadow became a third party in our interview. When I observed it, its presence disturbed me. Sometimes, as before, I fancied it the sprite of the sister dead, sometimes the double of the person before me,—her true self, or her false self, which she had dismissed for this occasion, while she made her impression upon me.

Strange fancies! faintly drifting across my mind. But I did not often observe that dim watcher in the mirror. My companion engaged me too closely. Now that Densdeth was gone, we sat in quiet mood, and let our old acquaintance renew itself.

Our talk was hardly worth chronicling. Words cannot convey the gleam of pleasure with which our minds alighted together on the same memory of days gone by, as we used to spring upon a flower in the field, or a golden butterfly by the wayside.

"Ah! those sorrowless days of childhood!" I said. "Not painless,—not quite painless!"

"There are never any painless days," said she.

"No. Pain is the elder brother of Pleasure. But the days when the sense of injury passed away with the tears it compelled; when the sense of wrong-doing vanished with the light penance of a pang, with the brief penitence of an hour, and left the heart untainted. Those days were sorrowless."

As I spoke thus, Emma Denman suddenly burst into tears.

I had not suspected her of any such uncontrollable emotion. She had seemed to me one to smile and flash, hardly earnest enough for an agony.

"Pardon me," she said, quelling her tears, "but since those bright days I have suffered bitter sorrow. As you, my old playmate, speak, all that has passed since we met comes up newly."

This was all she said, at the moment, of her sister's death. I respected the recent wound. I had no right to renew her distress even by sympathy. I changed the subject.

"I find myself," said I, "between two opposites, as guardians for my second childhood at home. Mr. Churm is to launch me upon my work. Mr. Densdeth introduces me at the club. Which shall my boyship obey?"

"Such opposites will neutralize each other. You will be left free for a guardian in my sex. Have you sought one yet?"

"Destiny selects for me. I am thrust into your hands. Will you take me in charge?"

The look she gave as I said this touched me strangely. It seemed as if her double had suddenly glided forward and peered at me through her evasive eyes. A mysterious expression. I could no more comprehend it from my present shallow knowledge of the lady, than a novice perceives why Titian's surface glows, until he has scraped the surface and knows the undertones.

"Will I take you in charge?" she rejoined, with this strange look, henceforth my controlling memory of her face. "Will you trust me with such grave office? What say the other guardians? Do they recommend me? Does Mr. Churm? Have you consulted him?"

"Churm has rather evaded forming a prejudice in your favor in my mind. He gave me no ideal to alter. I had no counter-charm of the fancy to oppose to your actual charm."

"Your other choice among mentors, Mr. Densdeth,—has he offered you any light upon my qualifications?"

"Not a word! But he is not my choice. He has chosen me, if our companionship is choice, not chance."

"You accept him?"

"I have not thought of rejecting a man of such peculiar power."

"Has he mastered you, too?"

"Mastered? I am my own master. He attracts my curiosity greatly. I cannot resist the desire to know him by heart."

"To know him by heart!" she repeated, with almost a shudder. "To know Densdeth by heart! Study him, then, for yourself! I will give you no help! No help from me! God forbid!"

I must have looked, as I felt, greatly surprised at this outburst, for she recovered her usual manner, with an effort, and said: "Pardon me, again! Do not let me prejudice you against Mr. Densdeth. He is our friend, our best friend; but sometimes I suddenly have superstitious panics when I think of him and my sister's death."

She seemed to struggle now against a flood of sorrowful recollections. The force of the struggle carried her over to the side of gayety.

Smiles create smiles more surely than yawns yawns. I yielded readily to Miss Denman's gay mood. She threw off the depression of the early moments of our interview. "This should be a merry hour," her almost reckless manner said, "be the next what it might."

All the while, as we sat in the crimson dimness of that luxurious room,—she eager, animated, flashing from thought to thought, talking as an old friend who has yearned for friendship and sympathy might talk to an old friend who has both to give,—all the while, as she held me bound by her witchery, her shadow in the distant mirror sat, a ghostly spy.

She was in the midst of a lively sketch of the society I was to know under her auspices, when all at once a blight came upon her spirits. She paused. Her color faded. Her eyes became flighty. Her smile changed to a look of pain. She shivered slightly. These were almost imperceptible tokens, felt rather than perceived.

Steps approached as I was regarding this transformation with a certain vague alarm, such as one feels at a doubtful sound, that may be a cry for help, by night in a forest. In a moment Densdeth entered the room. With him was a large man, of somewhat majestic figure, a marked contrast to the slender grace of Densdeth. This new-comer was following, not leading, as if not he, but Densdeth, were the master in the house.

Mr. Denman! As he came up the suite of parlors, I could observe him, form, mien, and manner.

Without any foreknowledge of him, I might have said, "An over-busy man,—a man overweighted with social responsibilities. Too many banks choose him director. Too many companies want his administrative power. Too many charities must have him as trustee. One of the Caryatides of society. No wonder that he looks weary and his shoulders stoop. No wonder at his air of uneasy patience, or perhaps impatient endurance and eagerness to be free!"

But Churm had told me of other burdens this proud, self-confident man must bear. I could not be surprised that Mr. Denman looked old beyond his years, and that as he spoke his eyes wandered off, and stared vaguely into his own perplexities.

He received me cordially. His manner had a certain broken stateliness, as of a defeated sovereign, to whom his heart says, "Abdicate and die." As he welcomed me to his house, he glanced at Densdeth. Did he fear a smile on that dark, cruel face, and a look which said, "O yes! you may keep up the pretence of lordship here a little longer, if you enjoy the lie!"

"You are an old friend, Mr. Byng. Robert, I am happy to see you again," said Mr. Denman. "You must be at home with us. We dine at six. You will always find a plate. Come to-day, if you have no pleasanter engagement."

Miss Denman's look repeated the invitation.

I accepted. The old intimacy was renewed. And renewed with a distincter purpose on my part, because I said to myself, "Who knows but I may, with my young force, aid this worn and weary man to shake off the burden that oppresses him, and frustrates or perverts his life,— be it the mere dead weight of an old error,—be it the lacerating grapple of a crime?"

And now the tale of my characters is complete. This drama, short and sad, marches, without much delay, to its close. If I have, in any scene thus far, dallied with details that may seem trivial, let me be pardoned!

It may be that I have flinched, as I looked down the vista of my story, and discerned an ending of its path within some sombre cavern, like a place of sepulture. It may be that I have purposely halted to pluck the few pale flowers which grew along my road, and to listen a moment to the departing laugh, and the departing echoes of the laugh, of every merry comrade, as he went his way, and left me to fare as I might along my own.

Chapter XVII

A Morning with Cecil Dreeme

Through Churm's active friendship, I at once found my place. I have mentioned my profession,—chemistry. I was wanted in the world. Better business came to me than a professorship at the Terryhutte University, salary Muddefontaine bonds, or a post at the Nolachucky Polytechnic, salary Cumberland wild lands.

Churm only waited to establish me, and then was off, north, south, east, and west. It was one of those epochs when mankind is in a slough of despond, and must have a lift from Hercules. It was a time when society, that drowsy Diogenes, was beginning to bestir itself after a careless slumber, and, holding up the great lantern of public opinion to find honest men, suddenly revealed a mighty army of rogues. Rogues everywhere; scurvy rogues in mean places, showy rogues in high places; rogues cheating for cents in cheap shops, rogues defrauding for millions in splendid bank parlors; princely rogues, claiming princely salaries for unprofitable services, and puny rogues, corrupted by such example, stealing the last profits to eke out their puny pay and give them their base pleasures; potent rogues, buttoning up a million's worth of steamships or locomotives in their fob, and rogues, as potent for ill on a smaller scale, keeping back the widow's mite, and storing the orphan's portion with the usurer. Rogues everywhere! and the great, stern, steady eye of public opinion, at last fully open and detecting each rogue in the place he had crept or strode into, marking him there in his dastard shame or haughty bravado, and branding him THIEF, so that all mankind could know him.

In this crisis, Society's great eye of Public Opinion turned itself upon Churm, and demanded him as The Honest Man. Society's unanimous voice called upon him to put his shoulder to the wheel. Society said, "Be Dictator! dethrone, abolish, raze, redeem, restore, construct! Condemn; forgive! Do what you please,—only oust Roguery and instate Honesty."

This gigantic task engaged Churm totally. I lost him from my daily life.

It was a busy, practical life,—the life of one who had his way to work; and yet not without strange and unlooked-for excitements, in the region of romance.

My comrades in Europe, countrymen and foreigners, had condoled with me on my departure for home.

"Going back to America!" said they, "to that matter-of-fact country, where everything is in the newspapers."

"You that have lived in Italy!" deplored my romantic friends,—"in Italy, where skeletons in closets are packed scores deep; where you can scarcely step without treading on a murder-stain; where if a man but sigh in his bedchamber, when he loosens his waistcoat, the old slumbering sighs, which chronicle old wrongs done in that palace, awake and will not sleep until they have whispered to each other and to the affrighted stranger their tale of a misery; where the antique dagger you use for a paper-cutter has rust-marks that any chemist will say mean maiden's blood; where the old chalice you buy at a bargain gives a mild flavor of poison to your wine;—you that have lived in richly historied Italy, where the magnificent past overshadows the present, what will you find to interest you in a country where there is no past, no yesterday, and if no yesterday, no to-day worth having,—but life one indefinitely adjourned to-morrow?"

"Poor Byng! Romantic fellow! Why, unless there should be a raid of Camanches or Pawnees from the Ohio country," said my European friends, with a refreshing ignorance of geography,—"unless there should come a stampede of the red-skinned gentry to snatch a scalp or a squaw in the Broadway of New York, you will positively pine away for lack of adventures."

"What a bore to dwell in a land where there are no *sbirri* to whisk you off to black dungeons! How tame! a life where no tyrannies exist to whisper against always, to growl at on anniversaries, to scream at when they pounce on you, to roar at when you pounce on them. Yes, what stupid business, existence in a city where nobody has more and nobody less than fifteen hundred dollars a year, paid quarterly in advance; where there is such simple, easy, matter-of-fact prosperity that no one is ever tempted to overstep bounds and grasp a bigger share than his neighbors; and so there is never any considerable wrong done to any one;—no wrong, and consequently hearts never break, and there can be no need of mercy, pity, or pardon."

"Why, Byng! life without shade, life all bald, garish steady sunshine, may do to swell wheat and puff cabbage-heads; but man needs something other than monotony of comfort, something keener than the stolid pleasures of deaconish respectability. Byng," said my Florentine, Heidelberg, or Parisian comrades, each in their own language and manner, "Byng, you will actually starve for poetry and romance in that detestably new country."

I confess that I had had some fears on this subject, myself.

I had made up my mind to drop into systematic existence, cut fancy, eschew romance, banish dreams, and occupy my digestion solely on a diet of commonplace facts.

I might have known that man cannot live on corporeal, mundane facts alone, unless he can persuade his immortality to forget him, and leave him to crawl a mere earth-worm, dirt to dirt, until he is dust to dust.

As to romance, I might have known, if I had considered the subject, that wherever youth and maiden are, there is the certainty of romance and the chance of tragedy. I might have known that the important thing in a drama is, what the characters are, and what they do, not the scenes where they stand while they are acting. In the theatre, people are looking at the lover and the lady, not at the balustrade and the tower.

But though I might have known that the story of Life and Love is just as potent to create itself a fitting background when it is acted anew on a new stage, as when it is announced for repetition with the old familiar, musty properties, I had, indeed, been somewhat bullied by the unreflecting talk just quoted. I had fancied that the play could not go on without antiquated stuff to curtain it, dry-rotted boards for it to tread, and a time-worn drop for it to stand out against. I was sceptical as to the possibility of a novel and beautiful development of romance under the elms of a new land, in the streets of its new cities. I had adopted the notion of Europe, and Europe-tainted America, that my country was indeed very big, very busy, very prosperous, but monstrously dull, tame, and prosaic.

Error! Worse,—mere stupid blindness!

My first plunge into life at home proved it. See how my very first day became over-crowded with elements of interest and romance,—nay, of mysterious and tragic excitement!

Even the ancient scenery, whether important or not to the progress of the drama, had packed itself up, and followed my travels. Stillfleet's chambers were an epitome of the whole Past,—that is to say, of the Past as leading to the Present and interpreting it. Stillfleet had concentrated the essence of all the ages in his informal museum. I had but to glance about, and I had travelled over all terrestrial space, and lived through all human centuries. He had relics from all the famous camps in the great march of mankind. He had examples, typical objects, to show what every age and every race had contributed to the common stock. By art on his walls, by books in the library, by objects of curious antiquity, even by the grotesque fabrics and contrivances of savages and transitory tribes of men, all distributed about in orderly disorder, I could study history at a glance, or rather absorb history with unconscious eyes.

Scenery! I need but to look into the Egyptian corner of my chamber, and, if I took any interest in the life of the Pharaohs, there it was in a pictured slab from the Memnonium; or in the dead Pharaoh, there himself was grinning in a mummy-case,—a very lively corpse,—unpleasantly lively, indeed, when nights were dark, and matches flashed brimstone and refused to burn.

Scenery! Greece and Rome, Dark Ages, Crusades, Middle Ages, Moorish Conquest, '88 in England, Renaissance, '89 in France, every old era and the last new era,—all were so thoroughly represented here, by model of temple, cast of statue, vase, picture, tapestry, suit of armor, Moslem scymitar, bundle of pikes, rusty cross-bow or arquebuse, model of guillotine,—by some object that showed what the age had most admired, most used, or most desired,—that there, restored before me, rose and spread the age itself, and called its heroes and its caitiffs forward in review.

If I preferred to live in the Past, I had only to shut myself up at home, and forget that eager Present about me,—that stirring life of America, urged on by the spirit of the Past, and unburdened by its matter.

Romance, too! Romance had come to me, whether I would or no. Without any permission of mine, asked or granted, I was become an actor, with my special part to play, perforce, among mysteries.

Cecil Dreeme.

Emma Denman.

Densdeth.

My connection with these three characters grew daily closer. I do not love mystery. Ignorance I do not hate; for ignorance is the first condition of knowledge. Mystery I recoil from. It generally implies the concealment of something that should not be concealed, for the sake of delusion or deception; or if not for these, because tragedy will follow its revelation.

Cecil Dreeme continued to me a profound mystery. He kept himself utterly secluded by day, working hard at his art. He knew no one but myself. No one ever saw him except myself and Locksley, or Locksley's children. Only at night, wrapped in his cloak, did he emerge from his seclusion, and wander over the dim city.

I became his companion in these walks whenever my engagements allowed; but such night wandering seemed unhealthy for him in his delicate state.

"Are you wise, Dreeme," said I to him, one morning, in his studio, after we had become intimate, "to live this nocturnal life? Sunshine and broad daylight are just as indispensable to man as they are to flower or plant. I might give you good chemical reasons for my statement."

"There are night-blooming flowers,—the Cereus, and others," said he, avoiding my question.

"Yes, but they owe their blossom to the day's accumulation of sunshine. Botany refuses to protect you."

"Plants grow by night."

"In night that follows sunny day."

"I accept the analogy. I have accumulated sunshine enough, I hope, for growth, and perhaps for a pallid kind of bloom, in my past sunny days. My rank growth went on vigorously enough in the daylight. I am conscious of a finer development in the dark."

"But I do not like this voluntary prison."

"Few escape a forced imprisonment, longer or shorter, in their lives. Illness or sorrow shut us in away from the world's glare, that we may see colors as they are, and know gold from pinchbeck. Why should I not go to prison, of my own accord, for such teaching, and other reasons?"

"And other reasons? Tell me, Dreeme, before our friendship goes further,—before I utterly and irrecoverably give you my confidence."

"Go on."

"No! I cannot go on."

"I understand, and am not insulted. You mean to ask whether I am hiding here because I have picked a pocket, or pillaged a till, or basely broken a heart, or perhaps because I have a blood-stain to wear out."

"My imagination had not put its suspicion, if any existed, into any such crude charges."

"So I saw, and stated the question blankly. You could not connect me with vulgar or devilish crime. At the same time, you had a certain uneasiness about me, undefined and misty, but real. You will not deny it," and he smiled as he spoke.

"No. Since you affront the fact with such cheerful confidence, I will not deny the vague dread."

"Be at rest, then! There is not a man or a woman in the world, whom I cannot look in the eyes without blenching. You need not be ashamed of me. You may trust me, without any fear of that harshest of all the shocks our life can feel, loss of faith in a friend's honor."

"Well, we will never speak of this again. Live by your own laws, in the dark or the light! I demand unquestioned freedom for myself. I am the last man to refuse it to another."

"Really," said Dreeme, "since your projection into my orbit, I no longer need personal contact with the outer world."

"You find me a good enough newsman."

"The artistic temperament does not love to bustle about in the crowd, to shoulder and hustle for its facts. You give me the cream of what the world says and does. But, by and by, when you tire of the novelty of a tyro-artist's society, you will drop me."

"Never! so long as you consent to be my in-door man. I often feel, now, as I stir about among men, collecting my budget of daily facts, that I only get them for the pleasure of hearing your remarks when I un-pack in the evening."

"I must try to be a wiser and wittier critic."

"You return me far more than I bring. I train my mental muscle with other people. You give me lessons in the gymnastics of finer forces. My worldling nature shrivels, the immortal Me expands under your artistic touch."

"I am happy to be accused of such a power," Dreeme said, with his sweet, melancholy smile. "It is the noblest one being can exercise over another, and needed much in this low world of ours."

"Yes, Dreeme, your fresh, brave, earnest character I begin to regard as my guardian influence. With you I escape from the mean ambitions, the disloyal rivalries, the mercenary friendships of men,—from the coarseness, baseness, and foulness of the world. You neutralize to me all the evil powers."

"That Mr. Densdeth, of whom you have once or twice spoken,—is he one of them?"

"Perhaps so."

"Are you still intimate with him?"

"Intimate? Hardly. Intimacy implies friendship."

"Familiar, then?"

"Familiar, yes. He seeks my society. We are thrown together by circumstances. He interests me greatly. I know no man of such wide scope of information, such knowledge, such wit, such brilliancy,—no one at all to compare with him, now that my friend Churm is absent."

"Those two fraternize, I suppose."

"Churm and Densdeth?"

"Yes; you seem to make one a substitute for the other."

"'How happy could I be with either!' O no! You strangely misapprehend Mr. Churm. The two are as much asunder in heart as in looks."

"Ah!" said Dreeme.

"You seem incredulous. But let me tell you that Churm's knowledge of Densdeth gives the same result as these clairvoyant intuitions of yours. I suppose I am a perverse fellow for not obeying everybody's 'Fœnum habet in cornu' of Densdeth; but I have Cato's feeling for the weaker side, or at least the side assailed. Besides, I have a scientific experiment with this terrible fellow. I let him bite, and clap on an antidote before the brain is benumbed. I play with Densdeth, who really seems to me like an avatar of the wise Old Serpent himself, and then, before he has quite conquered me with his fascination, I snatch myself away, and come to you, to be aroused and healed."

"I am glad to be an antidote to poison. But have you no fears of such baleful intercourse?"

"None. As a man of the world, I must know the perilous as well as the safe among my race. How am I to become as wise as the serpent, unless I study the serpent? I find Densdeth a most valuable preceptor. He has sounded every man's heart, in life or history, and can state the depth of evil there in fathoms, feet, and inches. I could no more do without him for that side of my education, than I could spare your dove-like teaching to make me harmless as a dove. Pardon my giving you this unmasculine office."

"You speak lightly, Mr. Byng. I fear you are a man who has not yet fully made up his mind."

"What? As to the great choice,—Hercules's choice? Virtue or Vice? O yes, I am absolutely committed. Virtue has me fast. In fact, I am deemed quite a Puritan, as men go; I should be so not to shame my ancestors."

"Forgive me if I ask, Do you know what Evil is?"

"I suppose so; as much as is to be known."

"O, you cannot! You would not trifle with it, if you dreamed how it soils. You would fly it."

"Not face it?"

"Never, unless duty commanded you to face and crush it. Those who know Evil best fly farthest, hide deepest, dread its approach, shudder at the thought of its pursuit. It is so terribly subtle. The bravest are not brave before it; the strongest are not strong; the purest are not pure. It makes cowards of the brave, it paralyzes the strong, it taints the pure. No one is safe,—no one, until personal agony has made him hate Evil worse than death. Mr. Byng, you have a noble soul; but no soul can safely palter with a bad man. Palter! I use strong words. I mean to use them. You have spoken lightly and pained me. To a bad man—to some bad men—every pure soul is a perpetual reproach, and must be sullied. You speak plainly of this Densdeth; you understand his bad influence, and yet you deal with him as if he were some inert chemical combination, which you could safely handle and analyze. Such a being is never inert; the less active he seems, the more he is likely to be insidiously at work to ruin. Forgive me, my dear friend, that I warn you so eagerly against this fatal curiosity!"

He had spoken with fervid energy and eloquence. In fact, there was in this strange young genius a passionate ardor, always latent, only waiting to flame forth, when his heart was touched. And when some deeper interest stirred him,—when he had some protest to utter against wrong,—his large, melancholy eyes grew intense, his voice lost its pensive sadness; color came to his thin, sallow cheeks. It was so now. For a moment, he was almost beautiful with this sudden evanescent inspiration.

I paused after his eager outburst, watching him with such admiration as we give to a great actor, and then—for I confess that my conceit was somewhat offended by this good advice, from one in years so much my junior—I said, with a confident smile: "You talk like a Cassandra. What do you foresee so very terrible, as about to befall me? Pray do not be uneasy! I am an old stager. I have managed to make my way thus far in my life without being worse than my fellows. 'I am indifferent honest.' I will try to remain so, despite of the seductions of Bugaboo. And then, you know, I cannot go far wrong with you for Mentor."

My tone seemed to pain him. He painted some moments in silence on his Lear.

While he painted, I observed him,—interested much in the picture of his creation, more in the creator. "Raphael-Angelico," I thought, "he merits the name fully. What a delicate being! The finest organization I have ever seen in man. How strangely his personality affects me! And every moment fancies drift across my mind that I actually know his secret, and am blind, purposely blind to my knowledge, because I promised him when we first met that I would be so."

CHAPTER XVIII

Another Cassandra

Dreeme went on slowly and carefully with his work, after my closing remark of the last chapter. I continued to observe him for some moments in silence. His palette and brushes were kept with extreme neatness. The colors on the palette were arranged methodically, with an eye to artistic gradation; so that the darker of the smooth, oily drops squeezed from his paint-tubes made, as it were, a horizon of shadow on the outer rim of the palette. Within this little amphitheatre of hillocks, black, indigo, and brown, the dashes of brighter hue were disposed in concentric arcs, shading toward pure white at the focus. All his utensils and materials betokened the same orderliness and refinement; nothing was out of place, nothing daubed or soiled. So careful too was his handling, that he needed no over-sleeve to protect his own. The delicate hand and the flexible wrist seemed incapable of an awkward or a blundering motion. He could no more do a slovenly thing, than he could dance a break-down or smoke a pipe. This personal neatness was specially beautiful to me. In my laboratory, at my task of splitting atoms and unbraiding gases, I learnt from the exquisite order and proportion that Nature never forgets in her combinations to require the same of men. I found it in Dreeme. His genius in art was not of the ill-regulated, splashy, blotchy, boisterous class. Nothing coarse could come from those fine fingers.

"You elaborate your work with great care," said I, after some moments' silence, while the painter had been touching in dots of light, and then pausing, studying, and touching again, here a point and there a line.

"I *must* be careful and elaborate. It is partly the timidity of a novice. I feel that my hand lacks the precision of practice,—the rapid, unerring touch of a master. But besides, now, as my work approaches completion, I perceive a failure in creative power. I work feebly and painfully."

"Creative power of course is temporarily exhausted by a complete consistent creation. Jove felt empty-headed enough when he had thought Minerva into being. Lie fallow for a season, and your brain will teem again with images!"

"Yes, that is the law; but you must remember that my case is solitary. My picture is a spasm. It came to me prematurely, as a purpose and a power come in the paroxysms of a fever. I have spent all my large force in it."

"Your picture is older, subject and handling, than you, as I have said before. But music, painting, and poetry are gifts of the gods to the young."

"Older than my years? Ah yes!" he said, drearily. "I was in the immortal misery when I poured out my soul there. It was sore, sore, sore work. I pray that I may never need to create tragedy again. I pray that no new or ancient experience may compel me to confess and confide it to the impersonal world. No, I have wreaked my anguish, my pity, my shame for the guilty, on that canvas, and the virtue is gone out of me."

"Essay another vein! You have worked off bitterness. Open your heart to sweetness! In brighter mood, you will do fairer things without the tragic element."

"Since you and Locksley compelled me to accept the sweet gift of a life more hopeful, I have made some sketches in a less severe manner than my Lear. That was cruel tragedy. These are only anecdotes."

"Pray exhibit!"

"To so gentle a critic, I venture. Do not expect passion,—that I wished to spare myself. The sentiment is simple and commonplace enough."

He placed before me three sketchy pictures, able and rapid.

"You see," said he, "I play upon one idea or its reverse."

The first sketch depicted a young girl, caught in a snow-storm, and sunk, a mere shapeless thing, among the drifts in a dreary pine-wood. A gentleman, in the costume of a Puritan soldier, stooped over her. Beside him stood a sturdy yeoman with a cloak and a basket. A few sunbeams cleft the pines, glinted on the hero's corslet, and warmed the group. It was a scene full of the pathos of doubtful hope.

"Thank you for my immortality," said I. "It was a pretty thought to put Locksley and myself in this scene of rescue,—me too in the steel and buff of that plucky old pioneer, the first Byng, with whose exploits I have bored you so often. I hope we were in time, before the maiden perished."

"The sunbeam seems to promise that," said he smiling, and handed me the next.

Second picture. Scene, the splendid salon of a French chateau. Through the window, a mad mob of *sans culottes* were visible, forcing the grand entrance. Within, myself—costume, purple velvet, lace, and rapier—and Locksley, in blouse and sabots, were bearing off a fainted lady, dark-haired, and robed in yellow.

"Twice immortal!" said I. "But why avert the heroine's face?"

"Good female models are hard to find. My heroine should be worthy of my hero. Have you one of your own, whose features I might insert?"

"Have I found my heroine? Not yet,—that is, not certainly."

Dreeme handed me the third picture. "My Incognita," said he, "is willing to encounter bad company out of gratitude to her benefactors. Please appreciate the compliment!"

Third picture. Scene, the same splendid salon of the same chateau. Without, instead of the *sans culottes,* a group of soldiers of the Republic stood on guard. Within, the same dark-haired lady,—costume, yellow satin (it reminded me of that coverlet of Louis Philippe's which had served Dreeme for wrapper),—the same heroine as in the second picture, sat with her back to the spectator. At a table beside her was an official personage, signing a passport. He was dressed with careful coxcombry in Robespierre's favorite color, and resembled that demon slightly, but enough to recall him. Behind him, I—yes, I myself again—could be seen through a half-opened closet-door, sullenly sheathing my sword in obedience to a sign from the lady. Locksley also was there, in blouse and stealthy bare feet, playing prudence to valor and holding me back.

"Ah!" said I, "another person with us in the pillory of your picture. Strange! Your Robespierre might almost be a portrait of Densdeth."

"Indeed! It is a typical bad face, and may resemble several bad men."

"Singularly like Densdeth!" I repeated. "The same cold-blooded resolve, the same latent sneer, the same suppressed triumph, even the coxcombry you have given to your gentle butcher of '93,—all are Densdeth's. May you not have seen and remembered his marked face?"

"Possibly." He evaded my inquiring look, as he replied.

"Perhaps he has stared at you for an instant in a crowd. Perhaps you have caught a look of his from the window of a railroad-car. He may at some moment, without your conscious notice, have stamped himself ineffaceably upon your mind."

"It may be. An artist's brain receives and stores images often without distinct volition. But you may lend my villain a likeness from your own memory."

"Yes; our talk about Densdeth, and your warnings against an exaggerated danger are fresh in my mind. Certainly, as I see the face, it is Densdeth's very self."

"Now," said Dreeme, "take your choice of my three sketches. Three simple stories,—which will you have? I painted them for your selection, and have taken much grateful pleasure in the work. One is for you, one for Locksley, one for myself,—a souvenir for each of us in happier days."

"Mine will be precious as a souvenir, apart from its great value as Art. And, let me tell you, Dreeme, in their manner, these studies are as able as your Lear. The anecdotes hold their own with the tragedy. I believe you are the man we have been waiting for."

"Your praise thrills me."

"Do not let it spoil you," said I, willing in my turn to act the Mentor.

"Mr. Byng," said he gravely, "my life has been so deepened and solemnized by earnest trial and bitter experience, that vanity is, I trust, annihilated. I shall do my work faithfully, because my nature commands me to it; but I can never have the exultant feeling of personal pride in it as mine."

"That too is a legitimate joy. You will have it when the world gives you its verdict, 'Well done.'"

Dreeme sighed, and seemed to shrink away.

"To face the world!" said he,—"how dare I? And yet I must. My scanty means will not last me many weeks longer."

"My dear Dreeme," said I, "my purse is not insolent with fulness; but it holds enough to keep two spiritual beings, like ourselves, in oysters and ale, slaw and 'Wing's pethy,'—crackers being thrown in."

"Thank you," said he, smiling; "but I suppose I must go out into daylight, brave my fate, and take my risk."

"There is no risk. You must succeed."

"Ah!" said he, and tears stood in his great sad eyes; "I speak of another risk. Of another danger, which I shudder at. Here I am safe, unharming and unharmed. How can I take up my life's responsibilities again?"

"Dreeme," said I, "in any other but you, I should almost say that these fancies were unmanly."

He evaded my eye, as I said this, but did not seem insulted.

"But," I continued, "there is a certain kind of courage in your working here alone,—enough to establish your character. If you want a rough pugilistic ally against this mysterious peril of yours, take me into your confidence. Here are my fists! they are yours. What ogre shall I hit? What dragon shall I choke?"

"You are neglecting my poor gift," said he, resolutely changing the subject; "make your choice of the three pictures, and I will show you my portfolio of drawings. You shall see what my fingers do when they obey the dictates of my careless fancy."

"I choose the third of the series. Neither of those where I or my semblance is the chief figure,—neither where I am doing, but where I am receiving the favor. My only regret is that I cannot look through the back of her head and see the features of the lady, whose gesture tells me, 'Sheathe sword and swallow ire!' Robespierre—Densdeth too, that adds to its value. I must hang it up where he can see it. I am curious to know whether he will recognize himself."

"O no! Promise me that you will not show it at present. No, not to any one!"

"What, not identify myself with the *début* of the coming man? May I not be your herald?"

"Wait, at least, till I am ready to follow up the announcement of my coming. No premature pæans, if you please!"

"I obey, of course. But I should vastly like to show it to Towers, Sion, and Pensal. You know I have a growing intimacy with that trio of great artists. They would heartily welcome your advent."

"Spare me the dread of their condemnation! Keep my little gift to yourself, at present! Here is my heap of drawings. Look at them, and judge with your usual kindness!"

"So these were the thoughts too hot for your brain to hold. These represent what you *must* say, not what you chose to say. I perceive that the bent of your mind is not toward tragedy."

Very masterly sketches they were! A fine fancy, a subtle imagination, a large heart, had conceived them, an accurate and severe artistic sense had controlled and developed the thought, and an unerring hand had executed it. Dreeme was a youth, certainly not more than twenty-one; and yet here was the maturity of complete manhood. Whether he had had opportunities for studying classic art, or whether his genius had seized in common life that fine quality which we name "classic," these drawings of his would have stood the test with the purest of the Italian masters, in the days before Italian art had suffered blight,—that blight which befell it when progress ceased in the land, and a tyrannical Church bade the nation pause and let the world go by.

Dreeme's female figures were not drawn with the liberal and almost riotous fancy of youth, which loves floating and flaunting draperies and a bold display of the nude. A chaster feeling had presided over the studies of this fine genius. There was a severe simplicity in his drawings of women. He seemed to have approached the purer sex with a loving reverence, never with that coarse freedom which debases the work of many able men, nullifying all spiritual beauty. One would say that the artist of these drawings had taken his mother and his sisters as models for the elevated and saintly beings, whom he had placed in scenes of calm beauty, and engaged in tender offices of mercy, pity, and pardon. I could safely name him Raphael-Angelico,—the title saves me longer criticism.

Strangely enough,—and here I recognized either a wound in Dreeme's life or a want in his character,—there was not one scene of love—that is, the love Cupid manages—in the collection. Not one scene where lovers, happy or hapless, figured. No pretty picture of consent and fondness. Not one of passion and fervor.

Now, a young man or a young maiden, in the early twenties, in whose mind love is not the primal thought, is a monstrosity, and must be studied and analyzed with a view to cure.

Either Dreeme's nature was still in the crude, green state, unripened by passion, or he had suffered so bitterly from some treachery in love that he could not reawaken the memory. Either he was ignorant of love's sweet torture, or he had felt the agony, without the healing touch.

I suspected the latter.

Often, recently, as my relations with Dreeme grew closer, I had been conscious of a peculiar jealous curiosity. I was now his nearest friend. But had he not had a nearer? If not in my sex, in the other? It was under the influence of this jealousy, that I said,—

"It seems almost an impertinence, Dreeme, to suggest a negative fault in this collection of admirable drawings; but I perceive a want. The subject of love,—the love that presses hands and kisses lips, the tender passion,—had you nothing to say of it?"

"No," said he, "I am too young."

"Bah! you are past twenty."

"Twenty-one—the very day of your coming."

"Too young! why, as for me, I was in love while my upper lip was only downy. The passion increased as that feature began to be districted off with hairs, stalwart, but sporadic. And ever since I have grown up to a real moustache, with ends that can be twirled, I have been in love, or just out and waiting to jump or tumble in again, the whole time."

"How is it now?"

"I hardly know. In love? or almost in? Which? In, I believe. I am tempted to offer you a confidence."

"I would rather not," said Dreeme, uneasily.

"O yes; you shall interpret my feelings. I admire a woman, whom it seems to me that I should love devotedly, if she were a little other than she is,—herself touched with a diviner delicacy,—her own sister self, a little angelized."

Dreeme evaded my questioning look, and made no reply. I paused a moment, while he painted a jewel, flashing on the white neck of his Goneril.

"Come," said I, "my Mentor, do not dodge responsibility! Your reply may affect my destiny."

He met my glance now, and replied, without hesitation, "Love that admits questions is no love."

"Perhaps I am suffering the penalty for the inconstant mood I have permitted myself heretofore. Perhaps I only want a steady and sincere purpose to love and trust, and I shall do so."

"Beware such perilous doubts!" said he earnestly. "With a generous character like yours, they lead to illusions. You will presently, out of self-reproach for at all doubting the woman you fancy, pass into a blind confidence, and so win some miserable shock, perhaps too late."

"Cassandra again! Cassandra in the other sex."

"Do not say Cassandra! that proves you intend to disdain my warning."

"Dear me! what solemn business we are making of my little flirtation!—a flirtation all on my side, by the way. In fact, I really believe I have cleared my head of my vague doubts of the unknown lady in question. They only needed to be put into words, in presence of a third party, to seem, as you say, utterly ungenerous."

"I am sorry that you forced the confidence upon me,—very sorry! But you would have it so."

"You talk as if you knew the lady, and considered her unfitted for me."

"Believe that I have discernment enough, knowing you, to know the class of woman who in this phase of your life will necessarily attract you. I can divine whom,—that is, what manner of person you will choose for a love, since you have characterized the man you are fascinated by as an intimate."

"Oh! you mean Densdeth."

"Yes; while you allow him to dominate you,—and mind, I take my impression from yourself,—you will naturally seek a counterpart of his in the other sex."

I grew ill at ease under this penetrating analysis of my secret feelings.

It was, of course, of Emma Denman that I had spoken.

Emma Denman was the woman I deemed myself on the verge of loving.

It was she whom I felt that I did not love, and yet ought to love. It was she whom I should have loved, without any shadow of hesitation, if she had been herself touched with a diviner feminineness, her own sister self, a thought more angelic.

I had sometimes had a painful lurking consciousness that if I were nobler than I was,—if my mind were more resolutely made up and unwavering on the side of virtue,—I should have applied the test of a higher and purer nature on my side to Emma Denman, and found her in some way fatally wanting. But whenever this injurious fancy stirred within me, I quelled it, saying, "If I were nobler, I should not have morbid notions about others. How can you learn to trust women while you allow yourself daily to listen, and only carelessly to protest, when Densdeth urges his doctrine, that women and men only wait opportunity to be base?"

In fact, in violation of an instinct, I was going through the process of resolving to love Emma Denman, because I distrusted her, and such vague distrust seemed an unchivalric disloyalty, a cruel wrong to a friend.

The strange coincidence of Dreeme's warning determined me to banish my superstitions. No more of this weakness! I would cultivate, or, as I persuaded myself, frankly yield to my passion for my childish flame, love her, and do my best to win her. I saw now how baseless were my doubts, when they came to be stated in words. Indeed, there was no name for one of these misty beings of the mind.

All this flashed across my mind as I continued mechanically turning over Dreeme's drawings. With the thought came the resolve. I would no more begrudge my faith. I would love Emma Denman, and by love make myself worthy of it.

> *"The fleeting purpose never is o'ertook*
> *Unless the deed go with it,"*

I half murmured to myself, and so, taking my leave of Dreeme for the morning, I passed to Denman's house.

From that time, I was the undeclared lover of Emma Denman, as I shall presently describe.

And you, Cecil Dreeme,—it was your warning that urged me so perversely to do violence to an unerring instinct.

How strangely and fatally we interfere, unconsciously, for one another's bliss or bale!

Churm away;

Densdeth my intimate;

Cecil Dreeme my friend of friends;

Emma Denman almost my love.

So matters stood with me and the other characters of this drama, two months from the day of my instalment in Chrysalis.

But let it not be understood that I had nothing to do except to study these few persons. My days were full, and often my nights, with hard and absorbing work I had undertaken in my profession. I touched the world on many sides. I came into collision with various characters. I had my daily life, like other men,—my real life, if you will, that handled substances, and did not deal in mysteries. This I am not describing. I am at pains to eliminate every fact and thought of mine which did not bear immediately upon the development of the story I here compel myself to write.

CHAPTER XIX

Can This Be Love?

Meantime my intimacy with the Denmans had been growing closer. With me Mr. Denman laid aside his usual manner, a mixture of reserve and uneasiness. He forgot his preoccupations, and talked with me frankly.

"If I had had a son, Byng," said he, "I could have wished him a young man like yourself. I suppose you will not quarrel with me if I expend a little fatherliness on you."

I was touched by this kindness. My distrust of him wore away. It is my nature to think gently and tenderly of others. I was in those relations with Mr. Denman where one sees the better side of character. I shared his liberal hospitality. I perceived that he did not love wealth for itself, but as power; and that he used this power often judiciously, always generously. The vanity of exercising power, the mistake of fancying himself a being of higher order than men of lesser influence, he seemed to have outgrown. And the power, with its duties attached, he often found a weary burden. I saw him a tired and saddened man, thankful for the freshening friendship of his junior. I gave him mine frankly.

Could such a man be called, as Churm had harshly called him, the murderer of his daughter? Surely not! I might believe him to have erred in that business; I could not deem him criminal. And, justifying him, I even did injustice to the memory of the dead Clara. Who knew what undiscovered or unpublished sorrowful motive she might not have had for a suicide? The dead have no friends to justify them.

But there was another reason for my favorable judgment on Mr. Denman. I loved, or thought I loved, or wished that I loved, his daughter.

Ever since my conversation with Cecil Dreeme, I had encouraged this passion. I had seen Emma Denman frequently, then constantly; it was now every day.

Her fascination grew in power. There was a certain effort in it; but what man disputes a woman's right to make effort to please him? With me her manner was anxious, and even agitated. Other men, now that the blackness of first mourning was past, began to be at the house. Them she treated with civil indifference, or indifferent cordiality, as they merited. With me she seemed always eagerly striving that I should not misapprehend her, always protesting against some possibility of a false impression.

Ah! now that I look back upon it all, how I pity her! No wonder that she grew thin and worn! No wonder that her gayety often struck me as forced or fantastic! When it did so seem, I said to myself that she was determined not to be crushed by that sad tragedy of her sister's death. I did not dream that her eager moods were tokens of the desperate struggle she was making against the inevitable tragedy of her own life.

Shall I go through all the history of the progress of my passion? Shall I say how, day by day, my sympathy for this motherless, sisterless girl deepened,—how I sorrowed for her that, amid all the splendor of her life, her heart was sad and empty, and so the life a vain show? how I, dreading what might be the fate of her father's wealth, pleased myself with the thought that, if disaster befell him, I could offer her the home and the heart of a hopeful working-man? Shall I re-edit such an old, old story, with the new illustrations drawn from my own experience?

I shrink from the task of opening an ancient wound.

I shrink, but yet I force myself to the anguish.

And time has changed that bygone grief into a lesson. I must write. No matter how dark, the story shall be told. Every man's precious or costly experience belongs to every brother-man. No man may be a miser of the sorrows by which he has bought the power to be strong, to be tender, to pardon the weak and the guilty. Perhaps by some warning I here utter I may persuade a young and hesitating soul to shudder back from the brink of sin. Often a timely trifle of a gentle word of admonition has struck a foully fair temptation dead. I know how the recurring fragrance of a flower that childhood loved, how the far-away sound of breakers on a beach where childhood wandered, how a weft of cloud, how the leap of a sunbeam, how the sudden jubilant carol of a bird, how a portrait of the pure Madonna on the wall, how a chance line on an open page,—how any such momentous trifle will save a wavering soul from a treachery or a crime,—will interpose an instant's check, and rescue the life from a remorse, guarding it for a repentance. Yes; whatever agony it costs me to revive this old history, I do now, after its lesson is fully thought out, of my sober judgment, revive it,—let who will murmur, "Bad taste!" let who will cry out, "Unhealthy!" let who will sigh, "Alas! have we not our own griefs? why burden us with yours?"

Did I, or not, love Emma Denman? Why could I not determine this question? I had my friends among men. Closest among these was Cecil Dreeme; his friendship I deemed more precious than the love of women. But among women, no other, none, was at all so charming to me as Emma.

She was to me far more beautiful than any beauty,—infinitely more beautiful, always, than any of those round, full, red beauties who are steadily supplied to the city market, overt or covert, for wives or mistresses to the men who pay money for either, and have nothing but money to give.

She was brilliant, frivolously brilliant perhaps; but we pardon a dash of frivolity in a young woman of fashion, all her life flattered and caressed, and untrained by daily contact with men of strong minds and women of strong hearts.

Emma Denman stood just on the hither brink of genius. It seemed that, if some magnificent emotion, some heart-opening joy or grief, could befall her, she would suddenly be promoted to become herself, and that self a genius. If she could be once in earnest, she would be a noble woman. Such a character has a mighty charm to a lover. He stirs himself with the thought that his love may give the awakening touch; that his passion may supply the ripening flame, and win the bud to bloom.

In music, in art, in thought, I felt that Emma Denman needed but one step to stand on the heights among the inspired. She seemed to feel this also, and to be always pleading tacitly with me to give her the slight aid she needed. She could not pass into the realms of the divine liberty of genius, for some gossamer wall, invisible to all but her, and against her strong as adamant.

I was terrified sometimes by her keenness of insight into bad motives, her comprehension of the labyrinthine causes of bad acts. It is a perilous knowledge. We must pay price for power. How had she bought this unerring perception of the laws of evil? How came she by this aged possession in her first youth?

How? I quelled my uneasiness with the thought that the sensitive touch of innocence is warned away from poisoned blossoms by the clammy airs that hang about them, and so recoils, and will not pluck the flower or gather the fruit. I said that the mere dread of evil will instruct a virgin soul where are those paths of evil it must shun. I said it is better to know sin and shun it, than to half ignore and half evade.

Since our first interview, our relations had grown more and more intimate without check. We named them brotherly and sisterly, as they had been in our childish days. She claimed the sister's privilege of presiding over my social life, and aiding me to make a choice in love.

Miss Denman led me about the grand round of society. She took me to see the belles for beauty, the belles for money, the belles for wit, the belles for magnetism, the belles for blood. And all of them she drew out to show their most attractive side, in fact, their better and more genuine nature. She persuaded each to reveal that the belle had not addled the woman.

And then she wondered that she could not persuade me to fall in love with one of these ladies.

I could not, of course, if only because her process made her appear superior to them all. I admired the kindliness with which she strove to put sparkle into the stupid girls, to dignify the trifling, to refine the vulgar,—and the teacher was to me an infinitely finer being than her scholars ever could become.

And so I told her,—but never yet with the words of a lover.

And so she insisted I should not think,—not craftily and with systematic coquetry. No, poor child! Ah, no! I acquit her of all such slight wiles and surface hypocrisy. But how could I know that she was sincerely striving to save us both from the tragedy of a mutual love?

And did I love her? The question implied a doubt, where there should be only undoubting conviction and compelling impulse.

Why doubt, Robert Byng?

There was surely no other affection in my heart that I was playing false. Surely none. My heart was free from any love of woman.

And my doubt was based upon a suspicion.

A suspicion! of what?

If I at all stated to myself, however faintly, what, it seemed to me such disloyalty that I despised myself for entertaining the unwholesome thought.

"You are not fit," I said, "for the society of a pure woman! Densdeth has spoilt you."

Thus I trained my affection the more tenderly for its weakness. Thus, ignorant and rejecting the sure law of nature, I strove to create the uncreatable, to construct what should have come into being and grown strong without interference, even without consciousness of mine. Thus I began to deem the sentiment I was manufacturing out of ruth and a loyal intention, as genuine, heart-felt love.

Bitter error! And to be punished bitterly!

CHAPTER XX

A Nocturne

Night! Night in the great city!

Night! when the sun, the eye of God, leaves men to their own devices; when the moon is so faint, and the stars so far away in the infinite, that their inspection and record are forgotten; when Light, the lawgiver and orderer of human life, withdraws, and mankind are free to break or obey the commands daylight has taught them.

Night! when the gas-lights, relit, reawaken harmful purposes, that had slept through all the hours of honest sunshine in their lairs; when the tigers and tigresses take their stand where their prey will be sure to come; when the rustic in the peaceful country, with leaves whispering and crickets singing around him, sees a glow on the distant horizon, and wonders if the bad city beneath it be indeed abandoned of its godly men, and burning for its crimes. Night! the day of the base, the guilty, and the desolate!

Every evening, when it was possible, of that late winter and wintry spring, I abandoned club, parlor, and ball-room, and all the attractions of the brilliant world, to wander with Cecil Dreeme about the gas-lit city, and study the side it showed to night. And yet the phenomena of vice and crime, my companion refused to consider fit objects of curiosity. Vice and crime were tacitly avoided by us. Dreeme's nature repelled even the thought of them. I was happy to know one solitary man whose mind the consciousness of evil could not make less virgin.

It chanced one evening, a fortnight after our conversation when Dreeme gave me the picture, that walking as usual, and quite late, we passed the Opera-House. Some star people were giving an extra performance on an off night. The last act of an heroic opera was just beginning. Dreeme hummed the final air,—a noble burst of triumph over a victory bought by a martyrdom.

"Your song makes me hungry to hear more," said I.

"I have been almost starving for music," he rejoined.

"Come in, then. You can take your stand in the lobby, with your mysterious cloak about you, and slouched hat over your eyes. I defy your best friend or worst foe to know you."

"No, no!" said he, nervously; "in the glare of a theatre I should excite suspicion. I should be seen."

"And pounced upon and hurried off to durance vile?" said I, lightly enough; for I began at last to fancy that his panic of concealment was the sole disorder of a singularly healthy brain. "Well, I will not urge it. I cannot spare you. I am selfish. I should soon go to the bad without my friend and Mentor."

"It is strange," said Dreeme, bitterly, "that I, with a soul white as daylight, should be compelled to lurk about like a guilty thing,—to be as one dead and buried."

"I thank the mystery that secludes you for my benefit, Dreeme," I said. "I dread the time when you will find a thousand friends, and many closer than I."

He dropped his cloak and took my arm. It was the first time he had given me this slight token of intimacy. We had been very distant in our personal intercourse. I am not a man to slap another on the back, shake him by the shoulder, punch him in the ribs, or indulge in any rude play or coarse liberties. Yet there is a certain familiarity among men, by which we, after our roughish and unbeautiful fashion, mean as much tenderness for our friends as women do by their sweet embraces and caresses. Nothing of this kind had ever passed between Dreeme and me. His reserve and self-dependence had made me feel that it would be an impertinence to offer even that kind of bodily protection which a bigger man holds ready for a lesser and slighter.

It surprised me, then, a little, when Dreeme, for the first time, took my arm familiarly.

"You have been a kind friend to me, Mr. Byng," said he; "there are not many men in the world who would have treated my retirement with such delicate forbearance and good faith."

"Do not give me too much credit. I have been a selfish friend. I know that I am a facile person, something of the chameleon; I need the fairer colors in contact with me to keep me from becoming an ugly brown reptile. Having this adaptability of character, I have had very close relations with many of the best and noblest; but of all the men I have ever known, your society charms me most penetratingly. All the poetry in my nature being latent, I need precisely you to bring it to the surface. The feminine element is largely developed in you, as a poetic artist. It precisely supplies the want which a sisterless and motherless man, like myself, has always felt. Your influence over me is inexpressibly bland and soothing. You certainly are my good spirit. I like you so much, that I have been quite content with your isolation; I get you all to myself. These walks with you, since that famous oyster supper, the very day of my return home, have been the chief feature of my life. I count my hour with you as the pay for my scuffle with the world. A third party would spoil the whole! What would become of our confidence, our intimate exchange of thought on every possible subject, if there were another fellow by, who might be a vulgarian or a muff? What could we do with a chap to whom we should have to explain our metaphysics, give page and line for our quotations, interpret our puns, translate our allusions, analyze our intuitions, define our God? Such a companion would take the sparkle and the flash of this rapid and unerring sympathy out of our lives. No, Dreeme, this isolation of yours suits me; and since you continue to tolerate my society, I must suit you. We form a capital exclusive pair, close as any of the historic ones,—Orestes and Pylades, for example,—to close my long discourse classically."

"Do not compare us to those ill-omened two. Orestes was ordained to slay his parent for her sin," my friend rejoined, in an uneasy tone.

"It was a judicial murder,—the guiltless execution of a decree of fate. And all turned out happily at last, you remember. Orestes became king of Argos, and gave his sister in marriage to his Pylades, the faithful. Who knows but when your tragic duty is over, whatever it be, and you have brought the guilty to justice, you will resume your proper crown, and find a sister for me, your Pylades, the faithful? If my present flame should not smile, that would be admirable. Your sister for me would make our brotherhood actual."

"My sister for you!" said Dreeme, with an accent almost of horror; and I could feel, by his arm in mine, that a strong shudder ran through him.

We had by this time passed from the side-front of the Opera-House, where this conversation began, had walked along Quatorze Street, and turned up into the Avenue. Quatorze Street, as only a total stranger need be informed, is named in triumphant remembrance of the minikin monarch whom we defeated in the old French war. The crossing of Quatorze Street and the Avenue was, at that time, the very focus of fashion. Within half a mile of that corner, Everybody lived—Everybody who was not Nobody.

It was mid-March. Lent was in full sigh. Balls were over until Easter. Fasting people cannot take violent exercise. One can dance on full, but not on meagre diet,—on turkey, not on fish. But in default of balls, Mrs. Bilkes, still a leader of fashion, had her Lent evenings. They were The Thing, so Everybody agreed, and this evening was one of them. I had deserted for my walk with Dreeme.

Mrs. Bilkes's house was just far enough above Quatorze Street, on the Avenue, to be in the van of the upward march of fashion. Files of carriages announced that all the world was with her that evening. The usual band discoursed the usual music within; but wanting the cadence of dancers' feet to enliven them, those Lenten strains came dolefully forth.

We were passing this mansion when Dreeme had last spoken. Before I had time to ask him what meant his agitation at the thought of me for possible brother-in-law, the factotum of the Bilkes party, the well-known professional, hailed me from the steps, where he stood in authority; for by the bright light from the house he could easily recognize me.

"What, Mr. Byng! You wont drop in upon us? They're packed close as coffins inside, but there's always room for another like yourself. Better come in,—Mrs. Bilkes will take on tremendous if she finds I let you go by without stopping."

I paused a moment, half disgusted, half amused by the privileged

man's speech. As I did so, a gentleman coming down the steps addressed me. And it is such trivial pauses as these that bid us halt till
Destiny overtakes our unconscious steps.

I turned with a slight start, for I had not observed the new-comer
as an acquaintance until he was at my side.

It was Densdeth.

He looked, with his keen, hasty glance, at my companion. He seemed
to recognize him as a stranger. He did not bow, but turned to me, and
said,—

"What, Byng! Are you not going in? It is very brilliant. All the fair
penitents are there, keeping Lent, in their usual severe simplicity of
penitential garb. I asked Matilda Mildood if I should give her a bit of
partridge and some chicken-salad. 'I'm quite ashamed of you, Mr.
Densdeth,' says Matilda, with the air of one resolutely mortifying the
flesh; 'don't you remember it's Lent. Oysters and lobster-salad, if you
please, and a little terrapin, if there is any.'"

While Densdeth made this talk, he glanced again at my companion.
Dreeme had withdrawn his arm, and stood a little apart, half turned
away from us, avoiding notice, as usual.

"Don't throw away your cigar, Byng," continued Densdeth, taking
out his case, and stepping toward the lamp-post, to make, as it seemed
to me, a very elaborate selection. "Give me a light first. Will you try one
of mine?"

"No, thank you. I have had my allowance."

Densdeth took my cigar to light his. The slight glow was sufficient
to illuminate his face darkly. Its expression seemed to me singularly
cruel and relentless. It was withal scornful and triumphant. Something
evidently had happened which gave Densdeth satisfacton. Whom had
he vanquished to-night?

The cigar would not draw.

"Bah!" said Densdeth, tearing it in two, with his white-gloved hands,
with a manner of dainty torture, as if he were inflicting an indignity
upon a foe. "Bah!" said he, taking out another cigar, with even more
elaborate selection, and as he did so glancing, quick and sharp, at my
friend, who had retreated from the lamp. "I don't allow cigars, any
more than other creatures, to baffle me. Excuse me, Byng, for detain-
ing you. The second trial must succeed; if not, I'll try a third time,—*that*
always wins. Thanks!"

He lighted his cigar. Again by the glow I observed the same relentless, triumphant look.

Densdeth turned down the Avenue. I rejoined Dreeme. He took my arm again and clung to it almost weakly.

"What is the matter, Dreeme?" I asked, my tenderness for him all awake.

No answer, but a nervous pressure on my arm.

"You are tired. Shall we turn back?"

"Not the way that man has gone," said he.

"Why not? What do you fear?"

"I heard him name himself Densdeth. I saw his face—that cruel face of his. Mr. Byng,—my dear friend, Robert Byng,—that man is evil to the core. You call me your Mentor, your good influence; take my warning! Obey me, and shun him, as you would a fiend. You say that I have a fresh nature; believe that my instinct of aversion for a villain is unerring."

"Is not this prejudice?" said I, somewhat moved by his panic, but still fancying so much alarm idle.

"It might before have been prejudice, derived from your own account of him; but now I have seen him, face to face."

"A glance merely, and in a dusky light."

"Yes, but one look at that face of his sears it into the heart."

"You seem to have been as inquisitive about him as he about you. He studied your back pretty thoroughly. In fact, I believe it was to observe you that he made such parade of breaking up his delinquent cigar. He evidently meant to know for what comrade I was abandoning the charms of the Bilkes *soirée.*"

"I shudder at the thought of such a man's observation. What ugly fate brought me here?"

Dreeme turned, and looked back.

I involuntarily did the same.

The Avenue, at that late hour, was nearly deserted of promenaders. As far away as two blocks behind us, I noticed the spark of a cigar, and as the smoker passed a gas-light, I could see him take the cigar from his lips with a white-gloved hand. He even seemed to brandish it triumphantly.

"He is following us!" cried Dreeme.

The painter whirled me about a corner, and dragged me, almost at a run, along several humbler streets. At last we turned into one of the avenues by the North River, for away from the beat of any guest of Mrs. Bilkes.

There Dreeme paused, and spoke.

"Good exercise I have given you by my panic," said he, with a forced laugh. "How absurd I have been! Pardon me! You are aware how nervous I get, being so much shut up alone. And then, you know, I was only hurrying you away from your devil."

"Strange fellow you are, Dreeme! I suppose this very strangeness is one element of your control over me. You excite my curiosity in degree, though not in kind, quite as much as Densdeth does. And now that you and he are brought together, I hope these two mysterious personages will explain each other by some flash of hostile electricity. I wait for light from the meeting of the thunder-clouds."

"It must be very late," said Dreeme in a weary tone. "What a dismal part of the city! This squalor sickens me. These rows of grog-shops infect me with utter hopelessness. Sin—sin everywhere, and the sorrow that never can be divorced from sin! How can we escape? How can we save others? These nocturnal wanderings of ours have told me of a breadth and a depth of misery that years of a charitable lifetime would never have revealed. If I ever have opportunities for action and influence, I shall know my duty, and how to do it. I see, Mr. Byng, as I have before told you, that you do not thoroughly share my sympathy for poverty and suffering and crime."

"Perhaps not fully. My heart is not so tender as yours. I cannot seem to make other people's distress my personal business, as you do. I endure the misfortunes of strangers with reasonable philosophy. Suffering, like pain, I suppose is to be borne heroically, until it passes off. Every man has his hard times."

"You are not cruel," said Dreeme, "but you talk cruelly on a subject you hardly understand. Wait until the hours of your own bitterness come, and you will learn the precious lesson of sympathy! You will soften to others, and most to those who suffer for no fault of theirs,—the wronged, driven to despair by wrong-doing in those they love,—the erring, visited with what we name ruin, for some miserable mistake of inexperience. But let us hasten home! I have never felt so sick at heart, so doubtful of the future, so oppressed by the 'weary weight of all this unintelligible world,' as I do at this moment."

"Dreeme, are you never to take your future into your own hands, and live a healthy, natural life, like other men? Think of yourself! Do not be so wretched with other people's faults! You cannot annihilate the troubles that have made you unhappy; but do not brood over them. Be young, and live young, in sunshine and gayety."

"Be young!" said he, more drearily than ever.

"Yes; make me your confidant! Face down your difficulties! If you do not trust my experience, and think me too recent in the country to give you practical help, there is my friend, Mr. Churm. He will be here to-morrow from a journey. Churm is true as steel. Trust him! He and I will pull you through."

"I trust no one but you. Do not press me yet. I am generally contented, as you know, with my art and your society. Only to-night the sight of that bad man has discomposed me."

"Discomposed is a mild term," said I, as I unlocked the outer door of Chrysalis.

"Well, I am composed now. But I wish," said he in a trepidating way, that belied his words, "that you would see me safe to my door."

I did so, and we parted, closer friends than ever.

Densdeth, Cecil Dreeme, Emma Denman,—these three figures battled strangely in my dreams.

CHAPTER XXI

Lydian Measures

I dined *en famille* at Mr. Denman's the day after that panic-struck night walk with Cecil Dreeme.

"You are looking pale and thin, Emma," said Mr. Denman, as his daughter rose to leave us to our claret. "You need more variety in your life. Why not let Byng take you to the opera to-night? Our box has stood vacant, now, these many weeks."

"Yes," said I, "it is the new opera to-night."

Emma glanced at her black dress.

"Go!" said Denman, with something of harshness in his tone, "that need not cloud your life forever."

"Do go," said I.

"I will," she said, with a slight effort. "But I shrink from appearing in public again."

"It is time you should get over that feeling. We shall soon be receiving company again," said her father. "So be ready when Byng and I have had our cigars."

She was ready, and we drove to the Opera-House together.

Her mourning was exquisitely becoming to her slight, graceful, refined figure. The startled and almost timorous manner I had noticed in our first interview had lately grown more marked. This shy, feminine trait excited instant sympathy. It recalled how her life had been shocked by the sudden news of a tragedy. She seemed to have learned to tremble, lest she might encounter at any moment some new disaster sadder than the first. This was probably mere nervousness after her long grief, so I thought. Yet sometimes, when I spoke to her with any suddenness, she would start and shrink, and turn from me; then, exercising a strong control over herself, she would return, smile away the fleeting shiver, and be again as self-possessed and gay as ever.

As we entered the Opera-House and took our places in Mr. Denman's conspicuous box, the glare of the lights and the eyes of a great audience making a focus upon her affected Emma with the panic I have described. She turned to me with the gesture of one asking protection, almost humbly.

"I must go," she said; "I cannot bear to have all the world staring at me in this blank, hard, cruel way. They hurt me,—these people, prying into my heart to find the sorrow there."

"In a moment it will be an old story," said I. "Do not think of going, dear Emma. The change and the excitement of the music will do you good. This nervousness of a *débutante* will pass away presently."

Dear Emma! The first time that any such tender familiarity had passed my lips. And my manner, too, I perceived, expressed a new and deeper solicitude. I perceived this; so did my companion.

She looked at me, with a strange, fixed expression, as if she were resisting some potent impulse. Then a hot blush came into her cheeks. She sank into her seat, and fanned herself rapidly. Her brilliant color remained.

"Emma," said I, bending toward her, "what splendid change has befallen you? You are at this moment beautiful beyond any possible dream of mine."

"Do not speak to me," she said; "I shall burst into tears before all these people. This crowd, after my seclusion, confuses and frightens me. Let me be quiet a moment!"

All the world, of course, was immediately aware of the reappearance of the beautiful Miss Denman. There was much curiosity, and some genuine sympathy. "Nods and becks and wreathed smiles" came to her from the boxes on every side. Her *entrée* was a triumph—as such triumphs go.

To avoid this inspection, she took her lorgnette and glanced about the house. I followed its direction.

I saw her pause a moment on the group of men in the lobby. At the same time we both recognized Densdeth, regarding us.

He was laughing with Raleigh and others. I seemed almost to hear the sharp tone of that cynical, faithless laugh of his.

All the color faded out of Emma Denman's face. She sank back, almost cowering. Cowering,—the expression does not exaggerate the effect of her gesture. She cowered into the corner of the box, and hid her face behind her fan.

I should have spoken to demand the reason of her strange distress, when the leader of the orchestra rapped; there was a hush, and the new overture began with a barbaric blare of trumpets.

So the opera went on, to the great satisfaction of all dilettanteism.

It was thoroughly debilitating, effeminate music. No single strain of manly vigor rose, from end to end of the drama. Never would any noble sentiment thrill along the fibres of the soul in response to those Lydian measures. It was music to steep the being in soft, luxurious languors; to make all effort seem folly, all ardor madness, all steady toil impossible;—music to lap the mind in somnolence, in a careless consent to whatever was, were it but bodily ease and moral stagnancy.

There was no epic dignity, no tragic elevation, no lyrical fervor, in the new opera. Passion it had; but it was a dreamy passionateness, not the passion that wakes action, nervous and intent. Even its wild strains, that meant terror and danger, came like the distant cry of wild beasts in a heavy midnight of the tropics,—a warning so far away, that it would never stir the slumbers of the imperilled.

Always this music seemed to sound and sing, with every note of voice or instrument,—"Brethren, what have we to do with that idle fiction of an earnest life? While we live, let us live in sloth. Let us deaden ourselves with soft intoxications and narcotic stupors, out of reach of care. Why question? Why wrestle? Why agonize? Here are roses, not too fresh, so as to shame the cheeks of revelry. Here is the dull, heavy sweetness of tropic perfume. Here is wine, dark purple, prostrating, Lethean. Here are women, wooing to languid joys. Here is sweet death in life. So let us drowse and slumber, while the silly world goes wearily along."

Emasculated music! Such music as tyranny over mind and spirit calls for, to lull its unmanned subjects into sensual calm. Such as an Italian priesthood has encouraged, to make its people forget that they were men, and remember that they were and would ever be slaves. Music that no tyrant need ever dread, lest it should nerve the arm of a tyrannicide. Music that would never ring to any song of freedom, or chime with any lay of tender and ennobling love.

The story was as base as the strain. There was tragedy, indeed, in it, and death. But a neat, graceful, orderly death, in white satin. Nothing ugly, like blood and pangs; nothing distressing, like final repentance with tears, or final remorse with sobs and anguish. The moral was, that after a life of revelry, not too frantic, to die by digestible poison, when pleasure began to pall, was a very proper and pretty exit.

Delicious music, and only soothing if music were simply a corporeal influence, but utterly enervating to the soul. I felt it. I was aware of a deterioration in myself. I passed into a Sybaritic mood,—a mood of consent,—of accepting facts as they were, and missing nothing that could give a finer joy to my sensuous tranquillity. In this frame of mind, the degree and kind of my passion for Emma Denman satisfied me wholly. I yielded to it.

And she, in the same lulled and dreamy state, lost the dignity of manner which had kept us apart. She no longer shrank as she had been wont to do when my voice or words conveyed a lover meaning. Her shyness was gone. She seemed to yield herself to me, fully and finally.

All the while the swelling, flowing, soothing strains of honeyed music hung around us, and when the movement of the drama paused, our minds pursued the same intention in our talk.

We agreed that all regret was idle; that sorrow was more idle than regret; that error brought its little transitory pang, and so should be forgotten; that mundane creatures should not be above mundane joys in this fair world, reeking with sights and sounds of pleasure, and all lavish with what sense and appetite desire. We agreed that it was all unwisdom to perplex the soul with too much aspiration; better not aspire than miss attainment, and so pine and waste, as one might sigh his soul away that loved a cloud.

Between the acts, I saw Densdeth moving about, welcome everywhere,—the man who had the key of the world. A golden key Densdeth carried. All the salable people, and, alas! that includes all but a mere decimation, threw open their doors to Densdeth. Opera-box and the tenants of the box were free to him.

The drama was nearly done, and he had not been to pay his respects to Emma Denman, though he had bowed and smiled in congratulation.

"Densdeth does not come to tell you how brilliantly you are looking to-night," I said.

"I do not need his verdict," she said, coldly enough;—and then, as if I might take the coldness to myself, she added, "since I have yours, and it is favorable."

"Yes; my verdict is this,—Guilty,—guilty of being your most fascinating self,—guilty of a finer charm to-night than ever before."

"Guilty!" she said, turning from me. "Guilty, thrice repeated! Do use some less ominous word."

The music ceased. The curtain slowly descended, and hid the sham death-scene. There was the usual formal applause. The conceited tenor in his velvet doublet, unsullied by his late despair, the truculent basso, now in jovial mood, the prima donna, past her prime, sidled along, hand in hand, behind the foot-lights, and bowed to the backs of two thirds of the audience, and to the muffled resonance of the white gloves of the other third.

The spiritual influence of the opera remained, mingled with a slight forlornness, the reaction after luxurious excitement.

I left Emma Denman in the corridor, and went to find the carriage.

CHAPTER XXII

———•———

A Laugh and a Look

In the lobby of the Opera-House was the usual throng,—fat dowagers, quite warm enough with their fat, and wretchedly red-hot under a grand exhibition of furs; pretty girls, in the prettiest of opera-cloaks, white and pink and blue, and with downy hoods; anxious papas, indifferent brothers, bored husbands, eager lovers, ineligible young men taking out mamma, while her daughter hung on the arm of the eligible.

Such was the scene within the Quatorze Street lobby. Without, in a raw, drizzly March night, was a huddle of coaches, and on every box a coachman, swearing his worst.

It was some time before, in the confusion, I could find the Denman carriage. At last I discovered it, and went up-stairs for Emma.

As I ran up the stairs, and was just at the top steps, whence I should turn into the corridor where the lady was waiting, I heard the ominous sound of Densdeth's laugh.

It came from where she stood. I paused.

Instantly, in answer, and in thorough sympathy with that hateful tone, I heard another laugh. It seemed even baser, more cynical and false, than Densdeth's; for threaded in it, and tarnished by the contact, were silver notes I had often heard in genuine merriment.

"Emma Denman!" I thought, with a shiver. "How dares she let herself respond to his debasing jests? How can she echo him,—and echo that jarring music familiarly, as if she had long been a pupil of the master?"

The pang of this question drove me forward. I turned into the corridor.

Only those two were standing there,—Densdeth and she. His back was turned toward me. The glare of a gas-light overhead fell full upon her.

The languor caused by that enfeebling music was visible in her posture and expression. Her manner, too, to a sensitive observer like myself, betrayed a certain drowsy recklessness.

And then, as I entered the corridor by a side-door, before she was conscious of my presence, she gave Densdeth a look which curdled my blood.

I may live long. I am not without a share of happiness. I am at peace. God has given me much that is good and beautiful. The atmosphere of my existence is healthy. But there is one memory in my heart which I have never ventured to recall until this moment,—which I bear down upon and crowd back whenever it stirs and struggles to burst up into daylight. There is one memory which has power to burn away my earthly bliss with a single touch, and to throw such a ghastly coloring over all the world, that my neighbor seems a traitor and my Creator my foe. That memory is the look I saw Emma Denman give to Densdeth.

It was my revelation of evil in the woman I had honestly and earnestly resolved to love and trust. It showed to me first, by the fiery pang of a personal experience, the curse of sin.

Sin,—I fancied that I knew it well enough.

Sin,—I had been wont to class myself lightly among its foes; to feel a transitory gloom when I heard of its harm; to wonder and protest, nonchalantly, at its existence; to believe that its power was broken, with the other ancient tyrannies, and that it would presently accept a banishment and leave the world to a better day.

Ah no! I had never dreamed a dream of what is sin. But now the revelation came to me.

I am a stalwart man. This blow aged and enfeebled me as might a sorrowful lifetime. The weight of the thousands of ill-doing years, all the accumulated evil of the old bad centuries, rose suddenly, like a mountain, and fell upon me.

I cannot describe this look of hers. I do not wish to. It is enough to say that it told me of a dishonorable secret between the two. It told me that at this moment, however it might be in a mood of stronger self-possession, she felt no compunction, no remorse, no agony, that such a secret existed,—nothing but an indolent acquiescence in the treason.

And this was the interpretation of so much mystery. This justified my instinctive suspicions. This punished my generosity and my resolve to quell the warnings of nature. This explained the inexplicable. In that one instant I learned my capacity for an immortal misery.

They heard my step. Densdeth turned, and bowed to me politely enough, smiling also, as if to himself, behind his black moustache.

It was not the first time that his scornful smile had seemed to me to take a cast of triumph as he regarded me. But such fleeting expression had always disappeared, stealing back like an assassin who has peered out too soon, and may awake his drowsy victim. I too had always had my own covert smile. For I was quite satisfied that Densdeth was never to win any very substantial victory over me. I could seek his society in perfect safety, so I fancied, against its debasing influence. He never should wield me as he did Raleigh, nor master me as he did that swinish multitude at the club, or those wolves in Wall Street.

But now his vanishing smile of triumph chilled me. This harm was a more deadly harm than aught I had dreamed of as in any man's power. If I was so wronged in my faith, what would hinder me henceforth from losing all faiths, and so becoming the hateful foe of my race, and being forced into detested alliance with this unholy spirit—this corruption—Densdeth!

I wrapped the lady's cloak about her. In this duty I by chance touched her arm. My hands had become icy cold,—so this touch revealed to me,—and I shivered. She felt the shock, and shivered also. Then she took my arm, and moved forward hastily, as if the spot had become hateful to her.

Densdeth bowed, and left us.

We walked down stairs. She clung to my arm wearily.

I pitied her with such deep and sorrowful pity for the seeming discovery of this evening, that I felt that I must speak kindly; I spoke, and my voice sounded to me like the voice of one unknown, so desolate it was.

"Emma, you are tired. Poor child!"

"Emma!"—there was no withdrawing into forms again. Ah, nevermore! Nothing done could be undone.

"You are very kind," she said, with an altered manner,—sadness instead of languor. "No one has ever been so tender with me. O Robert! why did you not come years ago?"

While my answer to this pleading question lingered, we entered the lobby.

A young lady, standing there alone and forlorn, pounced upon Emma Denman.

"Dear Emma!" cried Miss Matilda Mildood, "I'm so glad you are here. Do take me home. Our coachman is wild with drink, and my brother Pursy is in danger of his life."

"I shall be most happy," said Emma.

I put the ladies into the Denman carriage, rescued Pursy from his scuffle, and we drove off together.

Pursy Mildood was a compliment-box, Matilda a rattle-box. Pursy played his little selection of compliments to Miss Denman. Matilda rattled to me. They filled time and space, as it was their business to do. Triflers have their office in this world of racking passions and exhausting purposes.

I needed this moment's pause. I could not have endured the *tête-à-tête* with Emma in the carriage. The interval, while Matilda sprinkled me with a drizzle of opera talk and fashionable gossip, gave me time to bethink myself.

What must I do and say?

To-night, nothing.

To-night, if I spoke in my agony, I must accuse. Let me wait for a calmer moment. Let me reflect, and assure myself that my thought was not doing a pure heart a cruel and irreparable wrong.

The Mildoods' house was opposite the Denmans'. Compliments and prattle came to an end, unconscious of the emotions they had for a time diverted. We dropped brother and sister at their door, and drove across.

I handed Emma out, unlocked the door with her key, and stepped within to say good night.

CHAPTER XXIII

A Parting

"Your hands were like ice, when you touched my arm," said Emma Denman. "You have taken cold. Come in. I will play Hebe, and make you a goblet of hot nectar."

"No, I must go. Good night."

"Mr. Byng, Robert! What has happened?"

"Do not ask me?"

"You appall me with your voice of a Rhadamanthus. Have I offended you? Is it fatal?"

The light of a large globe in the hall fell full upon her face as she spoke. All the eager, triumphal look of the early evening had departed. All the languid acquiescence was gone. Gone was even the faintest shadow of the expression that had turned my blood to ice. Pale horror—yes, no less than horror—seemed suddenly to have mastered her. Was she too now first learning the sin and misery of sin?

She stood in the grand hall of the stately house, a slight, elegant figure in mourning, with the abundant drapery of her cloak falling about her. There were no other lights except the tempered brilliancy of the globe overhead. It was after midnight. We were quite alone, except that a white statue, severely robed from head to foot, and just withdrawn in a niche, watched our interview, as it might be the ghostly presence of Clara Denman dead.

As Emma stood awaiting my answer, her look of horror quieted. She seemed to me like one who has heard her death-sentence, and is resigned.

I could not force myself to answer, and she spoke again.

"Robert, if you have fault to find with me, do not tell me so to-night. To-morrow,—come to-morrow! Perhaps we may still be friends. Good night."

She gave me her hand. It was burning hot. I held it in mine.

There we stood,—the chaste and ghostly statue watching.

We could not separate. I trusted her again. I cursed myself for my doubts.

Should I, for the chance of one brief, passing look, sacrifice the woman whom I had maturely concluded that I loved, who loved me,—for so I was persuaded?

Should I stain a maiden's image in my heart with this foul suspicion,—a suspicion I dared not state to myself in terms?

Could I there erase from my mind all those pleasant memories of childhood, so sweetly anew revived, and all the riper confidences of our friendship, and believe that this brilliant creature's life was one monstrous lie, which she must daily, hourly, momently, harden herself to repeat?

Could I convince myself that her fascination was utter treachery,—that she, a grisly witch at heart, had carefully, with fairest-seeming spell, and lulling daily all my doubts away, entranced me until she deemed me wholly hers?

Had I not been for the moment under the sickly influence of that enervating music?

Had not my mind gained a permanent taint in the debasing society I had refused to resolutely shun? Was I not doing her foul injustice, and visiting it unfairly and cruelly upon her, that I had let myself be the comrade of ignoble and sensual people,—of Densdeth, to whom no purity was sacred?

Could she, my only intimate among women, be responsible for the lowering of my moral tone, so that I did not abhor, and had not been for these late months loathing, all contact with vice? It must be that a man who loves a pure and elevating woman will no more palter with evil. He is abashed by her whiteness of soul. He will not carry into her presence the recent taint of staining associates. He will strive to breathe no other but that sweet serenity of atmosphere where she dwells, and so refresh and recreate his holier being.

Ah, these bitter doubts! They did in my sinking heart justify themselves.

And so, as I could not speak the tender, trustful, joyful lover words, nor any words but sad reproaches and questions of distrust, I stood there, silent, holding fast her hand.

Then, in the silence, the terrible thought overcame me, that if by any syllable or gesture, or even by the dismay of an involuntary look, I should convey my suspicions to Emma Denman, there would be another tragedy in that ill-omened house, another despair, another mystery,—no mystery to me,—and all the sickening horror of a death.

"Good-night," said Emma again.

But still she did not withdraw her hand.

We did not hold each other with the close grasp of earnest, confident friendship, nor with that strong pressure of love which seems to strive to make the two beings one life. It was a nerveless, lifeless clutch. Her burning hand had grown icy cold in mine. She held me feebly, as a drowning woman might wearily, and every weary moment still more wearily, cling to the fainting shoulder of a drowning man, as the great solemn waves fell on him, one by one.

A dreary moment.

It tore something from my earthly life that never can return. My youth faded away from me, as we stood there miserably. My youth shrank and withered, never to revive again and be the same bright youth, whatever warmth of after sunshine came. The blight of sin was upon me. The sense of an unknown horror of sin grew about me, and I became a coward for the moment,—a coward, smitten down by the dread that for me, forever, faith was utterly dead, and so my heart would be imbittered into a vague and fiendish vengeance for its loss.

"Robert," said she, at last, "you will not speak. You are murdering me with this ominous silence. How have you learned all at once to hate me?"

"Hate you?"

"Worse then! Do you distrust me?"

"Why should I? We will not speak of this now. That music has taken all the manliness out of me,—that, or some power as subtle. I will see you to-morrow. By broad daylight, all the ugly fancies that beset me now will vanish."

"Yes," she said, more drearily than ever; "fancies fade with sunshine; facts grow more fatally prominent. Good night."

She withdrew her hand.

She moved wearily and sadly away,—a slight, graceful figure in mourning, draped with the heavy folds of a cloak.

Half-way up the stairs she paused and turned, grasping the massive dark rail with both her white hands. Light from the floor above threw her face and form into magical relief, hardly less a statue than that marble figure watching us.

"Good-bye," she said, in a tone mournful as a last adieu.

"Good night," I answered; and so we parted.

I walked hastily home to Chrysalis. It was a raw March night, with a cold storm threatening, and uttering its threats in melancholy blasts and dashes of sleet.

How chilly, lonely, ghostly it looked in the marble-paved corridors of Chrysalis! I opened the great door in front with my pass-key. The wind banged it after me with a loud clap. But no closed door could repel the urgent chase of that night's cruel thoughts.

I was wretchedly timorous and superstitious after these excitements. As I passed the padlocked door of Densdeth's dark room, next to mine, I fancied him lurking within, and leering triumphantly at me through the key-hole. And then in the sound of the storm, sighing along the halls and staircases, and shaking the narrow windows, I seemed to hear that mocking laugh of Densdeth's,—that hard, exulting laugh of his,—that expressive laugh,—saying, with all the cruelty of scorn, and proclaiming to the scoffing legions who love the fall of noble souls,—"Here, at last! here is another who trusted and is deceived. Now his illusions are over. He will join us frankly, and share our jolly joys. Welcome, Robert Byng, to a new experiment of life! Come; you shall have revenge! You shall spoil the happiness of others, as your own is spoilt. We offer you the delicious honey of revenge. Sweet it is! ah, yes! the sweetest thing! You shall be one of us,—a tempter. Come!"

Such sounds seemed to me to issue from that dark room of Densdeth's, to clothe themselves with those tones of his, which I had heard to-night echoed by the lips of the woman I longed to love, and to pervade the building, like a bat-winged flight of fiendish presences, claiming me as their comrade, whether I would or no.

I entered my great, dusky chamber. The fire had gone out; it was chilly and dark within. In the faint light from the street lamp, streaming through the narrow mullioned windows, the ancient furniture, carved with odd devices of griffins, looked grotesque and weird. All the pictures, statues, reliefs, and casts in the room stared at me strangely. Was I suddenly another man than the undejected person who had lived so many weeks under their inspection? The portrait of Stillfleet's mother, a large, dignified woman, gazed kindly and pityingly upon me, with a mother's look, as I lighted the gas.

On the table Locksley had deposited a parcel addressed to me. I unwrapped it. It was the frame I had ordered for my present, Cecil Dreeme's sketch.

I put it in the frame, and examined it again. Only a sketch; but very masterly, full of color, full of expression, full of sweet refinement not diminishing its power.

"If it were not for Dreeme," I said aloud, "I should despair. Him I trust. Him I love with a love passing the love of women. If I should lose him, if he should abandon me, I might be ready to take the world as Densdeth wishes. What can a soul do without one near and comrade soul to love and trust?"

Then the mocking wind through the corridors, and all along the wintry streets without, answered me with new scoffs of the same derisive laughter.

I lifted my eyes from the picture. That ancient tapestry caught my eye, where Raleigh had found Densdeth in the demon. That malignant face—Densdeth's, and no other—was looking at me with a meaning smile.

I tore down the tapestry, and slunk to bed. The blessing sleep, foreshadower of that larger blessing death, fell upon me. Sleep, the death after the brief cycle of a day, received me tenderly, and restored me, that I might be man enough to bear the keener pangs and sterner griefs of the morrow.

CHAPTER XXIV

Fame Awaits Dreeme

I was indisposed next morning to face my associates at the club, or any chance acquaintance at the Minedurt. I went off and took a dismal, solitary breakfast at Selleridge's. The place had a claim on my gratitude, since it had supplied the materials of our gentle orgie in Chrysalis.

As I walked forlornly back, I endeavored to prepare myself for my appointed interview with Emma Denman.

I knew that a woman may blind herself to the measure and quality of a man's admiration; I knew that she can even desperately accept his heart; but I also knew that only a woman thoroughly deteriorated by deceit can listen to a lover's final words of trust, and still conceal from him one single fact in all her history that might forbid his love. She must reveal, or let her lover know she cannot reveal. She will, unless she has grown base and shameless, scorn to be a lie—yes, even for a moment, after the avowal of love—a lie to one she loves, whatever the truth may cost. I believed that, if I went to Emma Denman, and said, "We are before God, I love you," she would be true, and, if the truth commanded, would say, "Robert, you must not." So waiting until our interview, I held my agony under, as one presses a finger upon a torn artery, while the surgeon lingers.

In the letter-box in my door at Chrysalis I found this note:—

"I am not well. I cannot see you this morning. I will write again,—perhaps to-day, perhaps to-morrow.

"EMMA DENMAN."

My finger on the bleeding artery a little longer.

While I stood reading and re-reading this billet, in the bewilderment of one thrust back into suspense from the brink of certainty, I heard a knock at my door.

I opened. It was Pensal, the artist.

Pensal occupied a studio in a granite house which continues the architecture of Chrysalis along Mannering Place. It had once been a residence for the President. But perhaps the salary of that official grew contingent,—perhaps it was paid in Muddefontaine bonds. Certain it was that no President now dwelt in this supplementary building; but, like the main Chrysalis, it was let to lodgers. Among these was Pensal. A friendship had begun to crystallize between us. He was a profound observer, as well as a great artist.

Pensal came in, and looked at me for a moment in silence.

"What is it?" said I. "What new do you find in my face?"

"Much. And you too have stepped into the Valley of the Shadow of Death? Well, a friend can only say, God help you! It comes to us all."

"Yes, Pensal, the shadow is upon me."

"It will pass away. You cannot believe it now; but the shadow will drift away. It cannot blight the immortal man. Be sure of that!"

"But there is immortal grief."

"While you think so, you have a right to look a hundred years older than you did yesterday. But, Byng, I came to ask you a favor, not to criticise you. I am in a sea of troubles."

"'Take arms, and by opposing end them.'"

"Very well for you to say, who know better this moment by your own experience. So far as taking arms—that is towels and sponges—against my sea can go, I have ended it; but its wet bottom remains. The fact is, that I am suffering from a vulgar misery. My Croton pipe burst in the thaw last night. My studio is the bed of a lake with all manner of drowned entomology, looking slimy and ichthyological."

"Do bring your work over here."

"Thank you. You have anticipated my request."

"You are a godsend to me. I could not tolerate this morning a fellow with a new treasure-trove of scandal, the last cynical joke or base story";—and I thought of Densdeth, and other men, the coarsened and exaggerated shadows of Densdeth, who sometimes lounged in upon me for a lazy hour.

"I will be a treble godsend," said Pensal. "I will bring you not only myself, but two friends, whose lips or hearts are never sullied with anything scandalous or cynical."

"A pair of plaster casts,—a pair of lay figures?"

"You are cynical yourself. No; two men, fresh and pure."

"*En avant,* with such sports of Nature!"

"With such types of manhood! Sion, the sculptor, is in town for a day or two. I caught him last night, and he promised to sit to me this morning. Towers, also, is to come and stir up Sion while he sits,—to put him through his paces of expression."

"Ah, Towers and Sion! I withdraw my doubts. If my great barn here will serve you, pray bring your tools and your men over at once."

Pensal went off for his friends.

I was delighted with this interruption. It was a tourniquet on the bleeding artery.

I had felt too forlorn to solace myself with Cecil Dreeme's society this morning. I was conscious, also, that I could not see him now without pouring forth the whole story of my doubtful love for Emma Denman, my hesitant resolve to be her lover, the shock of last night, and the suspense of to-day. All this, with only the name suppressed, I knew must gush from me when I saw my friend of friends. And yet, by a certain inexplicable instinct, I shrank from thrusting such confidence upon him. I loved him too much, and with too peculiar a tenderness, to tell him that I had fancied I loved even a woman better than him.

I had said to myself, "I will wait for my usual evening walk with Dreeme, and then, if my heart opens toward him, I will let the current flow. He cannot console; he will teach me to be patient."

Meantime I welcomed the visit of Pensal and our two friends, as a calm distraction in my miserable mood. I was too much shaken and unmanned to trust myself out in the world and at my tasks.

Presently Pensal arrived with the two gentlemen, and set up his easel before my window.

I need hardly describe men so well known as the three artists, Sion, Towers, and Pensal. Indeed, as their business in this drama is merely to hasten one event by a few hours, it would be impertinent to distinguish them as salient characters. I glance at them merely, as they enter, halt a moment, do their part and disappear.

It was a blessed relief to me that morning to have their society. And now that I compel myself to write this sorrowful history, the relief is hardly less, to pause here and recall how blessed then it was. I had never known fully until then what it was to have the friendship of pure and true hearts.

Pensal sat down and wielded his crayon with a rapid hand. Each of the party, artist, sitter, critic, began to scintillate, to flash and glow, according to the fire that was in him.

Stillfleet's collection suggested much of our conversation. It was, as I have said, an epitome of all history. My three guests took the American view of history; that, give the world results, the means by which those results were attained cease to be of any profound value or interest. Everything ancient is perpetually on its trial,—whether its day has not come to be superannuated, and so respectably buried. Antiquity deserves commendation and gratitude; but no peculiar reverence or indulgence. The facts and systems of the past are mainly rubbish now; what is precious is the spirit of the present, which those systems have reared, or at least failed to strangle, and those facts have mauled strong and tempered fine.

These three great artists act on this theory, adapted to art. Hence their vigor. Hence also their recognition by a nation whose principle is faith in the present,—the only healthy faith for a man or Man.

While the magnetic current of a lively conversation flowed, Pensal worked away at his paper.

Presently, on the blank surface, a semblance of a man's face began to appear, rather fancied than distinguished, as we behold a countenance far away, and say, "Who is it?"—the question implying the instant answer, as we approach, "It is he!"

Sion's head, mildly lion-like, grew forth from the sheet,—lion-like, with its heavy mane of hair and beard. A potent face, but gentle.

Slowly the creation grew more distinct. The face drew near, and demanded recognition for its spiritual traits.

It was Sion's self.

And yet it was not the Sion who sat there before us, in high spirits, making jokes, telling stories, laughing with a frank and almost boyish gayety of heart, as if his life was all careless jubilee, and never visited by those dreams of tender, nay, of pensive and of melancholy sweetness, which he puts into undying marble.

Yet it was this joyous companion too, and the other and many another Sion, whom we had always known, but never perceived that we had known, until this moment.

In fact, Pensal, a master, had not merely seized and combined the essence of all Sion's possible looks in all possible moods; but he had divined and created the inspiration the sculptor's face would wear, if changeful mortal features could show the calm and final beauty of the immortal soul. The picture was Sion's apotheosis.

"Come and look at yourself, Sion," said Towers, as this expression at last by a subtle touch revealed itself. "Pensal has drawn you as you will look in Valhalla, if you are a good boy, and don't make any bad statues, and so get your own niche there at last."

Sion stepped round to survey himself.

"I am lucky," said he, "Pensal, to have nothing to be ashamed of lurking in my heart. You would be forced to obey your insight, drag it out, and set it inexorably in full view, in my portrait. It's well for Byng, there, that you are not doing him this morning."

"Why?" said I.

"You look as if '*Et tu, Brute?*' had been giving you a deadly stab. But what a poor bungler, compared with Pensal, the sun is in picturing men!" continued Sion. "To say nothing of his swelling our noses and blubbering our lips, spoiling our lights and blackening our shades, he can only take us as we choose to look while he is having his little wink at us."

"And a man cannot choose to look his noblest on occasion. A got~up look is generally a grimace," says Towers.

"Well, Pensal," said Sion, "your picture convinces me that I am not a miserable failure and a humbug, who cannot see anything in marble or out. Now let me free for a moment. I am tired of sitting to be probed and flayed."

Sion took his furlough, and strayed about the room, glancing at Stillfleet's precious objects. I stepped aside to get a cigar for Pensal.

"Ah!" cried Sion. "Here is a fresh thing. This was never painted in Europe; and yet I do not know any one here who could do it."

He had found the sketch, my present from Cecil Dreeme. In my sickness of heart last night, I had neglected the painter's injunction, and left it exposed on my table, half covered by a newspaper.

Sion held it up for inspection.

Now that it had been seen, there was nothing to do, except to get the approval of these final authorities, and communicate it to Dreeme.

"It is a new hand," said I, "what do you think of it?"

"She has great power, as well as delicacy," said Pensal,—the others waiting for him to speak.

"She! Who?" I asked.

"The artist."

"Odd fancy of yours! It is a man."

"What! and paint only a back view of a woman? I supposed that being a woman, as the general handling too suggests, she took less interest in her own sex; or, on the other hand, fancied that she could not represent it worthily."

"O no!" said I. "He had no female model."

"Probably," said Towers, "he is too young to have a woman's image in his brain, which fevers him until he wreaks it on a canvas."

"Man or woman," said Sion, "and I confess it seems to me to have a somewhat epicene character, it is a very promising work,—a pretty anecdote well told. I should like to see what this C. D.—it seems to be so signed—can do in other subjects calling for deeper feeling."

"A friend of mine in the building has other drawings and sketches by the same hand. I will see if I can borrow them," said I.

"Do," said Sion. "If they are worthy of this, we must know him, and have him known at once. Fame waits him. Here is that fine something called Genius."

If Dreeme would only profit by this chance, and give his fame into the hands of my friends, his success was achieved.

I forgot my own sorrows, and ran up-stairs, eager to persuade the recluse to seize this moment, to terminate his exile and step forth into the light of day.

Chapter XXV

Churm Before Dreeme's Picture

Full of hope for my friend, I left the three artists below, and darted up to his studio.

I knocked lightly, thinking a quick ear listened, and a quick voice would respond.

No answer.

I knocked again, distinctly and deliberately, and listened with some faint beginning of anxiety. Yesterday I had not seen him. Was he ill again?

Still no answer.

All the remembrance of the night when Locksley and I first made entrance there rushed back upon me.

I knocked once more, and spoke my name.

Again no answer.

I thundered at the door, striking it hard enough to hurt the dull wood that was baffling me.

Profound silence within.

"Is it possible that he has ventured out into daylight? It would be an unlucky moment for his first absence, now when good-fortune waits to befall him. His Fame is here, holding her breath to trumpet him, and he is away."

At the same time I doubted much if he could have gone. His terror of exposing himself was still great, and would be more extravagant after his panic-struck flight from Densdeth.

An indefinable dread seized upon me. I resisted, and dashed down stairs to the janitor's room.

I knocked peremptorily.

Locksley peered out, holding the door ajar.

"Dreeme!" whispered I, panting, "do you know anything of Dreeme?"

"It's you, sir," says Locksley. "Come in. It was only strangers I was keeping out."

"Don't let any one enter," said a voice within,—a miserable voice, between a whimper and a moan.

"He won't hurt you, Towner," said Locksley. "This is Mr. Byng, a friend of Mr. Churm's."

The janitor looked worn and worried. By the stove, in a rocking-chair, sat, slinking, a miserable figure of a man. There sat Towner, a bloodless, unwholesome being, sick of himself,—that most tenacious and incurable of all diseases. There he sat, sick with that chronic malady, himself,—a self all vice, all remorse, and all despair. Himself,—his cowering look said that he knew the fatal evil that was devouring his life, and that he longed to free himself from its bane by one bold act of surgery, such as his evasive eyes would never venture to face, such as his nerveless fingers dared not execute.

My glance identified the man, but I did not pause to study him. I had my own troubles to consider.

"Locksley," I said, seizing him by the arm, "where is Cecil Dreeme?"

My perturbation communicated itself to the janitor.

"Yes," said he, "I hadn't given my mind to it; but he did not answer when Dora went up with his breakfast. Then Towner was brought in, and we've been so busy with him that I forgot to send her up again."

"He is not there. He does not answer my knock."

"Going out in the daytime is as unlikely for him as the sun's showing at midnight. I mistrust something's happened."

"Do not say so, Locksley. Disaster to him is misery to me. Yes, double misery to-day!"

"Did you have your walk together last night?"

"No. I was at the opera until late."

"We must try his door again."

"I can't be left here alone," feebly protested Towner.

"Dora will take care of you."

"But Densdeth might come," shuddered the invalid.

"He never comes here. He'd better not," said Locksley, bristling.

"Who keeps the key of his dark room?"

"His servant, I suppose. Come, Mr. Byng." Locksley led the way up stairs. "Towner isn't long for this world, you see," said he. "We thought he'd better die among friends. Mr. Churm will be back this morning to talk to him, and get his facts."

It was afternoon, and the boys of Chrysalis, the College, were skylarking in the main corridor. Their rumor died away as we climbed the stairs. It was as quiet at Cecil Dreeme's door as on the night when we first forced entrance,—as quiet without, and, when we knocked, as silent within.

Locksley tried the door. It was unlocked. He opened. We entered, in a tremor of apprehension.

My friend of friends was gone! Gone! and another, some unfriendly and insolent intruder, had been there desecrating the place. The picture of Lear was flung from the easel and lying on the floor. The portfolio was open, and its drawings scattered. Upon one—a sketch of two sisters tending a mild and venerable father—a careless heel had trodden. Even the bedroom the same rude visitor had violated, and articles of the young painter's limited wardrobe lay about. How different from the order that usually lent elegance to his bare walls and scanty furniture!

Locksley and I looked at each other in indignant consternation.

"My old scare has got hold, and is shaking me hard," said the janitor. "Some of them he was hiding from must have found him out, and been here rummaging, to pry into what he's been at all this time. When did you see him, Mr. Byng?"

"Not yesterday. Night before last,—can it be only night before last that we met Densdeth?"

"Densdeth!" said Locksley, bristling more than ever with alarm. "Is he in this business?"

"I dread to think so," said I, unnerved, and sinking into Dreeme's arm-chair. And then across my mind flitted my friend's warnings against Densdeth, the meeting at Mrs. Bilkes's steps, the covert inspection, Densdeth's triumphant, cruel look, the panic, the flight, the conversation,—all the mystery of Dreeme.

"What are we going to do?" said Locksley, staring at me, in a maze. "Henry Clay's ghost couldn't persuade me that Mr. Dreeme had got himself into a scrape. Something's happened to the lad. His enemies have taken hold of him. Why did you leave him, Mr. Byng?"

"Why did I leave him? Why? To be taught the bitterest lesson a soul can learn," said I; and again I seemed to hear that mocking sound of Densdeth's laugh, echoed from the lips of Emma Denman, in the corridor of the Opera-House; again I seemed to see that hateful look of hers. The blight fell upon me more cruelly. I could not act.

"If Mr. Churm were only here!" said Locksley, forlornly, seeing my prostration.

With the word, there came through the open door the sound of a heavy trunk bumping up the staircase, now dinting the wall, and now cracking the banisters, and presently we heard Churm's hearty voice hail from below: "Hillo, porter! that's the wrong way."

"There comes help," cried Locksley.

"Call him up," said I, and the janitor hurried after him.

In came Churm, sturdy, benevolent, wise. His moral force reinvigorated me at a glance. His keen, brave face solved difficulty, and cleared doubt.

"What is it, Byng?" said he. "What has come to this young painter?"

Before I could answer, his eye caught Dreeme's picture of Lear, resting against the easel, where I had replaced it. His calm manner was gone. He sprang forward, kneeled before the easel, stared intently. Then he looked eagerly at me.

"What does this mean?" he exclaimed.

"Mean!" repeated I, astonished at his manner.

"Yes. Who painted this?" He spoke almost frantically.

"Cecil Dreeme," I replied.

"Cecil Dreeme! Cecil Dreeme! Who is Cecil Dreeme?"

"The young painter who lives here."

"Where is he? Where?"

"Gone, spirited away, I fear."

"What are you doing here," said he, almost fiercely.

"Mr. Churm," said I, "I do not understand your tone nor your manner. What do you know of this recluse?"

I seemed faintly to remember how Dreeme had shown a slight repugnance, more than once, when I named Churm as a trusty friend.

"You,—what do *you* know," he rejoined, staring again at the picture. "Tell me, sir; what do you know?"

"In a word, this," replied I, resolved not to take offence at his roughness. "The evening I moved into Chrysalis, Locksley called me to go up with him to this chamber. He feared the tenant was dying alone."

"Poor child! poor child!" interjected Churm.

"We broke in, and found him in a death-trance. Locksley's thoughtfulness saved him. We soon warmed, fed, and cheered him back to life."

"God bless you both!" said Churm, fervently.

"Churm," I asked, "what does this mean? Do you know my friend?"

"Go on! Tell your story!"

"Little to tell of fact, much of feeling. There was a mystery about Mr. Dreeme. I took him, mystery and all, unquestioned, to my heart of hearts. He was utterly alone, and I befriended him. I befriended unawares an angel. He has been blue sky to me."

"I am sure of it," said Churm; "but the facts, Byng! the facts of his disappearance!"

"He kept himself absolutely secluded. He never saw out-of-doors by daylight. We walked together constantly in the evening. I made it my duty to force him to a constitutional every day. We were walking as usual night before last, when we met Densdeth."

"No!" exclaimed Churm, vehemently. "Densdeth! I have been waiting for that name. Has he put his cloven hoof on this trail?"

"Densdeth observed us. I noticed ugly triumph in his face. Dreeme was struck with a panic at this meeting. I thought it instinct. It may have been knowledge. Densdeth, we suspected, followed us. Dreeme dragged me away in flight. But it would be easy for Densdeth, if he pleased, to watch Chrysalis, see me enter, and identify my companion. I am all in the dark, Churm. Can you help me to any light?"

"Let us hope so! Locksley, is Towner here?"

"Yes sir; and ready to make a clean breast of it."

"Bring him up to Mr. Byng's quarters. I have no fire, and the poor creature must be coddled. I may take this liberty, Byng? You are interested. It may touch the question of Dreeme. It does so, I believe."

"Certainly; my room is yours. Pensal was there, drawing Sion; but he will be done by this time. But, my dear friend, do you penetrate this mystery of Cecil Dreeme's? Tell me at once. He is dearer to me than a brother."

"Robert," said Churm, with grave tenderness of manner, "look at that picture,—that tragic protest against a parental infamy. Have you ever seen those faces?"

"Dreeme womanized himself for his Cordelia. I have sometimes had a flitting fancy that I had seen people like his Lear and Goneril. They are types so vigorous that they seem real."

"They are real."

"Who? Churm, if you know anything of my friend, do not agonize me by concealment."

"Be blind until your eyes open!"

We were at my door as he spoke.

Artist, sitter, and critic were moving to depart. I made the apology of "business" for quitting them.

"Keep at such business," said Pensal, with a keen glance at me, "and you will knock off the other seventy-five years of your new century."

"Yes," said Towers (artist's insight again), "Byng has taken a dip into counter-irritation and mended his paralysis of this morning."

"A fair stab," says Sion, "has made him forget the foul one."

So they took their leave.

"Do you remember," Churm said, as he seated himself in a great arm-chair of black carved oak, "my fancy, when we first talked here, that this would be a fit chamber for a Vehmgericht?"

"It was prophetic. We are to try the very culprit you hinted then,—Densdeth."

"Not in person, unless he may be lurking there in his dark room, to listen."

"Do not speak of it! Now that I begin to know more of Densdeth, the thought of that place sickens me."

"He has harmed you, then, in my absence."

"I fear a bitter treachery," said I; and my cheeks burned as I spoke.

"Is it so?" said Churm, sadly. "I dreaded it, and warned you as clearly as I dared. But we will save Cecil Dreeme. Yes, the ruin is terrible,—but this last must be saved."

Here Locksley entered, with Towner following, wrapped in a great dressing-gown. It was plain, as Locksley had said, that the invalid was not long for this world. But yet there seemed to glimmer through the man's weakness a little remnant of force, well-nigh quenched. It might still burn hot for an instant, if a blast touched it; but such a flash would search out all the fuel, and leave only ashes when it expired.

CHAPTER XXVI

Towner

The invalid peered cautiously into my room, halting on the threshold to inspect.

"Who is there?" said he.

"Nobody but Mr. Churm," replied Locksley.

"Promise me that on your honor!"

"Certainly. But haven't you known me long enough to be sure that I'm always upon honor? Come on!"

He entered feebly, shrinking from the sound of his own footsteps.

"Is there nobody in those small rooms?" he asked. "Nobody listening?"

"Show him, Locksley, to satisfy him," said I.

Towner examined my bath-room, my bedroom, and then my lumber-room.

"Where does that door in the lumber-room open?" said he, tremulously. "Into Densdeth's dark room?"

"Yes."

"Take me down stairs again, Locksley. I can't stay here."

"Why, man!" said I, "the door is bolted solid; those heavy boxes are between us and it, and here is another door which we can close and lock. Three of us too to protect you. You are safe from Densdeth."

"You don't know him!" and Towner shuddered, and would have

fallen. Locksley dropped him into an arm-chair by the stove. He seemed hopelessly prostrated.

I poured him out some brandy. The antique flask and goblet touched his fancy. He examined them with a pleased, childish interest, and glanced about the room, observing the objects, while he sipped his restorative with feeble lips.

"Evidently not a bad man by nature," I thought. "Only an impressible one,—one who should cry daily and hourly, 'Lord, deliver me from temptation!' If his superior being and chosen guide had been a hero, and not a devil like Densdeth, he might never have become the poor dastard he is."

"You have a pretty place here, Mr. Byng," said Towner, revived by his brandy, and assuming the air of a welcome guest and patronizing critic. It sat strangely on him after his recent trepidation. The man had the small social vanity of connoisseurship. It was one of Densdeth's favorite weaknesses; he loved to make confident ignoramuses talk of horses, wines, pictures, subjects on which a little knowledge generally makes a man a fool. Densdeth had no doubt found Towner's ambition toward the tastes of a gentleman a mighty ally in mastering the man.

"Yes, quite a museum," replied I, humoring him. Talking a little, I thought, would tranquillize him for business,—the hard task of confessing himself a culprit.

"Very fine paintings!" he continued. "I have a taste for such things. Not a connoisseur! Only an amateur, with a smattering of knowledge! Art refines the character wonderfully. I wish I had been introduced to it younger. You wouldn't guess now, Mr. Byng, what kind of scenery surrounded my childhood."

"No," said I, growing impatient. "What?"

"My father was the county jailer of Highland County. Instead of pictures and statues, my earliest recollections are of thieves pitching pennies in the jail-yard. Bad schooling for a boy, was it not? I remember the first hanging I saw, as if it were yesterday. The man's name was Benton Dulany. He robbed and killed his father. In his dying speech he said, that he never should have got religion, if it hadn't been for his errors; but now he was going straight to Abraham's bosom. And then a man, up in an elm-tree outside the jail-yard, shouted, 'Say, Benton! tell old Abe to keep some bosom for me!' Everybody roared, and the drop fell."

"You know what you came here for, Towner," said Churm, sternly. "Not to babble about your youth."

"Yes, yes," said the invalid, uneasily. "But I don't want you to be too hard on me. I want you to see that I haven't had a fair chance. No one ever showed me how to keep straight, and naturally I went crooked."

"If I had not understood your character long ago, I should not have interfered to protect you," said Churm. "But come to the point!"

"You will keep me safe from Densdeth?"

"He shall never touch you."

"His touch on my heart is what I dread, Mr. Churm. The first time he saw me, he laid his finger on the bad spot in my nature, and it itched to spread. I've been his slave, soul and body, from that moment. God knows I've tried to draw back times enough. He always waited until I was just beginning to regain my self-respect. Then he would come up to me, in his quiet way, and look at me with his yellow eyes, and smile at me with that devilish smile, and say, 'Come, Towner, don't be a prig! Here's something for you to do.' It was always a villany, and I always did it. It would take me days to tell you the base things I have done to help Densdeth to his million and his power. He has been the malignant curse of my life. I feel him now in my very soul, whispering me not to make confidants of people that will only hate me for my guilt and scorn me for my weakness."

"Brother-in-law," said Locksley, "you ought to know better than to think of hate and scorn when you face Mr. Churm."

"I do know better. I know that those are only devil-whispers. If I had merely been in general a bad man, Mr. Churm, I could endure your just judgment, and if you said mercy and pardon, I could believe that God would approve your sentence. But I have wronged you and yours. Can you forgive that?"

"Try me," said Churm.

"Mr. Churm," said the invalid, "I have always lied to you about the death of Clara Denman."

"So I supposed," Churm said, quietly; "but do you know anything of her fate."

"Nothing. You may get some clew from what I tell you."

"Speak, then," said Churm; "I listen."

"I need not go through a long story to tell you how Densdeth mastered Mr. Denman. It is really a short story, and old enough. Denman had an uneasy feeling that, with all his money, he was Nobody. He fancied more money would make him Somebody. That was basis enough for Densdeth. What a child Denman was in his hands! It was Densdeth who suggested, and I who had to stand the odium of, that first scheme of Denman's, to trample on the rights of the minority, and get the property of his railroad company into his own hands."

"I remember your share in the business," said Churm. "I suspected Densdeth's. Poor Denman!"

"Poor Denman!" repeated Towner, peevishly. "I don't see why he should have more sympathy than others."

"No more, but equal pity," rejoined Churm.

"That transaction was Densdeth's first victory over Denman. From that time Denman, and whatever he had, was Densdeth's. If I am not wrong, there is another, still in that house, that he has harmed, if not spoiled."

I sat by, in agony, listening,—in sorrow first, to find the reconstructed fabric of my respect for my father's friend and my own on the way to ruin,—in agony, now, at this dark allusion, which my heart interpreted. I sat by, listening, in a crushed mood, for further revelations of guilt and sorrow. Pitiable! and I seemed to detect, even in the remorse and self-reproach of the pitiful object before me, a trace of vulgar triumph that he was not the only sinner in the world, nor the only sufferer from the taint of sin.

"Densdeth led Denman on, step by step," continued Towner, "deeper and deeper into his gigantic financial schemes. You know how vain Denman is. He began to fancy himself Somebody. 'Bah!' said Densdeth to me, 'the booby will try to walk alone presently. Then he will have to go on his knees to me to keep him up.' And so it was. Denman devised an operation. A crisis came. Denman delayed ruin—what money-men call ruin—by a monstrous fraud. We had expected it, and we alone discovered it. 'Now,' said Densdeth to me, 'I have got the man.' 'What more do you want,' said I, 'than you have already gained by him?' 'I want his daughter Clara,' he said. 'She is the most brilliant woman in the world,—the only fit wife for me. But she will not think so, and I shall have to use force. Force is vulgar. I don't like it; but no creature shall baffle me.'

"So, to be brief, Densdeth said, 'Denman, compel your daughter to marry me, or you go to prison!'

"Denman at once began to apply a father's force to the young lady. As he urged her more and more, she spoke of appealing to you, Mr. Churm."

"Poor child! and I was absent!" said Churm.

"'Ah!' said Densdeth," continued the sick man, "when Denman told him of this. 'Here is business for Towner, that accomplished penman. Now, Towner! Letter first from Mr. Churm, in London,—"My dear Clara: I have heard with heartfelt satisfaction of your approaching marriage with your father's friend and mine, Mr. Densdeth," &c. Letter second,— "My dear Clara: It gives me great pain to know from your father that your mind is not made up as to your marriage. It is impossible to find a more distinguished or worthier gentleman than my friend Densdeth, or one who will make you happier. Do not alienate me by folly in this important matter," &c. Letter third,—short, sharp, and cruel,—"Clara: Your conduct is unwomanly and immodest. Except you are my friend Densdeth's wife, I shall never write or speak to you again." '"

"You wrote such letters!" cried Churm, savagely, rising and tramping the room.

"Cut off my right hand," said the wretched man, holding out his wasted, trembling fingers. "It wrote and prepared, with all the circumstance of seal and stamp, those base forgeries."

"That was foul!" said Locksley, shrinking away.

"Don't leave me, William," the invalid prayed, feebly. "I was not myself. I was the hand of Densdeth. Who can resist him? All this is idle struggle. He will conquer us again. He will clutch me, body and soul, again, and drag me down, down, down."

He burst into miserable tears.

Churm strode about the room, with a patient impatient step.

"I have tried you, Mr. Churm," at last the guilty man was able to gasp. "Can you be merciful?"

Churm's face was as an angel's, as he came forward, and laid a benignant hand on Towner's shoulder. "In the name of God, I forgive you. Yes, and I pity and will befriend you still."

It was an impressive scene in my antique chamber. Churm spoke "like one having authority."

The invalid grew calmer, and presently went on with his story again.

"Those letters, I am afraid, broke the young lady's heart. Her best friend had joined the enemy. Her father pleaded, no doubt, without concealment, his imminent ruin. A daughter will do much to save her father from shame. They forced from her a kind of qualified, protesting consent to think of the marriage as a possibility. Then they treated it as a certainty. My treachery to the young lady soon began to gnaw at my heart. Consign such a woman to Densdeth! to the daily agony of a life with him! Little as I knew her, I felt that she was an exceptional soul, worthy of all tender loyalty from all men. I must do something to repair my wrong to her. I must at least inform her of the forgeries. I was too weak-spirited to do it myself. I called in a woman to help me.

"She was another that Densdeth had spoilt. She hated and dreaded him as much as I did. She naturally resented his marriage to another woman. I sent her to see Clara Denman. Densdeth found it out, and stopped it. He finds out everything, sooner or later. He suspected me of an attempt to revolt from his dominion. He suspected me of instigating the young woman to show herself to his future wife. He made me stand by and listen, while, in his cool, cruel way, he sneered the poor girl into utter despair. She went off and drowned herself."

"Ah!" cried Churm, "it was she whose body was found,—she, and not my dear child."

"It was she," replied Towner. "Nobody cared for her, or missed her. She was not unlike Miss Denman in person. The disappearance of a young lady of fashion had made a noise. A great reward was offered. Scores of people identified the body. It had been greatly injured by the chances of drowning."

"Did Denman believe it to be his daughter's?"

"Entirely. It was the easiest solution. And no doubt he felt more at peace to suppose her dead than living, and likely to return and reproach him with his tyranny."

"And Densdeth?"

"He did at first. He did not believe that any woman could have eluded the strict and instant search he instituted and conducted all over the country. I myself cannot believe that she escaped alive."

"Perhaps Densdeth searched too far away from home," said Churm, glancing at me.

"He went to Europe for that purpose. When he missed the real drowned woman, he came to me, and charged me with aiding Miss

Denman to escape, and substituting the body. He soon discovered that I knew nothing of it. 'Towner,' said he, 'I am convinced that Miss Denman, my future wife, is alive. She fancies she is free from me. Bah! Did you ever know any one baffle my pursuit? She shall not. I want her, and must have her,—beautiful, untamed creature! but silly, and not willing to adore me, as her sex does! In fact, she got idle fancies in her head at last, and was really rude. She talked about abhorrence. Abhorrence of me! She said our marriage would be an infamy, for reasons she would not soil her tongue to give. She actually faced me, and said that. She said it, facing me, looking me straight in the eyes, not sobbing off in a corner, as most women would have done. It was splendid! Fine tragedy! and real too. Nothing ever entertained me so much. I would rather have her point at me, and call me villain, than any other woman fondle me,—that I have had enough of. O yes, she is alive, and I must have her. What a fool I was to fancy for a moment that such a being would drown herself, or be drowned by an accident,—quite unworthy of my intelligence, such a belief! I have a clew now. I have no doubt she has gone off to Europe, disguised as a man. She cannot elude me there. There or here, I will find her. I must have some more scenes with her. I should like to have one every day. Everything bores me now. I hunger to see again the magnificent scorn with which she repelled me when she fancied she had reason to. I want to see that loathing recoil from my touch. Ah! nothing like it! I should like to trample on her moral sense every day. If I could only sully her, and make her hate herself as she does me, and then stand by to watch her convulsions of self-contempt,—that would be worth living for. Perhaps I can manage even that. Who knows? But I must get her in hand first. My cue of course is that she is mad. The simplest methods are the best. Let me once have her in some uninquisitive madhouse, like Huffmire's here at Bushley, and something can be done. At least I can put her in a straight-jacket, and see her chafe, or sit, too proud to chafe, facing her fate with those great eyes, solemn and passionate. Denman will back me in whatever I do. If it gives you any satisfaction, Towner, to know that there is a wretcheder scrub than you, Denman is the man. I love to joke him about the State's prison, and make him grovel and implore. He is delightfully base. He will swear his daughter into a madhouse, and keep her there half a century, if I will only let him live in his house, and be pointed at as the great Denman. Pah!'"

Towner sank back in his chair, exhausted. It had cost him a giant effort to be free from his ancient allegiance to his fiend.

We three sat silent a moment, appalled by the depth of evil revealed to us in one human heart.

In this pause all the events and scenes of my life in Chrysalis drifted across my mind, and all my history for the past three months, culminating in last night's horror and to-day's agony, passed before me. Again I saw, as in a picture, Emma Denman standing, a slight, elegant figure in mourning, in the dimly lighted hall of the stately house. Again I marked on her pale face the deepening look of despair and pitiless self-abhorrence. Again I felt the blighting touch of her cold hand. Again there smote me the same throb of anguish I had perceived when I entered Cecil Dreeme's chamber and found him fled.

And Densdeth was in all this. The thought cowed me. I was ready to say, with Towner, "Why struggle vainly any more with this demon?"

Even as I uttered this hopeless cry within my soul, there came a quick step along the corridor, and a knock at my door.

Chapter XXVII

———◆———

Raleigh's Revolt

At this sound Towner half raised himself from the arm-chair, where he sat, cowering. "Don't let him in! Don't let anybody in!" he breathed, in an alarmed whisper.

The knock was repeated urgently. I stepped to the door and opened it a crack. Raleigh was without,—the man about town, of noble instincts and unworthy courses, who has already passed across these pages.

"Pray, drop in again, Raleigh," said I; "I have some people here on business."

"I must see you now. It may be life and death."

"To whom?" I asked, eagerly. He too had been a friend of Densdeth's. He might have knowledge of these mysteries.

"To one worth saving."

I observed him more particularly. All his usual nonchalance had departed. He was pale and anxious; but withal, his face expressed his better self, the nobler man I had always recognized in him.

"What is it?" said I, stepping out into the corridor.

"Not here!" said Raleigh in a whisper. And he pointed to the door of Densdeth's dark room.

"What?" I also whispered, with an irrepressible dread stealing over me, "Densdeth again!"

"Come in then," I continued; "we are already trying and condemn-ing him."

"Who are these?" said Raleigh, bowing slightly to Churm, and pointing to Locksley and Towner. The latter sat with his face covered by his hands.

"Foes of Densdeth, both! Sufferers by him!"

"Mr. Churm," said Raleigh, "I know you do not trust me much. But I came here to find you and Byng. Meeting you saves precious time. I have wasted hours already, struggling in my heart to throw off the base empire of Densdeth. I have done it. I am free of him forever. I can speak. I have seen your ward, Clara Denman!"

"Speak! speak!" cried Churm, seizing his arm.

"Alive, and in danger! I was riding home this morning before dawn, from Bushley,—never mind on what unworthy errand I had been. Go-ing down a hill, my horse slipped on the ice, and fell badly. I was getting him on his legs again, when a carriage came slowly climbing up the slope beside me. You know what a night it was,—stormy, with bursts of moonlight. There was light enough to give me a view of the people in the carriage. Two women, one a hag I well know, the other veiled. Two men, Densdeth and that black rascal, his servant. I knew them. They could not recognize me kneeling behind my horse. 'Mischief!' I thought. It was none of my business, but I got my horse up, and followed. Do you know Huffmire's Asylum?"

"Locksley!" said Churm, "quick! Run to my stable, and have the bays put to the double wagon! Quick, now! Have them here in five minutes!"

Locksley hurried off.

"Right!" said Raleigh, "you understand me. Yes, Densdeth had Clara Denman in that carriage."

"My poor child!" said Churm. "Her innocent life bears all the bur-den of others' sins."

"I rode after the carriage until I saw it stop at Huffmire's gate. Then I dismounted, let my horse go, and ran up in the shelter of some cedars by the road-side. I knew that Huffmire's Insane Asylum is no better than a private prison for whoever dares to use it. No one was stirring at that early hour, and it was some time before the bell was answered. At last, Huffmire himself came to the gate. Densdeth got out to parley with him. While they talked, the veiled lady managed, by a rapid movement with her tied hands, to strike aside her veil and look out. I saw her. I cannot be deceived. It was Clara Denman!"

"Is Locksley never coming with those horses?" muttered Churm.

"It was she, strangely dressed, altered, and pale, but firm and resolute as ever. I had but a glimpse. The hag and Densdeth's servant dragged her back. Huffmire undid the gate. They drove in. I caught my horse and rode off."

"Why did you not tear her away from that villain?" said Churm, fiercely.

"Mr. Churm, hear me through! I said to myself, 'This is none of my business. Clara Denman, whom the world thought dead, has come to light, mad, and Densdeth, the friend of the family, her betrothed, has very naturally been selected to put her into a madhouse.'"

"But the hour, the place! And Densdeth!"

"Yes; these excited my suspicions. I remembered the impression that Miss Denman had committed suicide rather than be forced into a marriage with Densdeth. Intimate as I have been with him, I can comprehend how to a nature like hers he would be a horror."

"But," said I, "this seems almost incredible, this audacious abduction of a young lady."

"Densdeth knew that she had no friends," said Churm, bitterly. "He knew that the manner and place of her hiding would favor his charge."

"It is audacious," said Raleigh, "and so is Densdeth. Success has made the man overweening. If it is true that Clara Denman baffled him for a time, I believe she is the only one, woman or man, who has done so, when he had fairly tried to conquer. Who knows but he feels that, once beaten, his prestige to himself is gone? He no doubt considers himself safe against Denman, and supposes, too, that the lady's flight and concealment have put her out of the pale of society."

"But what does he intend?" said I, looking at them both by turns.

"Will Locksley never come?" said Churm, striding to the window. "Towner has told us what he intends."

"Basely, I fear," replied Raleigh. "At least to compel her to a hateful marriage, if no worse. At least to have her where he can insult and scoff at her, and beat down her resistance. He means to master her, soul and body, and take some cruel revenge, such as only a fiend could devise."

"Your eyes seem to be opened, Mr. Raleigh," said Churm, "to the character of your bosom friend."

"They are opened, thank God! It has cost me a great and bitter struggle, this day, to tear that man out of my heart, to overcome my pride and inertia, and come and tell you, Mr. Churm, that I miserably despise myself; yes, and to say that I need the help and countenance of men like you to aid me to be a true man again,—to abandon Densdeth, and set myself forever against him and all his kind."

"Is that your purpose? My poor help you shall have," said Churm.

"Yes; I have been all day resisting my impulse to come and betray the man,—if this is treachery. But the remembrance of Miss Denman's pale face, as she looked friendlessly out of the carriage, has been shaming me all day, commanding me to break my fealty to sin, and obey my manly nature,—what there is left of it. I have obeyed at last."

"You have done well and honorably, Mr. Raleigh," said Churm, grasping his hand.

"Yes," said I, "Raleigh, I knew it was in you, and would come out."

"Thank you, Byng. Thank you, Mr. Churm," said he, gravely. "And now to help the lady! What are you going to do?"

"I am going to drive straight to Huffmire's, and demand her."

"Will he give her up without legal proceedings?"

"Probably not. I must take them, in time. I am convinced that Denman does not know of this. He still believes his daughter dead. But he would act with Densdeth. I mean to-day to let Huffmire know that the lady has friends, who are not to be trifled with, and that he is held responsible for her safety. Perhaps I shall set Byng sentinel over the house, to see that she is not spirited away again."

"Are we to be rough or smooth?" said I. "Do we want arms?"

And I glanced toward the table, where, at Towner's elbow, lay a long, keen, antique dagger, out of Stillfleet's collection. Its present peaceful use was to cut the leaves of novels, or the paper edges of a cigar-box.

"No arms!" said Churm, following my eye. "We might meet a wrong-doer, and be tempted to anticipate the vengeance of God."

I had forgotten, and did forget, in this excitement, to ask Towner what use Densdeth made of his dark room.

Chapter XXVIII

———◆———

Densdeth's Farewell

"The carriage is here," said Locksley, at the door. What with indignation at Densdeth, the janitor had got far beyond his usual bristly porcupine condition. He presented a spiky aspect. I hope no boy of the Chrysalids tried a tussle with him that day.

"Will you allow me to join your party?" Raleigh asked. "I may make myself of use."

"Certainly. Well, Towner, we leave you with friend Locksley. But, man!" continued Churm, in surprise, "what have you been doing to yourself?"

Well he might be astonished! Towner had risen, and was standing erect and vigorous. His manner was eager, almost to wildness. His little, unmeaning eyes were open wide, as if he saw something that made him young and unwrinkled again. There was a hot, hectic spot in his cheek, just now mere pale parchment.

"Embers ablaze at last!" thought I. "The man has struck a blow for freedom, and now he begins to hunger for vengeance. He has shaken off Densdeth; he looks as if he could turn and tear him."

"I should like to go with you, Mr. Churm, if you please," said Towner. "The drive will do me good. Huffmire knows me. He might open his doors to me, as Densdeth's friend, when he would exclude you."

"Very well," said Churm; "come, if you feel strong enough. But you must let Locksley fit you out with clothes."

Towner hurried off with the janitor. He had skulked into my room, at the beginning of the interview, like a condemned spy; he moved away like a brave and a victor.

"I take him," said Churm, "because I doubt his resolution. The old allegiance might prove too strong. He might confess to Densdeth that he had confessed to us. That would baffle us. We must not lose sight of him."

"Churm," said I, "I go with you, of course, through thick and thin. But Cecil Dreeme,—I feel that *my* first duty is to seek and succor him. I long to aid the young lady. But she is a stranger, and has you. Dreeme is part of my heart, and has no one."

"Patience, Robert! One thing at a time. Let us but run Densdeth to earth, and I dare promise you will find your friend. You for yours, and I for mine, and both against the common foe, we must prevail. If I doubted one moment of my child's safety, I should not be searching for her now, but chasing him."

"Not to impose upon him the mild sentence you spoke of long ago? Not to condemn him to bless as many lives as he has cursed?"

"I fear it is too late for such gentle treatment. Do you suppose, Towner, a life so cursed as his will be contented with that indirect application of the *lex talionis?* No; Densdeth must be stopped and punished."

The boys of Chrysalis, the College, were swarming in the corridor and upon the staircase under the plaster fan-tracery as we passed. Little enough of the honey of learning had they sucked from their mullein-stalk of a professor that day, and they buzzed indignantly or bumbled surlily about. Far different was the kind of education and discipline I was getting in the same cloisters. The great book of sin and sorrow, that time-worn, tear-marked, blood-stained volume, had been opened to me here, and I was reading it by the light of my own experience. And as I read, I felt that there were pages awaiting my record,— pages that I could already fill, and others that the future would sternly teach me to fill, before my story ended.

At the great western door we found Churm's drag, with the bays. Towner came out, muffled in an old blue camlet cloak,—a garment that the moths had disdained for a score of years, when in Locksley's prosperity they had choice pasturage of broadcloth to graze over. This queer figure and the elegant Raleigh took the back seat. Churm and I were on the box.

Churm's bays are not known to the Racing Calendar; but there are teams of renown that always pull up on the road, when they hear the accurate cadence of their coming hoofs, and recognize Churm's peculiar whistle as he signals, "More seconds out of that mile!" We drove fast through town to the nearest ferry, crossed, and presently, off the stones across the water, bowled along the Bushley turnpike, as merrily as if we were on our way to a country wedding festival. Little was said. We knew the past, and that was too painful to talk of. We did not know the future, and could not interpret its omens.

From time to time I turned to glance at Towner. He sat erect and alert, with cheeks burning and eyes aflame. The inner fire had kindled up his manhood again. "I would not give much for Densdeth's life," thought I, "if his late serf should meet him now. The man is capable of one spasm of vengeance. He looks, with his twitching face and uneasy fingers, as if he could rend the being that has debased him, and then die."

So we drove on, mile after mile, in the chilly March afternoon, and at last pulled up at a door, in a white stuccoed wall,—a whited wall, edging the road like a bank of stale snow. Within we could see an ugly, dismal house, equally stuccoed white, peering suspiciously at us over the top of the enclosure, from its sinister grated windows of the upper story.

A boy was walking up and down the road at a little distance a fine black horse, all in a lather with hard riding, and cut with the spurs. The animal plunged about furiously, almost dragging the lad off his feet.

"You will see Huffmire, Towner," said Churm, "and tell him that I want to talk with him."

"Yes," cried Towner, eagerly, "let me manage it!"

He shook off his cloak, sprang down with energetic step, and rang the bell. A man looked through a small shutter in the door, and asked his business, gruffly enough.

"Tell Dr. Huffmire that Mr. Towner wishes to see him."

The porter presently returned, and said that Dr. Huffmire would see the gentleman, alone.

"Huffmire will know my name. Send him out here to me, Towner, if he will come; if not, do you make the necessary inquiries," said Churm.

Towner passed in. The porter closed the outer door upon him, and then looked through the shutter at us, with a truculent stare, as if he were accustomed to inquisitive visitors, and liked to baffle them. He had but one eye, and his effect, as he grinned through the square port-hole in the gate, was singularly Cyclopean and ogre-ish. He probably regarded men merely as food, sooner or later, for insane asylums,—as morsels to be quietly swallowed or forcibly choked down by the jaws of Retreats.

"What!" whispered Raleigh to me, as the boy led the snorting and curvetting black horse by us. "That fellow at the eye-hole magnetized me at first. I did not notice that horse. Do you know it?"

"No," said I. "I have never seen him. A splendid fellow! His rider must have been in hot haste to get here. Perhaps some errand like our own!"

"Densdeth," again whispered Raleigh, "Densdeth told me he had been looking at a new black horse."

We glanced at each other. All felt that Densdeth's appearance here, at this moment, might be harmful. Churm's name brought Huffmire speedily to the door. Churm, the philanthropist, was too powerful a man to offend. Huffmire opened the door, and stood just within, de-fending the entrance. He was a large man, with a large face,—large in every feature, and exaggerated where for proportion it should have been small. He suffered under a general rush of coarseness to the face. He had a rush of lymphatic puffiness to the cheeks, a rush of blubber to the lips, a rush of gristle to his clumsy nose, a rush of lappel to the ears, a rush of dewlap to the throat. A disgusting person,—the very type of man for a vulgar tyrant. His straight black hair was brushed back and combed behind the ears. He was in the sheep's clothing of a deacon.

"You have a young lady here, lately arrived?" said Churm, bowing slightly, in return to the other's cringing reverence.

"I have several, sir. Neither youth nor beauty is exempt, alas! from the dreadful curse of insanity, which I devote myself, in my humble way, to eradicate. To e-rad-i-cate," he repeated, dwelling on the sylla-bles of his word, as if he were tugging, with brute force, at something that came up hard,—as if madness were a stump, and he were a cog-wheel machine extracting it.

"I wish to know," said Churm, in his briefest and sternest manner, "if a young lady named Denman was brought here yesterday."

"Denman, sir! No sir. I am happy to be able to state to you, sir, that there is no unfortunate of that name among my patients,—no one of that name,—I rejoice to satisfy you."

"I suppose you know who I am," said Churm. I saw his fingers clutch his whip-handle.

A rush of oiliness seemed to suffuse the man's coarse face. "It is the well-known Mr. Churm," said he. "The fame of his benevolence is co-extensive with our country, sir. Who does not love him?—the friend of the widow and the orphan! I am proud, sir, to make your acquaintance. This is a privilege, indeed,—indeed, a most in-es-ti-ma-ble pri-vile-age."

"Do you think me a safe man to lie to?" said Churm, abruptly.

"I confess that I do not take your meaning, sir," said Huffmire, in the same soft manner, but stepping back a little.

"Do you think it safe to lie to me?"

"I, sir! lie, sir!" stammered Huffmire. The oiliness seemed to coagulate in his muddy skin, and with his alarm his complexion took the texture and color of soggy leather.

"Yes; the lady is here. I wish to see her."

As Churm was silent, looking sternly at the pretended doctor, there rose suddenly within the building, a strange and horrible cry.

A strange and horrible cry! Two voices mingled in its discord. One was a well-known mocking tone, now smitten with despair; and yet the change that gave it its horror was so slight, that I doubted if the old mockery had not all the while been despair, suppressed and disguised. The other voice, mingling with this, rising with it up into silence that grew stiller as they climbed, and then, disentangling itself, overtopping its companion, and beating it slowly down until it had ceased to be,— this other voice was like the exulting cry of one defeated and trampled under foot, who yet has saved a stab for his victor.

They had met—Towner and Densdeth!

We three sprang from the carriage, thrust aside the Doctor, and, following our memories of the dead sound for a clew, ran across the court and through a half-open door into the hall of the Asylum.

All was still within. The air was thick with the curdling horror that had poured into it. We paused an instant to listen.

A little muffled moan crept feebly forth from a room on the left. It hardly reached us, so faint it was. It crept forth, and seemed to perish at our feet, like a hopeless suppliant. We entered the room. It was a shabby parlor, meanly furnished. The stained old paper on the walls was covered with Arcadian groups of youths and maidens, dancing to the sound of a pipe played by a shepherd, who sat upon a broken column under a palm. On the floor was a tawdry carpet, all beflowered and befruited,—such a meretricious blur of colors as a hotel offers for vulgar feet to tread upon. So much I now perceive that I marked in that mean reception-room. But I did not note it then.

For there, among the tawdry flowers of the carpet, lay Densdeth,— dead, or dying of a deadly wound. The long, keen, antique dagger I had noticed lying peacefully on my table was upon the floor. Its office had found it at last, and the signet of a new blood-stain was stamped upon its blade, among tokens of an old habit of murder, latent for ages.

Beside the wounded man sat Towner. His spasm was over. The freed serf had slain his tyrant. All his life had been crowded into that one moment of frenzy. He sat pale and drooping, and there was a desolate sorrow in his face, as if his hate for his master had been as needful to him as a love.

"I could not help it," said Towner, in a dreary whisper. "He came to me while I was waiting here. He told Huffmire to send you off, and leave me to him. And then he stood over me, and told me, with his old sneer, that I belonged to him, body and soul. He said I must obey him. He said he had work for me now,—just such mean villany as I was made for. I felt that in another instant I should be his again. I only made one spring at him. How came I by that dagger? I never saw it until I found it in my hand, at his heart. Is he dead? No. I am dying. Shall I be safe from him hereafter? I haven't had a fair chance in this world. What could a man do better—born in a jail?"

Towner drooped slowly down as he spoke. He ended, and his defeated life passed away from that worn-out body, the comrade of its ignominy.

I raised Densdeth's head. The strange fascination of his face became doubly subtle, as he seemed still to gaze at me with closed eyelids, like a statue's. I felt that, if those cold feline eyes should open and again turn their inquisition inward upon my soul, devilish passions would quicken there anew. I shuddered to perceive the lurking devil in me, slumbering lightly, and ready to stir whenever he knew a comrade was near.

"Spare me, Densdeth!" I rather thought than spoke; but with the thought an effluence must have passed from me to him.

His eyes opened. The look of treachery and triumph was gone. He murmured something. What we could not hear. But all the mockery of his voice had departed when in that dying scream it avowed itself despair. The tones we caught were sweet and childlike.

With this effort blood gushed again from his murderous wound. He, too, drooped away and died. The soul that had had no other view of brother men than through the eyes of a beast of prey, fled away to find its new tenement. His face settled into marble calm and beauty. I parted the black hair from his forehead.

There was the man whom I should have loved if I had not hated, dead at last, with this vulgar death. Only a single stab from another, and my warfare with him was done. I felt a strange sense of indolence overcome me. Was my business in life over, now that I had no longer to struggle with him daily? Had he strengthened me? Had he weakened me? Should I have prevailed against him, or would he have finally mastered me, if this chance, this Providence, of death had not come between us?

I looked up, and found Churm studying the dead man.

"Can it be?" said I, "that a soul perilous to all truth and purity, a merciless tempter, a being who to every other man was the personification of that man's own worst ideal of himself,—can it be that such an unrestful spirit has dwelt within this quiet form? What was he? For what purpose enters such a disturbing force into the orderly world of God?"

"That is the ancient mystery," said Churm, solemnly.

"Can it never be solved in this world?"

"It is not yet solved to you? Then you must wait for years of deeper thought, or some moment of more fiery trial."

Chapter XXIX

Dreeme His Own Interpreter

We left the dead, dead.

"Where is Huffmire?" Churm asked.

A sound of galloping hoofs answered. We saw him from the window, flying on Densdeth's horse. Death in his house by violence meant investigation, and that he did not dare encounter. He was off, and so escaped justice for a time.

The villanous-looking porter came cringing up to Churm.

"You was asking about a lady," said he.

"Yes. What of her?"

"With a pale face, large eyes, and short, crisp black hair, what that dead man brought here at daybreak yesterday?"

"The same."

"Murdoch's got her locked up and tied."

"Murdoch!" cried Raleigh. "That's the hellcat I saw in the carriage."

"Quick," said Churm, "take us there!"

I picked up my dagger, and wiped off the blood; but the new stain had thickened the ancient rust.

The porter led the way up-stairs, and knocked at a closed door.

"Who is there?" said a voice.

"Me, Patrick, the porter. Open!"

"What do you want?"

"To come in."

"Go about your business!"

"I will," said the man, turning to us, with a grin. He felt that we were the persons to be propitiated. He put his knee against the door, and, after a struggle and a thrust, the bolt gave way.

A large, gipsy-like woman stood holding back the door. We pushed her aside, and sprang in.

"Cecil Dreeme!" I cried. "God be thanked!"

And there, indeed, was my friend. He was sitting bound in a great chair,—bound and helpless, but still steady and self-possessed. He was covered with some confining drapery.

He gave an eager cry as he saw me.

I leaped forward and cut him free with my dagger. Better business for the blade than murder!

He rose and clung to me, with a womanish gesture, weeping on my shoulder.

"My child!" cried Churm, shaking off the Murdoch creature, and leaving her to claw the porter.

I felt a strange thrill and a new suspicion go tingling through me as I heard these words. How blind I had been!

Cecil Dreeme still clung to me, and murmured, "Save me from them, Robert! Save me from them all!"

"Clara, my daughter," said Churm, "you need not turn from me. I have been belied to you. Could I change? They forged the letters that made you distrust me."

"Is it so, Robert?" said the figure by my heart.

"Yes, Cecil, Churm is true as faith."

There needed no further interpretation. Clara Denman and Cecil Dreeme were one. This strange mystery was clear as day.

She withdrew from me, and as her eyes met mine, a woman's blush signalled the change in our relations. Yes; this friend closer than a brother was a woman.

"My daughter!" said Churm, embracing her tenderly, like a father.

I perceived that this womanish drapery had been flung upon her by her captors, to restore her to her sex and its responsibilities.

"Densdeth?" she asked, with a shudder.

"Dead! God forgive him!" answered Churm.

"Let us go," she said. "Another hour in this place with that foul woman would have maddened me."

She passed from the room with Churm.

Raleigh stepped forward. "You have found a friend," said he to me; "you will both go with her. Leave me to see to this business of the dead men and this prison-house."

"Thank you, Raleigh," said I; "we will go with her, and relieve you as soon as she is safe, after all these terrors."

"A brave woman!" he said. "I am happy that I have had some slight share in her rescue."

"The whole, Raleigh."

"There he lies!" whispered Churm, as we passed the door where the dead men were.

Cecil Dreeme glanced uneasily at me and at the dagger I still carried.

"No," said I, interpreting the look; "not by me! not by any of us! An old vengeance has overtaken him. Towner killed him, and also lies there dead."

"Towner!" said Dreeme, "he was another bad spirit of the baser sort to my father. Both dead! Densdeth dead! May he be forgiven for all the cruel harm he has done to me and mine!"

Cecil and I took the back seat of the carriage. I wrapped her up in Towner's great cloak, and drew the hood over her head.

She smiled as I did these little offices, and shrank away a little.

Covered with the hood and draped with the great cloak, she seemed a very woman. Each of us felt the awkwardness of our position.

"We shall not be friends the less, Mr. Byng," said she.

"Friends, Cecil!"

I took the hand she offered, and kept it. For a moment I forgot old sorrows and present anxieties in this strange new joy.

Churm had now got his bays into their pace. He turned and looked with his large benignancy of expression upon his daughter. Then tears came into his eyes.

"I have missed you, longed for you, yearned after you, sought you bitterly," he said.

"Not more bitterly than I sorrowed when I saw in your own hand that you had taken the side of that base man, and abandoned me."

"My brave child! My poor, forlorn girl!"

"Never forlorn after Mr. Byng found me," said Cecil. And when I looked at her she flushed again. "He has been a brother,—yes, closer than a brother to me. I should have died, body and soul, starved and worn out for lack of affection and sympathy, unless he had come, sent by God."

"And I, Cecil,—all my better nature would have perished utterly in the strange temptations of these weeks, except for your sweet influence. You have saved me."

"We have much to tell each other, my child," said Churm.

"Much. But I owe it to Mr. Byng to describe at once how I came to be under false colors, unsexed."

"Never unsexed, Cecil! I could not explain to myself in what your society differed from every other. It was in this. In the guise of man, you were thorough woman still. I talked to you and thought of you, although I was not conscious of it, as man does to woman only. I opened my heart to you as one does to—a sister, a sweet sister."

"Well," said Dreeme, "I must tell you my little history briefly, to justify myself. I cannot make it a merry one. Much of it you know; more perhaps you infer. You can understand the struggle in my heart when my father said to me, 'Marry this man, or I am brought to shame.' How could I so desecrate my womanhood? Here was one whom for himself I disliked and distrusted, and who was so base, having failed to gain my love, as to use force—moral force—and degrade my father to be the accomplice of his tyranny."

Dreeme—for so I must call him—spoke with a passionate indignation. I could comprehend the impression these ardent moods had made upon Densdeth's intellect. It was, indeed, splendid tragedy to hear him speak,—splendid, if the tragedy had not been all too real, and yet unfinished.

"Dislike and distrust, repugnance against him for his plot,—had you no other feeling toward Densdeth?" Churm asked.

"These and the instinctive recoil of a pure being from a foul being. Only these at first. Then came the insurrection of all my woman's heart against his corruption of my father's nature and compulsion of me through him. Mr. Densdeth treated me with personal respect. He left the ugly work to my father, his slave. Ah, my poor father!"

"And your sister,—what part did she take?"

"My sister!" said Cecil Dreeme, with burning cheeks, and as she spoke her hand grasped mine convulsively. "My sister kept aloof. She offered me no sympathy. She repelled my confidence, as she had long done. I had no friend to whom I could say, 'Save me from him who should love me dearest, who should brave whatever pang there is in public shame, rather than degrade his daughter to such ignominy.' Ah me! that Heaven should have so heaped misery upon me! And the worst to come!—the worst—the worst to come!"

"And I was across seas!" said Churm, bitterly.

"I had said to my father at the beginning, 'If Mr. Churm were here, you would not dare sacrifice me.' 'Mr. Churm,' he replied, 'would have no sympathy for this freak of rejecting a man so distinguished and unexceptionable as Mr. Densdeth.' And, indeed, there came presently a letter from you to that effect. It was you,—style, hand, everything, even to the most delicate characteristic expressions. How could I suspect my own father of so base a forgery? Then came another, sterner; and then another, in which you disowned and cast me off finally, unless I should consent. That crushed my heart. That almost broke down my power of resistance."

"My poor child! my dear child!" Churm almost moaned; "and I was not here to help!"

"I might have yielded for pure forlornness and despair," Dreeme went on, "when there was suddenly revealed to me, by a flash of insight, a crime, a treason, and a sin, which changed my repugnance for that guilty man, now dead, into utter abhorrence and loathing. Do not ask me what!"

We need not ask. All divined. And now, in the presence of these two who had warned me, their neglected cautions rushed back upon my mind. All were silent a moment, while Churm's bays bowled us merrily over the frost-stiffened road,—merrily as if we were driving from a rural wedding to the city festival in its honor.

"When this sad sin and shame flashed upon me," said Dreeme, "I did not wait one moment to let the edge of my horror dull. I sent for Densdeth. Was that unwomanly, my father?"

"Unwomanly, my child! It was heroic!"

"I sent for him. I faced him there under my father's roof, which he had so dishonored. For that moment my fear of him was vanished. I said to him but a few words. God's angel in my breast spoke for me."

God's angel was speaking now in Dreeme's words. With the remembrance of that terrible interview,—that battle of purity against foulness,—his low deep voice rang like a prophet's, that curses for God.

"But the man was not touched," continued the same solemn voice. "Strange power of sin to deaden the soul! He was not touched. No shudder at his sacrilege! No great heart-breaking pang of self-loathing! He answered my giant agony with compliments. 'A wonderful actress,' he said, 'I was. It was sublime,' he said, 'to see me so wrought up. The sight of such emotion would be cheaply bought with any villany'; and he bowed and smiled and played with his watch-chain."

Dreeme's voice, as he repeated these phrases, had unconsciously adopted the soft, sneering tone of their speaker. It was as if Densdeth were called back, and sitting by our side.

"Forget that man, if man he were, Cecil," I breathed, with a shiver. "Let his harm to us die with him! Let his memory be an unopened coffin in a ruined and abandoned vault!"

"Ah Robert! his harm is not yet wholly dead; nor are the souls he poisoned cured. The days of all a lifetime cannot heap up forgetfulness enough to bury the thought of him. He must lie in our hearts and breed nightshade."

"It was after this interview, I suppose," said Churm, "that the thought of flight came to you."

"The passion—the frenzy—of those terrible moments flung me into a fever. I went to my room, fell upon my bed, and passed into a half-unconscious state. I was aware of my father's coming in, and muttering to himself: 'Illness will do her good. This wicked obstinacy must break down,—yes, must break down.' I was aware of my sister looking at me from the door, with a pale, hard face, and then turning and leaving me to myself. While I lay there in a half-trance, with old fancies drifting through my mind, I remembered how but yesterday, in passing Chrysalis, I had marked the notice of studios to let, and how I had longed that I were some forgotten orphan, living there, and painting for my bread."

"They never told me, Cecil," said I, "that you had been an artist."

"I had not been, in any ripe sense, an artist. No amateur can be. I was a diligent observer, a conscientious student, a laborious plodder. I had not been baptized by sorrow and necessity. Power, if I have it, came to me with pangs."

"That is the old story," said I. "Genius is quickened, if not created, by throes of anguish in the soul."

"Such is the history of *my* force. Well, as I said, that fancy of an artist's life in Chrysalis came back to me. It grew all day, and as my fever heightened,—for they left me alone, except that the family physician came in, and said, 'Slight fever,—let her sleep it off!'—as the fever heightened, and I became light-headed, the fancy developed in my mind. It was a mad scheme. In a sane moment I should not have ventured it. But all the while something was whispering me, 'Fly this house: its air is pollution!' Night came. I rose cautiously. How well I remember it all!—my tremors at every sound, my groping in the dark, my confidence in my purpose, my throbs of delirious joy at the hope of escape,—how I laughed to myself, when I found I had money enough for many months,—how I dressed myself in a suit of clothes I had worn as the lover in a little domestic drama we played at home in happier days! Do not think me unwomanly for this disguise."

"Unwomanly, my child!" said Churm. "It was the triumph of womanhood over womanishness!"

"I wrapped myself," Dreeme continued, "in a cloak, part of that forgotten costume; I stole down the great staircase, half timorous, half bold, all desperate. I looked into the parlors. They were brilliantly lighted. In the distant mirror, at the rear, I could see the image of my sister, sitting alone, and, as I thought, drooping and weary. Ah, how I longed to fling myself into her arms, and pray her to weep with me! But I knew that she would turn away lightly and with scorn. I shrank back for fear of detection. You know that draped statue in the hall?"

"I know it," replied I, remembering what misery of my heart it had beheld, in its marble calm.

"In my fevered imagination it took ghostly life. It seemed to become the shadow of myself, and I paused an instant to charge it to watch over those who drove me forth,—to be a holy monitor in that ill-doing house. It was marble, and they could not harm it."

"That statue has seemed to me your presence there," I said, "and a sorrowful watcher."

I could not continue, and describe that fatal interview of last night. I was silent, and in a moment Cecil Dreeme went on.

"The rest you mostly know. You know how my rash venture succeeded from its very rashness. I won Locksley. The poor fellow had had troubles of his own, and I felt that I was safe with him, even if he discovered my secret. He gossiped to me innocently of my own disappearance, and how they were searching for me far and wide; but never within a stone's throw of my home."

"It was an inspiration," said I, "your concealment there,—such a plan as only genius devises."

"A mad scheme!" Dreeme said, musingly. "I hardly deem myself responsible for it. And who can yet say whether it was well and wisely done?"

"Well and wisely!" said Churm. "You are saved, and the tempter is dead."

"Ah!" Dreeme sighed, "what desolate days I passed in my prison in Chrysalis! I felt like one dead, as the world supposed me,—like one murdered,—one walled up in a living grave; and I gave myself no thought of ever emerging into life again. Why should I love daylight? What was there for me there? Only treachery. Who? Only traitors. I had no one in the world to trust. I dwelt alone with God."

Dreeme paused. The tears stood in those brave, steady eyes. How utterly desolate indeed had been the fate of this noble soul! How dark in the chill days of winter! How lonely in his bleak den in Chrysalis! Stern lessons befall the strong.

"Painting my Lear kept me alive, with a morbid life. It was my own tragedy, Robert. I am the Cordelia. When you did not recognize my father and sister on that canvas, I felt that myself was safe from your detection."

"How blind I have been!" I exclaimed; "and now that I recall the picture, I perceive those veiled likenesses, and wonder at my dulness."

"Not veiled from me," said Churm. "You saw me recognize them, Byng. Ah, my child! how bitter it is to think of you there pining away alone, and I under the same roof, saddening my heart with sorrow for your loss!"

"Yes, my father; but how much bitterer for me, who had loved and trusted you like a daughter, to believe that you were as cruel a traitor as the rest,—that you too would betray me in a moment. So I lived there alone, putting my agony into my picture. There was a strange relief in so punishing, as it were, the guilty. And when I had punished them, I forgave them. The rancor, if rancor there were, had gone out of me. I was ready for kindlier influences. They did not come. I could not seek them. I was no longer sustained by the vigor of my revolt. My days grew inexpressibly dreary. The life was wearing. And then I was starving for all that my dear friend and preserver, Mr. Byng, has given me,— starving to death, Robert; and there I should have died alone but for you. I knew you as my old playmate from the first moment."

I pressed her hand. "It is a touching history," I said, "but strange to me still,—strange as a dream."

"Yes, and my name, when I abandon it, will make the whole seem dreamier. My name was a sudden fancy, in reply to Locksley's query, what he should call me. Cecil; I did not quite give up my womanhood, as Cecil. And Dreeme,—it occurred to me that, if ever in life I should escape danger and be at peace, my present episode of disguise and concealment would be recalled by me only as a dream. And from such a fancy, half metaphysical, half mere girlishness, I named myself. My danger must excuse the alias."

A girlish fancy! Every moment it came to me more distinctly that Cecil Dreeme and I could never be Damon and Pythias again. Ignorantly I had loved my friend as one loves a woman only. This was love,—unforced, self-created, undoubting, complete. And now that the friend proved a woman, a great gulf opened between us. And as in my first interview with Emma Denman, I had fancied that form in the mirror the spirit of her sister regarding us, now again I seemed to see, projected against a lurid future, a slight, elegant figure in deep mourning, watching me, now with a baleful, now with a pleading look.

Thinking thus, I let fall Cecil's hand, and drew apart a little. Meantime Churm's bays whirled us merrily over the frozen turnpike, through the brisk air of that March evening. We might, for all the passers knew, have left a warm and kindly fireside, and now were speeding back to our own cheerful homes, talking as we went of rural hospitality, and how wealthy with content was life in a calm old country-house.

But thinking of what might start up between Cecil Dreeme and me, and part us, I let fall the hand I held.

"No, Robert!" said Cecil, reaching out that slight hand again, and taking mine. "I cannot let my friend go. You were dear and true to me when I was alone. Do not punish me, that I was acting an unwilling deceit with you. I longed to give you all my confidence. But how could I?"

How could she, indeed? To me, of all other men, how could she? To me, the friend of her father, the comrade of Densdeth, the disciple of

Churm, perhaps the lover of her sister, the ally of all whose perfidy had wronged her,—how could she offer to me the confidence that would compel me to choose between her and them? How could she, alone in that solitude of Chrysalis, cover her face with her hands and whisper,— "Robert, I am a woman!"

"Now, my child," said Churm, "we strike the pavements in a few moments. The bays will give me my hands full in the crowded streets, and across the ferry. Tell us how you came at last into Densdeth's power."

"You remember my terror, Robert, when at last I encountered that evil spirit again. He knew me. He must have watched Chrysalis, and seen me enter with you. Last night you did not come. I went out alone, not without some trepidation, to take my walk. By and by I perceived a carriage following me. I turned into a side street. It drove up. Densdeth's black servant—that Afreet creature—sprang out with another person. They dragged me into the carriage, and smothered my screams."

"O Cecil," I cried, "if I could have saved you this!"

No wonder that Densdeth smiled triumphant in the corridor of the opera,—smiled in double triumph over me!

"I had no fears, Robert. I felt that you would miss me. I hoped that you would trace me. At the ferry Densdeth got into the carriage. He treated me simply as an insane person, and was gentle enough. I do not think he had given up the thought that he could master my mind,— that he could weary out my moral force, and triumph over me by dint of sheer devilishness. He left me in peace last night. He had but just entered to-day, and began to address me quietly, as if I were in my father's parlor, and he were again my allowed suitor, when the woman burst in with the news of a hostile arrival. He ran out, and presently I heard that dreadful scream of exultation and despair. There seemed to me two voices mingled,—the cry of a mocking fiend baffled, and the shout of a rebel slave."

"It was so," said Churm. "How calmly you speak of all this, my child!"

"It is the life of Cecil Dreeme, and fast becoming merely historic to me, passing away into my dark ages. These will be scenes never to be forgotten, but never recalled. And now, a word of my father. Will the shame he feared come upon him at last?"

"It may not. Only Densdeth knew the crime. But Densdeth gone, poverty and sudden defeat of all his ambitious schemes must befall him."

"Better so! Poverty, shame even, are better for the soul than a life that is a lie. Only harsh treatment will teach a nature like my father's the sin of sin. Poor and ashamed, he will learn to prize my love."

"You can love him still, Cecil,—so cruel, so base?" I asked.

"Love does not alter for any error of its object."

"Error? I name it guilt, sacrilege!"

"Justice tells me that he must suffer. To every sin is appointed its own misery. An inevitable penalty announces the broken law. The misery is the atonement for the sin. I sorrow for the sufferer. Not that he suffers,—but that he should have sinned. The fiery pangs will burn away the taint, and leave the soul as white and pure as any most unsullied."

"Cecil," said I, after a silence, "you do not ask of your sister."

"No," she said, turning from me. She would have withdrawn her hand. I held it closer than before.

Chapter XXX

—◆—

Densdeth's Dark Room

We were now upon the pavements. Conversation ceased. The broad facts had been stated. The myriad details must wait for quieter hours. We were grave and expectant, for in the mind of each was an unspoken dread that all our sorrow was not over.

Churm drove hard. It was chilly sunset, a melancholy lurid twilight of March, when we turned out of Mannering Place and drew up in front of Chrysalis. Alternate thaw and freezing had fouled the snow in Ailanthus Square. It lay in patches, streaked with dirt of the city, and between was the sodden grass, all trampled uneven and stiffening now with the evening frost.

"The world never looked so dreary," said I.

"This is the very end of bitter winter," said Cecil; "let us hope now for brighter spring at hand. We will create it in ourselves."

"Yes," said Churm, whistling for his groom. "We must not let forlornness come upon us now, after this great mercy of my child's return. Byng, you had better take your friend Cecil Dreeme up to your palace-chamber, while I go round to the Minedurt, with Locksley, and have dinner brought. We all need it, after the drive and the day."

Dreeme and I climbed the broad staircase. We walked those few steps along the corridor to my door. It was almost dusk. As we passed the door of Densdeth's dark room, each was conscious anew how death had freed the world from that demon influence. We seemed to breathe freer.

We entered my great chamber. It was already sombre with the shades of evening. Only a dim light came through the mullioned and trefoiled windows. I established my guest in an arm-chair. She dropped the hood of her cloak. I smiled to notice the masculine effect of her crisp curling black hair. She perceived my feeling, and smiled also. A quiet domestic feeling seemed to grow up between us. I busied myself in reviving the fire from its ashes.

Cecil sat silent. Neither was yet at home in our new relation. I made occupation, to fill a silence I shrank from breaking with words, by examining the letter-box at my door.

There was the evening paper in the box. To-morrow it would be filled with staring capitals, and all this sorry business of the execution of Densdeth and the exposing of Huffmire.

There were sundry cards in the box; cards of lounging men about town, who had come to kill a half-hour at my expense; a card from a friend of Stillfleet's from Boston, asking permission to recover his dress coat and waistcoat, deposited in some drawer of Rubbish Palace when he came last a-wooing; a card from Madame de Nigaud, with—"Oysters and Frezzaniga at ten. Come, or I cut you!"—cards to the balls after Lent; a tailor's bill; a club notice; a ticket for a private view of Sion's new statue of Purity.

There was also a billet addressed to me in a hand I seemed to know.

"There is what the world had to say to me this afternoon," I said, handing the cards to Cecil Dreeme.

I walked toward the window for more light to read my billet; also to hide my face while I read. For I knew the hand of the address.

It was Emma Denman's.

It cost me a strong effort to tear open that slight missive. I knew not what I dreaded; but I was aware of a miserable terror, lest the sister should come between me and Cecil Dreeme, blighting both.

So I opened the letter, and began to read it, with hasty intentness, by that dim light through the narrow windows. Presently, as I divined its inner meaning, and anticipated some sorrowful, some pitiful confession at the close, I read more slowly, not to lose the significance of a word. The light faded rapidly, and each syllable was harder to decipher; and yet each, as I comprehended it, seemed to trail away and write itself anew on the dimness before me, in ineffaceable letters of fire.

This was the letter.

"Robert, good-bye! I could not see you face to face again,—I that have almost betrayed you with my sin.

"But you shall be safe from any further treachery of mine, and for the deep dread I have of myself, lest I again become a traitor to some trusting soul, I shall put any further evil work in this world out of my power.

"I tried—God knows I tried for myself and you—to keep away from between us any other sentiment than liking and simple good-will. But I could not withhold myself from loving you. It was my destiny first to be taught what love meant through you, and so to learn that I must never hope for love—for true love—in this waste misery of my ruined earthly life. I could not check you from loving me with that hesitating love you have given. I knew, O Robert! I knew why you could not love me with frank abandonment. I felt the want in myself you dimly and far away perceived. I was conscious in my whole being of the taint that repelled you.

"And yet sometimes—forgive me, for I hate myself, I loathe myself—I was willing to accept the success of my lie, my acted lie. I knew my power over you, and saw that it was greater because you had a doubt to overcome. Alas for me for such dishonor! But I yielded to the sweet delusion that I could repair the past, that by future truth to you I could annihilate the falsehood in me, upon which any love of yours must be based.

"And then, too, Robert,—for such is the cruel despotism of deceit,—I have found a base joy in my power to charm you, so that you forgot everything in my society. I have even felt a baser pleasure in keeping higher and holier aspirations away from your soul, lest you should become too sensitive, and so know me too well. Ah, how terrible is this corruption of a hidden sin! It has made me the foe of purity, eager to drag others down to my level.

"And yet I have agonized against it. More steadily, Robert, since you came. Why did you not come years ago? Why were

you ever away? I do not feel my nature wholly base. It seems to me that I might have been noble, if I had been guarded better in the innocent days. But I will be guarded, self-guarded, when this life I loathe is past, and that other life begun, with all my stern experience.

"You will not despise me. I know that it is braver to speak than to be silent; and then this struggle to be true with you helps me in the greater struggle to be true with God. Do not despise me, Robert! I saw what was in your mind when we parted. It is so. I might deceive you now. I might trifle away your suspicions; I might repel them with indignation. I will not. They are just.

"It is said. I shall die happier. I must die. I cannot trust myself. I cannot bear to act my daily lie before the world. I might again deceive, and again see the same misery in another I have seen in you,—again see a look of love grow cold,—again see doubt creep in and murder faith. I cannot trust myself. I might love you with all my heart, and yet go miserably yielding to a temptation. And so good-bye to my life, and all my womanly hopes!

"Ah Robert, if I could but have escaped that prying spirit of evil,—that one fatal being who mastered me with the first look, who saw the small germ of a bad tendency in me, and nurtured it!

"But do not believe that I was to be so base as it may seem to my sister. I did not love her ever. Her nature was a constant reproach to mine. But I should have saved her from the infamy of her marriage. I should,—O yes! I thank God that I had emancipated myself enough for that. I should have saved her; but while I was struggling with my dread of shame, my pride, and all the misery of an avowal,—while I was weeping and praying, and gaining strength to be as sisterly as I could be so late,—she was drowning! And so her sweet, innocent life perished, and the fault was mine,—the fault was mine, that I had not long before told her such a marriage would be sacrilege.

"I have had a bitter burden to bear since then,—a wearing weight of repentance. Ah! if my sister could have lived, I might have shown her that I was worthy of her love. I might have wrought her to forget those years of alienation,—all my fault, and never fault of hers,—my noble, hapless sister! A heavy

burden of shame and self-disgust! And heavier, heavier, since you came;—heavier, because, as I have learned to know what true love means, and to despair of ever being worthy of it, the reaction of hopelessness has almost driven me to utter self-abandonment, and that miserable comfort of recklessness. And so I die, lest I might fail my nobler nature, and pass into the ranks of the tempters.

"My father will not miss me. You will think pityingly of me, Robert. It is not for a dread of a lonely and sorrowful life that I die, but to save others from the contamination of my sin.

"I shall not sully this innocent roof with my death. I die in a place where I have the right to enter. My death there shall atone for my crime there. It is near you, Robert, and I could wish, if you can forgive and pity me, that you first would find me, in the dark room next to yours, and be a little tender with the corpse my purified spirit will have abandoned. Good-bye!

*"*EMMA DENMAN.*"*

"Oh, Cecil!" I cried, "your sister!"

I sprang toward the door of my lumber-room. Beside it stood a suit of ancient armor, staring with eyeless eyes, and in its iron fingers it held a heavy mace of steel,—a terrible weapon, with its head studded with spikes, and rusty with old stains, perhaps of Paynim blood. I snatched it, drew my bolts, and smote with all my force at the inner lock of the door of Densdeth's dark room.

A few such blows, the fastenings tore away, and the door flung open. I entered, and Cecil Dreeme was at my side.

It was a small room, but lofty as mine. By that faint light of impeded twilight, coming through my narrow windows, I could see that its furniture was a very dream of luxury.

But it was not the place that we noticed,—for there in the dimness we could discern the figure of a woman, seated in an arm-chair, gazing at us with a pale, dead face.

"Emma, Emma!" cried Cecil Dreeme.

She did not speak,—that dead form had given up its last words in the letter to me. The sickly odor of a deadly drug filled the room, mingling with the perfume I had noticed. She seemed to have been some hours dead, and sitting there alone, unforgiven by man.

We stood looking at her. It was pitiful. Her beauty wasted thus! Her life self-condemned to this drear death, lest her soul perish with the taint of sin!

I kissed her forehead; then pressed my lips chilled to Cecil's cheek.

"She is our sister, Cecil," I whispered.

"Our sister, Robert,—our sister, forgiven and beloved."

And so with clasped hands we knelt beside our sister, and in silence prayed for strength in the great battle with sin and sorrow, through the solemn days of our life together.

THE END.

NOTES

INTRODUCTION

1. Henry Blake Fuller, "A Legacy to Posterity," leaf 20 (entry for Jan. 10, 1875). Henry Blake Fuller Papers, Newberry Library, Chicago. Series 4, Box 9, Folder 294. My thanks to Joseph Dimuro for drawing my attention to this passage.
2. Henry Blake Fuller, *Bertram Cope's Year*, ed. Joseph Dimuro (Peterborough, Ontario: Broadview Press, 2010). Originally published in 1919.
3. Nathaniel Hawthorne, *The Blithedale Romance* (New York: Penguin, 1983), 53.
4. Margaret J. M. Sweat, *Ethel's Love-Life: A Novel* (New York: Rudd and Carleton, 1859), 92, 82, 92. For a brilliant reading of the vagaries of desire in *Ethel's Love-Life* see Dorri Beam, "Transcendental Erotics, Same-Sex Desire, and *Ethel's Love-Life*," in *Toward a Female Genealogy of Transcendentalism*, ed. Jana L. Argersinger and Phyllis Cole (Athens: University of Georgia Press, 2014), 327–47. An earlier version of this essay appeared in *ESQ* 57 (2011): 1–27.
5. In an excellent discussion of this novel Axel Nissen calls *Cecil Dreeme* "a paradigmatic example of romantic friendship fiction," even "the ultimate fiction of romantic friendship." Axel Nissen, *Manly Love: Romantic Friendship in American Fiction* (Chicago: University of Chicago Press, 2009), 57–88 (quotations at 58). Other valuable critical discussions of *Cecil Dreeme* include Robert K. Martin, "Knights-Errant and Gothic Seducers: The Representation of Male Friendship in Mid-Nineteenth-Century America," in *Hidden from History: Reclaiming the Gay and Lesbian Past*, edited by Martin Duberman, Martha Vicinus, and George Chauncey Jr. (New York: New American Library, 1989), 162–89, and Michael Millner, "The Fear Passing the Love of Women: Sodomy and Male Sentimental Citizenship in the Antebellum City," *Arizona Quarterly* 58, 2 (Summer 2002): 19–52.
6. For the "invention" of homosexuality and heterosexuality, see, among many

other works, Jonathan Ned Katz, *The Invention of Heterosexuality* (New York: Dutton, 1995); Siobhan Somerville, *Queering the Color Line: Race and the Invention of Homosexuality in American Culture* (Durham, N.C.: Duke University Press, 2000); and Hanne Blank, *Straight: The Surprisingly Short History of Heterosexuality* (Boston: Beacon Press, 2012).

7. Michel Foucault, *The History of Sexuality, Vol. 1: An Introduction*, translated by Robert Hurley (New York: Vintage, 1990), 43.

8. Peter Coviello, *Tomorrow's Parties: Sex and the Untimely in Nineteenth-Century America* (New York: New York University Press, 2013), 20.

9. Foucault, *The History of Sexuality*, 75ff.

10. See, among many other general sources, Kim M. Phillips and Barry Reay, *Sex Before Sexuality: A Premodern History* (Cambridge: Polity Press, 2011).

11. Katz, *The Invention of Heterosexuality*, 10; Blank, *Straight*, xiv.

12. Judith Butler has described in several places what she calls "heterosexual melancholy," the way that normative heterosexuality is constituted via the prohibition of same-sex desires—desires whose loss is neither acknowledged nor mourned, thus instituting and maintaining heterosexuals as perpetual melancholics. See Butler, *Gender Trouble: Feminism and the Subversion of Identity* (New York: Routledge, 1990), 70; see also Butler, *Bodies That Matter: On the Discursive Limits of "Sex"* (New York: Routledge, 1993), 235. One way to gloss my argument about *Cecil Dreeme* would be to say that the novel offers a startling premonition of heterosexual melancholy.

13. William Congreve, *The Way of the World and Other Plays*, edited by Eric S. Rump (London: Penguin Books, 2006), 380.

14. Adam Goodheart, "In Death, a Young Author Is Born," Opinionator, *New York Times* (June 19, 2011). http://opinionator.blogs.nytimes.com/2011/06/19/in-death-a-young-author-is-born/?_php=true&_type=blogs&_r=0. Accessed Aug. 31, 2015.

15. This language appears on a website, "NYU and the Village: An Urban University in Bohemia," presented by the NYU Archives and Fales Library of the NYU Division of Libraries. www.nyu.edu/library/bobst/collections/exhibits/bobst/washsq/voices/cd.html. Accessed Aug. 31, 2015.

16. Julian Hawthorne, *Confessions and Criticisms* (Boston: Ticknor, 1887), 176.

17. Hawthorne, *Confessions and Criticisms*, 180. He adverts to the story's "morbidness" once more at p. 181.

18. Theodore Winthrop, *Edwin Brothertoft* (Boston: Ticknor and Fields, 1862), 106. Further page references will be given parenthetically.

19. Theodore Winthrop, *John Brent* (Boston: Ticknor and Fields, 1862), 34. Further page references will be given parenthetically.

20. Theodore Winthrop, "Love and Skates," *Atlantic Monthly* 9, no. 51 (January 1862): 70–85 and 9, no. 52 (February 1862): 223–40; also reprinted in Theodore Winthrop, *Life in the Open Air, and Other Papers* (Boston: Ticknor and Fields, 1863), 123–215 (quotation at 181). Further page references will be to the latter version and will be given parenthetically.

21. Eve Kosofsky Sedgwick, *Between Men: English Literature and Male Homosocial Desire* (New York: Columbia University Press, 1992), 16 et passim; Sedgwick,

Epistemology of the Closet, updated with a new preface (Berkeley: University of California Press, 2008), 188–89.

22. Oliver Wendell Holmes, "The Stereoscope and the Stereograph," *Atlantic Monthly* 3, no. 20 (June 1859): 738–48. See also Holmes, "The American Stereoscope," *Image: Journal of Photography of the George Eastman House* 1, no. 3 (March 1952), 1 (repr. from *Philadelphia Photographer*, Jan. 1869); Edward W. Earle, ed., *Points of View, the Stereograph in America: A Cultural History* (Rochester, N.Y.: Visual Studies Workshop Press, 1979).

23. Roland Barthes, *Image-Music-Text*, translated by Stephen Heath (New York: Hill and Wang, 1978), 159.

24. Roland Barthes, *S/Z: An Essay*, translated by Richard Miller (New York: Hill and Wang, 1975), 15.

25. There is another image in the text that appears to want to give out this secret, too: the image of the wine that "had two flavors" because it was made from grapes that seemed to have been "drinking two kinds of sunshine all the long afternoons of ripe midsummer," the direct sunlight hitting them from above and also the reflected "sunshine shining back from the glassy bay its vineyard over-hung" (148–49).

BIOGRAPHICAL SKETCH OF THE AUTHOR

This biographical sketch first appeared as "Theodore Winthrop," *Atlantic Monthly* 8, no. 46 (Aug. 1861): 242–51.

1   **George William Curtis:** Curtis (1824–92) was a writer, speaker, and magazine editor, and a personal friend of Theodore Winthrop's. He helped see *Cecil Dreeme* and other writings by Winthrop into print after the author's death.

2   **"Washington as a Camp":** Theodore Winthrop, "Washington as a Camp," *Atlantic Monthly* 8, no. 45 (July 1861): 105–18.

2   **Sir Philip Sidney:** Sidney (1554–86), an English poet, courtier, and soldier, like Winthrop combined literary production with military action. Sidney died as the result of being shot during the Battle of Zutphen, fighting for the Protestant cause against the Catholic Spanish.

2   **Hubert Languet:** Languet (1518–81), French diplomat and reformer, advocate of religious and civil liberty.

2   **Paul Veronese:** Paolo Veronese (1528–88), Italian Renaissance painter.

3   **John Winthrop:** Sometimes referred to as John Winthrop, the Younger (1606–76), he was the son of John Winthrop, founding governor of the Massachusetts Bay Colony, whom he followed to America in 1631.

3   **His mother was . . . President Edwards:** Winthrop's mother was Elizabeth Dwight Woolsey, great-granddaughter of Jonathan Edwards (1703–58), early American theologian and president of the College of New Jersey (Princeton).

4   **W. H. Aspinwall:** William H. Aspinwall (1807–75), a merchant who founded the Pacific Mail Steamship Company, a key mover of people, goods, and gold during the California Gold Rush (1848–55).

4   **Dalles:** The Dalles, or Fort Dalles (Oregon), was the end of the Oregon Trail.

4   **expedition of Lieutenant Strain:** Isaac Strain (1821–57) led an expedition in

1854 to the Isthmus of Darien (present-day Panama) to explore the possibility of constructing a shipping canal to connect the Atlantic and Pacific Oceans. Winthrop accompanied the expedition, which was ill fated due to unreliable native guides, bad information, malnourishment, parasites, and disease.

5　　**Fremont campaign:** John C. Frémont (1813–90), an explorer, politician, and military officer, ran for president in 1856 as the first candidate of the anti-slavery Republican Party.

5　　**Church . . . Heart of the Andes:** Frederic Edwin Church (1826–1900) was an American landscape painter. He was a close friend of Winthrop's, who published a celebratory essay about one of Church's most admired canvases, *The Heart of the Andes* (1859). See Theodore Winthrop, *A Companion to the Heart of the Andes* (New York: D. Appleton, 1859).

5　　**Robinson Crusoe:** Daniel Defoe, *Robinson Crusoe* (1719), a fictional autobiography of a castaway and his adventures on a remote tropical island.

5　　**first published writing:** "New York Seventh Regiment: Our March to Washington," *Atlantic Monthly* 7, no. 44 (June 1861): 744–56. Reprinted in Theodore Winthrop, *Life in the Open Air, and Other Papers* (Boston: Ticknor and Fields, 1863), 217–52.

6　　**Bacon:** Francis Bacon (1561–1626), "Of Death" (1612, 1625): "Death hath this also, that it openeth the gate to good fame, and extinguisheth envy."

7　　**last election:** Presidential election in 1860 that brought Abraham Lincoln into office. Many Northern abolitionists were, like Winthrop, less trustful of Lincoln's commitment to end slavery than they had been of Frémont's.

7　　**Fort Sumter:** Sea fort in Charleston Harbor (South Carolina), fired upon by Confederate forces on April 12, 1861, precipitating the Civil War.

7　　**President's proclamation:** In the wake of the attack on Fort Sumter, Lincoln and his secretary of state, William Seward, issued a proclamation calling for seventy-five thousand volunteers to help retake the fort and put down the Confederate insurrection.

8　　**Fortress Monroe . . . General Butler:** Fort Monroe (in Hampton, Virginia) was Winthrop's military posting, where he was an aide to Major General Benjamin Butler (1818–93). Winthrop wrote about his detachment there for the *Atlantic Monthly* in "Washington as a Camp," and in its sequel, "Fortress Monroe," begun for the magazine but left unfinished at Winthrop's death. Both are included in Winthrop, *Life in the Open Air,* 255–90, 293–301.

9　　**Viele's quarters:** Egbert Ludovicus Viele (1825–1902), captain of engineers, New York 7th Militia.

9　　**snowballs:** Snowball viburnum, sometimes confused with hydrangea, a bush with large, round, white flower heads.

9　　**Cadmus:** In Phoenician mythology, Cadmus was instructed by Athena to sow the teeth from the dragon that he had slain; a gang of ferocious warriors sprang up and turned on each other.

9　　*Nil admirari***:** Latin, "to be excited by nothing," to possess equanimity.

9　　**Scott's Fabian policy:** General Winfield Scott (1786–1866), briefly the general-in-chief responsible for Union Army during the Civil War, devised the

Anaconda Plan, a strategy for blockading the Southern ports and cutting the South in two by passing down the Mississippi River.

9   **Cunctator:** Latin, "delayer" or procrastinator, indicating an impatience with President Lincoln's slowness to prosecute the war.

9   **neat jobs in Missouri:** Likely a reference to the capture of secessionist Camp Jackson, St. Louis, Missouri (where pro-Southern militia groups had been gathered for training), by Unionist forces on May 10, 1861.

9   *Quod faustum sit*: Latin, "May that be a good omen."

10   **Virgil's ". . . puer!":** From Virgil's *Aeneid*, VI.882, "Alas, boy to be pitied!"

10   **Walsingham:** Francis Walsingham (1532–90), secretary of state to Queen Elizabeth I of England; his daughter Frances married Philip Sidney.

11   **Great Bethel:** Sometimes known as the Battle of Big Bethel, or the Battle of Bethel Church, where Winthrop was killed on June 10, 1861, while trying to rally the troops.

CECIL DREEME

13   **Arago:** The steamship *Arago*.

13   **Despond:** Allusion to John Bunyan, *The Pilgrim's Progress* (1678), in which the protagonist, Christian, under the burden of sin and guilt, falls into the Slough of Despond, a deep miry bog fed by the "scum and filth that attends conviction for sin."

13   **"Entrez":** French, "enter."

13   **"Herein":** German, "enter."

13   **Patrick:** Shorthand for any Irish waiter or servant.

14   **"What's Hecuba . . . to Hecuba?":** Shakespeare, *Hamlet*, II.ii.497–98, "What's Hecuba to him, or he to her, / That he should weep for her?" In a general sense the expression has come to mean "It's of no importance to me."

14   **handsome as Alcibiades:** Alcibiades, an ancient Athenian politician and general, was reputed to be strikingly handsome and attracted the admiration of his teacher Socrates. In Plato's *Symposium* Alcibiades hopes to use his beauty to seduce Socrates.

14   **Absalom:** Biblical figure, described in 2 Samuel 14:25: "But in all Israel there was none to be so much praised as Absalom for his beauty: from the sole of his foot even to the crown of his head there was no blemish in him" (King James Version). This is the first of several suggestions that Densdeth may be Jewish (see also note at 85). Elsewhere he is variously racialized as having "Oriental hues" (73), an "Orientalism of face" (75), speaking with a "Spanish softness" (74), and displaying a "dark face" (173).

14   *de profundis*: Latin, "from the depths." May refer to Psalm 130, known as "De profundis" from its opening words, "Out of the depths have I cried unto thee, O Lord" (King James Version).

14   **Midas:** King of Phrygia, renowned in Greek mythology for his ability to turn everything he touched into gold.

15   **Sibylline soul:** A sibyl is a priestess or oracle in ancient Greece or Rome.

16   *pou stô*: Greek, "vantage point" or "standing place."

16 **"as I sailed"**: Alluding to a well-known broadside ditty "The Ballad of Captain Kidd" (1701), about the sailor and pirate William Kidd (1645–1701), which begins "My name was William Kidd, as I sailed, as I sailed."

17 **Young Americanism**: Political and cultural movement of the mid-nineteenth century, embracing cultural independence from European standards, social reform, continental expansion, technological progress, and other forms of modernization.

17 *nous autres*: French, "we others" or "the rest of us."

17 **Sybaris**: Ancient Greek city of great wealth, renowned for its hedonism. Mentioned again at 153.

18 **'En avant, marrche!'**: French, "Forward, march!"

19 **Chuzzlewit**: Named after the protagonist of Charles Dickens, *The Life and Adventures of Martin Chuzzlewit* (1843–44), a novel well known in the United States (the title character travels to America) and resented for its severe satire on American manners and morals.

19 *café au delay*: French, presumably a pun on *café au lait*, implying slow service at the Chuzzlewit.

19 à *discrétion*: French, "to discretion," i.e., as much as you like.

20 **Damon and Pythias**: In Greek mythology, their mutual devotion and loyalty made them epitomes of true friendship. This is the first of two references in the novel (see also 204).

20 **Ailanthus Square**: Fictional name for Washington Square in New York City, where New York University is located. According to Henry James, *Washington Square* (1880), ailanthus trees "formed the principal umbrage of the Square."

20 **Chrysalis College**: Fictional name for New York University, founded in 1831.

21 **Timon without gall:** Timon of Athens, inspiration for Shakespeare's drama of that name, was famous for his misanthropy.

21 **magnifique**: French, "magnificent."

22 **Brunelleschi and Giotto:** Artists of the Italian Renaissance, Filipo Brunelleschi (1377–1446) is best known for his engineering of the dome of the cathedral in Florence and Giotto di Bondone (1266/7–1337) for his advances in realism in painting.

22 **King's College Chapel:** Chapel to King's College, University of Cambridge, dating from the fifteenth century and considered one of the finest examples of late gothic architecture.

23 **Palazzo Sforza:** Sforza Castle, in Milan, Italy, one of the largest citadels in Europe.

23 **Columbus cracked the egg:** Legend has it that Columbus, after completing his voyages to the Americas, was challenged to defend his accomplishment, since it was said that the discovery could have been made by anyone; he asked his challengers to stand an egg on one end; when they could not do so, he took the egg, cracked the shell a bit on one end to flatten it, and stood it up, thereby showing that once something was demonstrated, it was easy, but not until then.

24   *'Sic vos non vobis ædificatis ædes'*: Latin, "Thus you build buildings not for yourselves."

24   **Dantesque, Byronic, Victor Hugoish:** References to the Italian Renaissance poet Dante Alighieri (1265–1321), the English Romantic poet George Gordon, Lord Byron (1788–1824), and the French novelist Victor Hugo (1802–85); named together, they imply that Stillfleet's quarters are a mix of dark and hellish, romantic, and gothic.

24   **Marshal Soult:** Marshal-General Jean-de-Dieu Soult (1769–1851), French general and statesman.

24   **Louis Philippe:** Louis Philippe I (1773–1850), king of France.

24   **Citizen Sabots:** Sabots are heavy work shoes, sometimes wooden clogs; peasants and unskilled workers were often called "sabots" metaphorically. They appear again at 129, in one of Cecil Dreeme's painted sketches. *Sabotage* derives from this word.

24   **'Raphaels, Correggios, and stuff':** Oliver Goldsmith, the final lines of "Retaliation: A Poem" (1774): "To coxcombs averse, yet most civilly staring, / When they judged without skill he was still hard of hearing: / When they talk'd of their Raphaels, Corregios and stuff, / He shifted his trumpet, and only took snuff."

24   **Rachel:** Mademoiselle Rachel (1820/21–1858), born Élisa Félix, French classical tragedienne famous for the intensity of her acting at the Comédie-Française.

24   *'Le flambeau fume encore'*: French, "the candle smokes yet." From Victor Hugo's play *Angelo, tyran de Padoue* (1835), II.v.

24   **Lady Macbeth:** In William Shakespeare, *Macbeth* (1606), V.i, The sleepwalking Lady Macbeth has an anguished dream that she cannot wash the blood off her hands, i.e., cannot erase the guilt of the murders she and her husband have committed.

25   **Otrantoish:** Reference to the early gothic novel, *The Castle of Otranto* (1764), by Horace Walpole.

25   *concierge*: French, doorman or caretaker of a hotel.

25   **Daggeroni, De Bogus, or Mademoiselle des Mollets:** Witty names for fictional potential visitors, evoking various disreputable social or literary types. *Daggeroni* may suggest the villain of a gothic melodrama, someone who carries a dagger. *De Bogus*, perhaps, indicates a swindler or other charlatan. *Mollet* is French for "calf," so presumably "Mademoiselle des Mollets" is a young woman not reluctant to exhibit those attractive parts of her anatomy, i.e., a coquette.

25   **Tubal Cain:** Biblical figure, mentioned in Genesis 4:22 as "an instructer of every artificer in brass and iron" (King James Version).

26   *objets*: French, "objects," knickknacks, decorations.

26   **Crœsus:** King of Lydia from 560 to 547 BCE, renowned for his incomparable wealth.

28   **Spitzbergen:** Large island in Norway, bordering the Arctic Ocean; it has many mountains, glaciers, and fjords.

29   **Peter Funk:** Colloquialism for a swindler or a by-bidder at an auction (one who deceptively runs up the bidding in cahoots with the auctioneer).

29   *manet*: Latin, "remains."

29   *bête noir*: French, literally, "black beast," more loosely, a person or thing strongly detested or avoided.

30   **Prometheus:** In Greek mythology, a Titan who steals the heavenly fire for humanity.

30   **Romulus . . . Remus:** Twin brothers, and the central characters of Rome's foundation myth. Abandoned to die in a river, they survive when they are suckled by a she-wolf.

30   **Garden of Eve:** The biblical Garden of Eden.

30   **Garden of Armida:** In Torquato Tasso's epic poem *Gerusalemme liberata* (1581), Armida, a Saracen sorceress, creates an enchanted garden and there holds Rinaldo, a crusading Christian soldier, as her lovesick captive.

31   **things of beauty, joys forever:** John Keats's poem "Endymion" (1818) begins: "A thing of beauty is a joy for ever."

31   **Venus of Milo:** One of the most famous ancient Greek statues, a marble sculpture depicting Aphrodite, now on display at the Louvre Museum in Paris.

32   **Vehm:** Type of secret medieval German court. The form "Vehmgericht" is used at 50.

33   **breakdowns:** A breakdown in nineteenth-century America usually referred to a lively, shuffling dance, often associated with the plantation celebrations of slaves or the stage performances of blackface minstrels.

33   **a cave of Adullam:** Adullam is an ancient ruin in present-day Israel, characterized by cisterns carved into the rocks.

34   **Valhalla:** In ancient Norse mythology, a magnificent hall in which the heroic dead are honored.

34   **Peris:** In Persian mythology, a peri is a good or graceful genie or fairy.

35   **Raphael:** Raphael Sanzio da Urbino (1483–1520), Italian Renaissance painter and architect.

35   **Fra Angelico:** Fra Angelico (c. 1395–1455), early Italian Renaissance painter.

37   **Muddefontaine Railroad:** Probably a fictional railroad swindle.

37   **Terryhutte University:** A play on Terre Haute, Indiana, where Indiana State University was established in 1865.

37   **Nolachucky State Polytechnic School:** The Nolichucky River is a large stream draining the Blue Ridge Mountains of western North Carolina and eastern Tennessee.

38   **Cumberland Mountains:** Mountain range in the southeastern section of the Appalachian Mountains, in southern West Virginia, western Virginia, eastern Kentucky, and eastern middle Tennessee.

38   **Comus,— . . . crystal bounds!:** John Milton, "Comus: A Mask Presented at Ludlow Castle" (1634), ll. 672–73.

38   *Après, le déluge*: French, "Afterward, the flood." A phrase denoting an attitude of carelessness about the future. Popular legend has it that Louis XV of France (1710–74) said, "Après moi, le déluge" ("After me, the deluge").

38   **Afreet:** In Arabian and Muslim mythology, a powerful demon or monstrous giant.

39   **the real Mumbo Jumbo:** The phrase "Mumbo Jumbo," as it is used here, probably refers to an African god or idol.

40   *mêlée*: French, "tussle" or "dispute."

41   **Acheron:** In ancient Greek mythology, the Acheron was the river that souls had to cross to reach the empire of the dead.

41   **flamboyant demirep:** *Demirep* is an archaic noun (deriving from "demi-reputable") meaning a woman whose virtue or chastity is compromised or in doubt.

43   **Tract Society:** American Tract Society, an evangelic organization founded in New York in 1825, dedicated to distributing Christian literature.

44   **Pleiads:** Known as the Seven Sisters, a constellation visible to the naked eye in the night sky, named after the seven sisters of Greek mythology.

44   **lanterns to search for an honest man:** Diogenes the Cynic, an ancient Greek philosopher, was reported to have carried a lantern in the daylight, explaining that he was in search of an honest man.

44   **Rhadamanthine:** In Greek mythology Rhadamanthus was a wise and just king, a man of inflexible integrity.

45   **Chartreuse:** French liqueur made by Carthusian monks near Grenoble, France.

45   *"Au revoir!"*: French, literally, "till seeing again," i.e., "goodbye."

47   *perdu*: French, "lost" or hidden.

49   **Kamtschatka:** Peninsula in the Russian far east.

50   **Wandering Jew:** Legendary figure who allegedly taunted Jesus on his way to the crucifixion and was then cursed to walk the earth until the Second Coming.

50   *Fiat lux!*: Latin, "Let there be light!"

51   *dramatis personæ*: Latin, "persons of the drama," i.e., the characters in a play.

51   *'se ranger'*: French, "to rank."

51   *'Hoc erat in votis!'*: Latin, "This was in my prayers," from Horace's *Satires*, VI.1.

53   *de rigueur*: French, "in fashion," or required by etiquette.

54   **Ophelia's song:** Ophelia is a character in Shakespeare's *Hamlet*, V.v, who sings mad songs after her father's death and Hamlet's betrayal.

55   **'marriage of true minds':** Shakespeare's Sonnet 116 begins, "Let me not to the marriage of true minds / Admit impediments."

55   *in posse*: Latin, "in potential" but not in actuality.

55   *esse*: Latin, "in being," actually existing.

56   **sent first to Coventry:** British idiom meaning to ostracize or exclude someone.

56   **St. Helena:** Tropical island in the South Atlantic where the British imprisoned Napoleon from 1815 until his death in 1821.

56   **the Russian campaign:** Napoleon led his army into Russia in 1812, but it was essentially destroyed because it was undersupplied and ill equipped for harsh winter conditions.

56   **out-Herod Herod:** Herod the Great (74/73 BCE–4 BCE), Roman client king of Judea, was often depicted in medieval mystery plays as a bloodthirsty tyrant; in Shakespeare's *Hamlet* III.ii, Hamlet uses the phrase "out-herods Herod."

The colloquial expression means to exceed in violence even someone famously violent.

56   **massacre the Innocents:** In Matthew 2:16, Herod, when the wise men failed to inform him of the location of newborn King of the Jews, "was exceeding wroth, and sent forth, and slew all the children that were in Bethlehem, and in all the coasts thereof, from two years old and under" (King James Version).

56   **dogma of original sin:** Christian doctrine of man's sinfulness resulting from Adam's rebellion in Eden.

56   *redivivus*: Latin, "revived" or "renewed."

58   **shirt of Nessus:** In Greek mythology, the poisoned shirt (daubed with the tainted blood of the centaur Nessus) that kills Heracles.

59   **pachydermatous:** Thick-skinned, like a pachyderm (e.g., an elephant or rhinoceros).

60   **the new truths . . . the new oracles:** Possibly a reference to the new ideas associated with Transcendentalism, or, more generally, to new religious ideas associated with progressive Christianity.

62   **South Ferry:** Name of a ferry between the southern tip of Manhattan and what was then the separate city of Brooklyn.

62   **Greenwood:** Green-Wood was one of the first rural cemeteries in the United States, founded in 1838 in Brooklyn, New York.

70   **'Cut behind':** If a nonpaying rider surreptitiously mounted the rear of a coach, malicious bystanders were wont to call out to the driver to "cut behind," i.e., look behind and use his whip to force the freeloader off.

70   **Hellgate:** May refer to the vicinity of Hell Gate, a narrow and treacherous tidal strait between Manhattan and Long Island; perhaps "hiding in Hellgate" was an idiom suggesting suicide by drowning.

71   **Quincy quarry:** Quincy, Massachusetts, was the location of the first great granite quarries in the United States.

71   **Sing-Sing:** Prison in Ossining, New York, opened in 1825.

71   **single-action cockroach:** An obscure idiom, also appearing in an anecdote from "a lady" reported in the "Editor's Drawer" of *Harper's New Monthly Magazine* 47, no. 279 (Aug. 1873), 474: when she didn't finish her meal on a train the conductor chided her, "Well, ma'am, I declare *you don't eat enough to keep a single-action cockroach going!*"

72   **opodildoc:** Medicinal preparation, a strong liniment.

73   **Ginevra:** Ginevra de' Benci (born c. 1458), a Florentine aristocrat painted by Leonardo da Vinci; behind her in the portrait is a juniper tree.

73   *Genièvre*: French, juniper berry, the principal botanical flavorant of gin.

73   **'Come, my lad, and drink some beer!':** From James Boswell, *The Life of Samuel Johnson* (1791), part of an anecdote under the date of Sept. 18, 1777.

73   **Borgia:** Infamous family during the Renaissance in Italy, patrons of the arts but suspected of many crimes, including murder by poisoning.

74   **Remorse or Despair:** The Giant Despair is a figure in John Bunyan, *The Pilgrim's Progress*; more generally, this adduces the tradition of literary allegory involving personification of emotions or states of mind.

74 *oubliette*: French, "forgotten place," i.e., a dungeon.

83 *tour de force*: French, "impressive performance," achieved with great skill.

83 **blind man's writing a Paradise Lost:** John Milton (1608–74), the author of *Paradise Lost* (1667, 1674), was blind.

83 **deaf man's composing a symphony:** Ludwig von Beethoven (1770–1827) became almost totally deaf by the end of his life but continued to compose music.

83 **Lear and his Daughters:** In Shakespeare's *King Lear*, the title character requires his three daughters to attest their love for him as a condition of receiving shares of his kingdom; the two eldest, Goneril and Regan, eagerly and fulsomely do so, but the youngest, Cordelia, refusing to flatter her father as her mercenary sisters have done, is disinherited.

84 **Pyrrhic breakdown:** *Pyrrhic* refers to an ancient Greek war dance, performed with weapons; for breakdown, see note at 33 above.

85 **Fortunatus's purse:** A legendary hero in German folklore, Fortunatus was said to have met the goddess of Fortune and to have received from her a magical purse that replenished its contents as often as he drew from it.

87 **Bassanio . . . Portia:** In Shakespeare's *Merchant of Venice* the young nobleman Bassanio wishes to woo the wealthy heiress Portia.

88 **Louvre . . . Pitti Palace:** The Louvre is an art museum in Paris; the Bernese Oberland a picturesque region of the Swiss Alps; the Coliseum, a ruined amphitheater in Rome; St. Peter's Basilica, a magnificent late Renaissance church in Vatican City; the Café Doné, perhaps a coffeehouse in Paris; the Pitti Palace in Florence an enormous museum of art.

88 **Magnificent Mafra:** The Mafra National Palace, a monumental palace/monastery in Mafra, Portugal.

89 **posset:** British hot drink of milk curdled with wine or ale, considered a remedy for illness.

89 **Shylock:** Character in Shakespeare's *Merchant of Venice*, a Jewish moneylender.

89 **Phœbus-like benignity:** Phoebus is the Latin epithet for Apollo, the Greek god of the sun.

91 **Lusitanian:** Lusitania was an ancient Iberian province of the Roman Empire. The modern meaning of Lusitanian is Portuguese.

92 *tête-à-tête*: French, literally "head-to-head," meaning a private conference.

93 **permutation lock:** Today called a combination lock.

93 **Shrewsburys . . . Blue-Pointers . . . Wilson's sweets . . . Wing's pethy:** Varieties of oysters.

95 **volcano:** Alcohol lamp, used for cooking or warming in the absence of a regular kitchen.

96 **commodore:** Style of hat worn by a naval commander.

99 *protégé*: French, a person who is guided or supervised by an older or more experienced person.

100 **Serbonian bog:** Herodotus (c. 484–25 BCE), in his *Histories* III.5, alluded to the legend that Typhon, cast out of heaven by Zeus, was buried in lake Serbonis; metaphorically a "Serbonian bog" has come to refer to a messy situation from which it is difficult to extricate oneself.

100   *'main de fer, sous patte de velours'*: French, a "hand of iron in a velvet glove" (cf. 44, "there was a claw curled under the velvet").

100   *'qui dort dine'*: French, "he who sleeps, dines," i.e., proverbially, he who sleeps forgets his hunger.

100   *'qui déjeune dort'*: French, "he who lunches, sleeps," i.c., he who lunches has had a good rest.

101   **fine old Madeira:** Fortified Portuguese wine, made in the Madeira islands.

101   **coarse old Monongahela:** American rye whiskey, made in western Pennsylvania's Monongahela River valley.

102   **Tittlebat Titmouse:** Protagonist of Samuel Warren's popular 1841 novel, *Ten Thousand a-Year*, Titmouse is a poor London dandy who comes unexpectedly into a fortune.

104   **sport oak:** To "sport the oak" or "sport one's oak" is a colloquial expression meaning to shut one's door (i.e., to exclude an unwelcome visitor).

106   **Mephistophiles:** Alternate spelling of Mephistopheles, a demon in German folklore.

107   **Michael Angelo:** Today more often spelled Michelangelo, Italian Renaissance sculptor, painter, architect, and poet (1475–1564) who painted seven prophets on the ceiling of the Sistine Chapel in the Vatican Palace.

107   **Murray Hill:** Neighborhood on the east side of Manhattan above Thirty-fourth Street, an "uptown" district at the time.

107   *dies non*: Latin, short for *dies non juridicus*, a nonjuridical day (a day on which no legal business can be conducted).

107   *dies perdita*: Latin, lost day.

107   **seven bells:** In naval parlance this means 11:30 a.m.; eight bells would be noon.

107   *gobemouches*: French, "flycatchers."

108   **unknightly knights of the Long Table:** Alluding to legends of King Arthur's court, where the worthy knights sit at a round table, implying the equal status of all of them. The "knights" here ("loungers" at the club), with their "blunted lances" (billiards sticks), are not worthy to be admitted to the Round Table, thus they gather at a "Long Table" (billiards table), implying their debasing admiration for their superior, Densdeth.

108   **Phelan:** Michael Phelan (1819–71), an Irish-born American billiards player and expert, billiards parlor owner, and billiards table manufacturer.

108   *entrée*: French, "entrance," access.

108   *vice versa*: Latin, "conversely."

108   *Apropos*: French (à propos), "by the way."

114   **Titian:** Titian (c. 1488/90–1576) was an Italian painter of the Venetian school, known for vivid, luminous tints.

116   **Caryatides:** Sculpted female figures serving as architectural supports, taking the place of columns or pillars.

118   **Hercules:** Roman name for the mythological Greek hero Heracles, renowned for his great strength and his many adventures.

118 **Diogenes:** Also known as Diogenes the Cynic, this ancient Greek philosopher practiced and espoused cynicism, or indifference.

119 **Camanches:** More often spelled Comanche, a Plains Indian tribe of hunter-gatherers with a horse culture and a practice of taking captives from weaker tribes and from Spanish, Mexican, and American settlers.

119 **Pawnees from the Ohio country:** One of the most powerful tribes on the Great Plains in the nineteenth century; the Ohio country (sometimes called Ohio Territory) was a region west of the Appalachian Mountains in the vicinity of the upper Ohio River.

119 *sbirri*: Italian, "ruffians" or henchmen.

121 **Pharaohs:** Kings of ancient Egyptian dynasties.

121 **Memnonium:** A name used in the nineteenth century to refer to the Ramesseum, or mortuary temple of Pharaoh Ramesses II (Ramesses the Great), the hieroglyphs of which were identified by Jean-François Champollion following his visit in 1829.

122 **Cereus:** Night-blooming cereus refers to a number of cereus cacti whose short-lived blossoms appear at night.

123 **pinchbeck:** Form of brass, an alloy of copper and zinc that resembles gold.

124 **'How happy could I be with either!':** From John Gay, *The Beggar's Opera* (1728), II.ii: Matt sings, "How happy could I be with either, / Were t'other dear charmer away!"

124 *Fœnum habet in cornu*: Latin, literally, "he has hay on his horns," figuratively meaning "beware, he shows signs of madness." From Horace, *Satires*, 4.34.

124 **Cato's feeling for the weaker side:** Possibly a reference to a story told by Plutarch about Cato the Younger, who instinctively rescued a child who was convicted by other children in a mock trial and was being carried away.

124 **Old Serpent:** Epithet for Satan. *Revelation* 12:9, "And the great dragon was cast out, that old serpent, called the Devil, and Satan, which deceiveth the whole world" (King James Version).

125 **Hercules's choice:** In his youth Hercules was sent to tend cattle on a mountain, where he was visited by two nymphs, Pleasure and Virtue, who offered him the choice of a pleasant and easy life or a severe but virtuous and heroic life; Hercules chose the latter.

126 **Cassandra:** In Greek mythology, a princess of Troy who had the power of prophecy but was cursed not to be believed.

126 **'I am indifferent honest.':** Shakespeare, *Hamlet*, III.i.122, "I am myself indifferent honest."

126 **Bugaboo:** A bogeyman, a legendary scary creature.

126 **Mentor:** A character in Homer's *Odyssey*, into whose care Odysseus commits his son Telemachus; generally, a term for a wise and experienced older person who gives sage advice.

128 **Jove . . . Minerva:** Minerva, the Roman goddess of wisdom (identified with the Greek Athena), was born from the head of Jupiter (or Jove), the king of the gods.

129 **Robespierre:** Maximilien de Robespierre (1758–94), one of the most influential figures of the French Revolution.

131 *début*: French, "first appearance."

135 **"The fleeting purpose . . . with it,":** Slightly altered from Shakespeare's *Macbeth*, IV.i.167–68: "The flighty purpose never is o'ertook / Unless the deed go with it."

136 **friend of friends:** A common expression in the nineteenth century, roughly what we mean by "best friend," but carrying a stronger connotation of deep loyalty and spiritual devotion. In Nathaniel Hawthorne's *The Blithedale Romance* (1852), Hollingsworth implores Coverdale to join his reform movement, to "devote yourself, and sacrifice all to this great end," to be his "friend of friends, forever." In some Christian contexts the "Friend of friends" would be a reference to God or to Jesus Christ. The phrase is used twice more in *Cecil Dreeme*, at 166 and 172.

139 **more precious than the love of women:** An echo of the lament of David over the dead Jonathan in 2 Samuel 1:26, "I am distressed for thee, my brother Jonathan: very pleasant hast thou been unto me: thy love to me was wonderful, passing the love of women" (King James Version).

142 **bad city . . . burning for its crimes:** Alluding to the story of the destruction of Sodom and Gomorrah in the book of Genesis; when not even ten righteous men can be found, the Lord rains "brimstone and fire" upon the sinful cities (Genesis 19:24). "And he overthrew those cities, and all the plain, and all the inhabitants of the cities, and that which grew upon the ground" (Genesis 19:25, King James Version).

144 **Orestes and Pylades:** In Greek mythology, Orestes and Pylades were cousins renowned for their intense lifelong devotion to one another.

145 **Opera-House:** Academy of Music, 126 East Fourteenth Street, New York; not far from "the Avenue" (Fifth Avenue).

147 *soirée*: French, evening party.

148 **'weary weight of all this unintelligible world':** From William Wordsworth, "Lines Composed a Few Miles Above Tintern Abbey . . ." (1798), ll. 39–40.

150 *en famille*: French, literally, "in family," i.e., at home, informally.

151 *débutante*: French, a young woman making her first appearance in fashionable adult society.

151 **"Nods and becks and wreathed smiles":** From John Milton, "L'Allegro" (1645). The narrator requests that Mirth appear with "Jest and youthful Jollity, / Quips and Cranks, and wanton Wiles, / Nods, and Becks, and wreathed Smiles" (ll. 26–28).

152 **Lydian measures:** A particular musical scale, a rising pattern of pitches; more loosely, "Lydian measures" refers to softly sweet, sensuous music, suggested here and in the following paragraphs to have a powerfully emasculating effect on its listeners.

152 **Lethean:** In classical mythology the Lethe was a river in Hades whose water induced forgetfulness of the past.

153 **Sybaritic:** Fond of sensuous luxury, pleasurable self-indulgence; the residents

of the ancient city of Sybaris were legendary among the Greeks for the hedonism. (Sybaris is mentioned at 17.)

160   **Hebe:** In Greek mythology Hebe was cupbearer to the gods.

165   **Valley of the Shadow of Death:** Psalm 23:4, "Yea, though I walk through the valley of the shadow of death, I will fear no evil; thy rod and thy staff they comfort me" (King James Version); in John Bunyan's *The Pilgrim's Progress* (1678), the hero, Christian, must traverse a Valley of the Shadow of Death.

165   **sea of troubles . . . by opposing end them:** Shakespeare, *Hamlet*, III.i.59–60: "Or to take arms against a sea of troubles / And by opposing end them."

165   **Croton pipe:** The Croton Aqueduct, constructed 1837–42, distributed fresh water from the Croton River in Westchester County to New York City reservoirs.

166   *En avant*: French, "forward."

168   *'Et tu, Brute?'*: Latin, "And you, Brutus?" Purportedly the last words of Julius Caesar to one of his assassins, Marcus Brutus; spoken in Shakespeare's *Julius Caesar*, III.i.77.

173   **Henry Clay's ghost:** Henry Clay (1777–1852), a senator and congressman from Kentucky, famously eloquent and persuasive.

178   **'Lord, deliver me from temptation!':** Matthew 6:13, the model for the Lord's Prayer: "And lead us not into temptation, but deliver us from evil" (King James Version).

181   **"like one having authority":** Mark 1:22, "And they were astonished at his doctrine: for he taught them as one that had authority" (King James Version).

190   *lex talionis*: Latin, law of retaliation or principle of retributive justice, epitomized in Exodus 21:24, "Eye for eye, tooth for tooth, hand for hand, foot for foot" (King James Version).

192   **Cyclopean:** In Greek and Roman mythology, the Cyclopes were a primordial race of giants, each with a single eye in the middle of his forehead.

211   **Paynim:** Archaic, "pagan," non-Christian.